Confessions of a Murdered Pope

Lucien Gregoire *friend/biographer* Albino Luciani

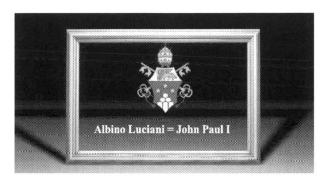

"Insofar as it defines the human soul, this book is a great comfort to the aging and those who contemplate death. Insofar as it traces the evolution of Christianity from the Neanderthals to Christ, it is most important to the young and those who contemplate life."

Howard Jason Smith, *Boston Globe*

authorHOUSE®

AuthorHouse™
1663 Liberty Drive
Bloomington, IN 47403
www.authorhouse.com
Phone: 1 (800) 839-8640

Published by AuthorHouse   09/15/2015

ISBN: 978-1-5049-1772-8 (sc)
ISBN: 978-1-5049-1773-5 (hc)

Library of Congress Control Number: 2015914677

Print information available on the last page.

Any people depicted in stock imagery provided by Thinkstock are models, and such images are being used for illustrative purposes only. Certain stock imagery © Thinkstock.

This book is printed on acid-free paper.

A bit about the Author

Lucien Gregoire was a NATO intelligence officer when he made the acquaintance of Albino Luciani in the nineteen-sixties when the little known bishop of Vittorio Veneto was leading the priest-worker movement which eventually gave rise to the Communist Party in Italy.

He is the author of the only biography of Albino Luciani written by an acquaintance of the 33-Day Pope.

The Vatican Murders: The Life and Death of John Paul I

Preface

As a bishop, Albino Luciani ordered his priests to melt down their golden chalices and other implements of idol worship to build an orphanage.[1] As a Pope, he lifted a chalice to world television cameras:

> *"This chalice contains one hundred and twenty of the world's most pristine diamonds. Do you really think this is what Christ meant by His Church?"* [2]

The little boy Albino Luciani had grown up in a tug-of-war.

His mother, a devout Catholic, prayed before crucifixes made of bits of wood. She told him, the only path to heaven was on his knees asking for selfish favors in this life and the reward of an afterlife.

His father, an atheist, burned his mother's crucifixes in the stove. He told him, the only path to heaven was on his feet helping others.

Under his father's guidance, he grew up free of prejudices peddled by religion. He reasoned atheists have a better chance of heaven than do the faithful. He wondered how faith had come about to begin with.

When his father placed him in a seminary with the commission to bring change to the Church, he traced the evolution of Christianity from the Neanderthal to the Eucharist.

His investigation culminated in his doctoral thesis dissertation:

> *"If we are ever to determine what happens to us after we are gone—we must first determine the truth of the God we are born into. Then, we must define the human soul. Precisely what is this thing we are trying to save? These things we will do now..."* [3]

The reincarnated Albino Luciani—in the voice of a precocious ten year old boy—in a wealth of entertaining chats with his bewildered father, traces the evolution of Christianity from the Neanderthals, to the Grecians, to the Egyptians, to the Jews, to those who wrote of Jesus. He finds that religion evolves just like any other social practice, each prophet building on the creativity of those who came before him.

---

[1] *Corriere delle Alpi* 2 Jun 1959, Albino Luciani, Bishop of Vittorio Veneto
[2] *Associated Press* 27 Sep 1978, John Paul I Public Audience
[3] *Gregorianum Journal Rome* 27 Mar 1947, Albino Luciani - *The Origin of the Human Soul*

Contents

The Reincarnation of Albino Luciani

I remember them all

> *Many times, many places*
> *Many people, many faces*
> *Many friends, many foes*
> *Many joys, many woes*
> *Many losses, many gains*
> *Many mates, many names*
> *Many ups, many downs*
> *Many smiles, many frowns*
> *Many struggles, many scenes*
> *Many hopes, many dreams*

Yet, always me

On Christmas day 1945, Albino Luciani eulogized General Patton in the Belluno Cathedral. A year earlier, Luciani and Patton had served jointly at the grave of a gay American soldier who had given his life to save twenty-eight Italian school children. Patton believed in reincarnation.

5

Pinocchio

Come, take his hand. Touch the sun, sniff the wine, taste the honey, peek the chartreuse, march the song. Come walk with him in the enchanting forests of the hinterland.

Come, walk in the woods with the little boy Albino, together with Pinocchio and the Cat and the Fox and the Poodle Medoro.

Let him take you out of the black and white chaos of yesterday into the technicolor world of tomorrow.

Let him give you a breathtaking glimpse of the human soul.

Let him reveal what he meant, when he told us:

"Don't knock yourself out over smart monkeys and Adam and Eve. Each of us is responsible for our own evolution. We can choose to remain as mortal men, or, we can evolve as Gods."

Quote is from Albino Luciani's doctoral dissertation, February 27, 1947, Rome

The Moth and the Butterfly

I would like to tell you of Audrey, of my friend Audrey.

She was in my class in high school, as homely as they come. Horned-rimmed glasses and all. Not a hint of a personality. Seemed to have been born without the instinct to smile.

Nothing, no, not a thing that could attract a friend, let alone a boyfriend. A sad state of affairs that each time I looked at her would touch my heart, as when one sees a sad-faced dog.

As for me, I had no trouble attracting friends. Though I was no Cary Grant, I was one of the smartest kids in the class and a four-letter man in the field.

I will remember my junior prom all of my life, for as long as I live, every day of my life. Not so much for what was there; but for what was not there.

On my arm, was the prettiest girl in the class, and we danced all night. Later that evening after I dropped her off, I drove home and sat in my car for a bit.

I thought not of the prettiest girl at the dance, but of the homeliest.

Audrey had not been there. No one, not a soul, had made it his responsibility to let her, too, have her time.

One of those things one calls tears climbed up out of my heart, started from the crevice of my eye, and crept toward the lid... I looked, first, to the right, then, to the left, then, again, to the right, and, finally, to the left, once more.

Not quite yet a man, I let it slip out onto my cheek.

In my heart, nothing, no, not a thing, was left in its place.

The following winter had come and gone and it was the week of the senior prom. As I came down the sidewalk, as was often the case, she was coming the other way.

Where normally we would pass with a downcast "Hi" I walked straight into her as to block her path.

Frightened, she asked, "What's wrong? I don't understand?"

I cut her off, "I was wondering... I was wondering if you would go to the dance with me this Friday."

With her lips quivering, "Why... why me?"

I told her, "I thought I would start at the top, this time!"

So, we went to the prom and we danced all night and I still have with me, today, one of the fondest memories of my life.

Taking her home, I kissed her, no, not a real kiss, but a noble kiss, as if we were sharing a great honor of some kind.

I drove home and sat in my car for a bit. I thought not of the prettiest girl at the dance, but of the homeliest.

One of those things one calls tears climbed up out of my heart, started from the crevice of my eye, and crept toward the lid... I looked, first, to the right, then, to the left, then, again, to the right, and, finally, to the left, once more.

Not quite yet a man, I let it slip out onto my cheek.

In its place, in my heart, was left something that would be with me all the remaining days of my life.

That year she went off to the university, and I, at the beginning of a rags-to-riches story, went to work to save for college. When I arrived at the university, she was a class ahead of me.

The first time I saw her, I didn't know her.

She was, no, not pretty. She was beautiful. Even the horned-rimmed glasses were gone. Her smile now relentless, as if she had not been born with the instinct to frown.

It was as if the fairy godmother had touched a common moth and there appeared a magnificent butterfly.

Except for a few 'hellos' when we would pass each other, I never really got to talk to her as she was forever surrounded by friends.

Now, she was the four-letter girl, and I, not much more than another spectator in the stands.

In her senior year, at the big dance, the reigning homecoming queen opened an envelope, and I, like the rest of the onlookers, waited anxiously for the name.

Audrey was handed two scepters, one for herself, the other for her king. In a crowd of ten thousand, it took her an hour to find me.

As she led me to the stage, I asked her, "Why… why me?"

She told me, "I thought I would start at the top, this time."

That night, I kissed her, no, not a noble kiss for the great honor we shared, but a real kiss. And she kissed me back.

So for me, my dream had come true. And, it can, too, for you.

All you need do, is to take a chance, and have on your arm, the homeliest girl at the dance.

'Not Quite yet a Man' (men don't cry) is the title of the author's award winning short story published in this book. Events in this book are told to the best of the author's recollection as they occurred. In those cases, they have been materially embellished by the author, a qualifying notation is made at the end of the episode.

The Interplanetary Visitor

I remember the first time Audrey told me of him.

She spoke of him as if he were some sort of foreign bigwig, some sort of interplanetary dignitary.

Early the day before, he had boarded a spaceship, and, although he would be traveling at the speed of light, it would take him several months to get here.

I remember the day he arrived. I remember all seven pounds of him. Yes, I remember each and every one of them.

I remember his first frown. His first smile. His first tear. His first laugh. His first step. His first word. His first day at school. His first communion. His first baseball mitt. His first home run.

Yet, of all the things I remember of him, was his first hug.

It came from deep within him—an electric communication of some sort or other—his first hug. One that could have only come from royalty. Perhaps, divinity. For it was heaven you see.

I recall, as if it was yesterday, the many talks I had with him. My many conversations with Justin.

Here, I want to share some of them with you.

From the day he sold his bike, to the day he got a 'D' on his term paper, to our talk of the birds and the bees, to that time we visited the *New Jerusalem* for the very first time.

To that time we checked into the golden hotel that sits at the crossroads of *Faith* and *Reality*. To that time we found ourselves caught up amid the make-believe world of yesterday, the real world of today, and the hope of a better tomorrow.

In this book, 'Justin' is the reincarnation of Albino Luciani

The Bike

"Love Thy Neighbor as Thyself."   The Universal God

By the time of his tenth birthday; biking, swimming, hiking, climbing, baseball, basketball, football, hockey, soccer and a somersault or two, had claimed half of him.

Curiosity, scrutiny, intellect, impulsiveness, or just simply the need to know, had taken over the other half. He had at this early age in life emerged as the Sherlock Holmes of our household.

Yet, unlike his celebrated predecessor of the nineteenth century, his investigation was not of this world, but of the next.

It was late in the afternoon when I went down the steps into the family room to see what the little rascal was up to.

As I entered the room, he looked up and exclaimed, "I sold my bike. I got two hundred dollars for it."

He was sitting at the table surrounded by a dozen books, hunched over one of them. I took it that he was reading from the book. I asked, "Who sold his bike?"

"I sold my bike." he asserted.

Suddenly, it struck me, he was speaking of himself. "Justin, you sold your bike for a couple hundred dollars? Are you crazy? That bike cost your mother and I more than a thousand dollars."

"That's the most I could get for it. I tried to get more. But that's the most I could get for it."

He took on a tone of utter conviction, "It makes no difference how much it cost you. All that counts is what I got for it."

"But you don't have any right to sell your bike," I fired back, raising my voice just short of a shout.

"Yes I do," his voice even more buoyant than before.

11

"It says right here: 'Sell all that thou hast...'"

"What do you mean, right here?" I began my interrogation.

"Here in Luke." He repeated: "'Sell all that thou hast...'" As I peered closer, I saw he was reading from the New Testament.

"What did you do with the money?" I questioned, taking on a tone of frustration. "Where is the money?"

"Mrs. Jackson has it," he shot back.

"Mrs. Jackson?" raising my voice, "What is she doing with it?"

"I don't know. But she needs it much more than we do.

"As you know, her husband died last month. She is losing the house and has four children to bring up. It is Christmastime. They will have nothing to eat and no presents under the tree."

"But you don't have any right giving her that kind of money," I tried to reason with him.

"Yes, I do." He completed the verse he had just read: "'Sell all thou hast and give to the poor.'"

"But... but..." I continued my onslaught, "she shouldn't have taken it from you. You're just a child."

Bouncing back with a whimsical smile. "She doesn't know where it came from. I sealed it up in an envelope and slid it under her door."

"You slid it under her door?" I shrieked.

He went on now more confident than ever. "Yes, it says here: 'Take heed ye do not give your alms before men, to be seen of them: otherwise ye have no reward of your Father who is in heaven. When thou dost give, do not sound the trumpet before thee, as do the Hypocrites in the synagogues.'

"Just think. If anything should happen to me, God forbid, I will have a bike in heaven. I will be able to get around.

"I will be able to go over to Grandma and Grandpa's place and visit them. I might even be able to visit with Mr. Jackson. I will be able to tell him his children did not go hungry."

He wiggled the key into the lock: "Again, in Matthew: 'Lay not up for yourselves treasures upon this earth, where moth and rust corrupt. But lay up for yourselves treasures in heaven, where neither moth nor rust corrupt. For where your treasure is, will be your heart also...If thou wilt be perfect, go and sell all thou hast, and give to the poor, and thou shalt have treasure in heaven.'"

He turned the key: "'It is easier for a camel to pass through the eye of a needle than it is for a rich man to enter the Kingdom of Heaven.'

"Even if he makes it, he will have nothing there. He won't be able to get around and visit his friends."

Conspiracy of the Gods

The little rascal pulled another one of his books forward. "Jesus' message is consistent with Muhammad's Koran in the Muslim world: 'Give all thou hast to your neighbor. For I am your neighbor. If the wealth ye have gained, and the merchandise ye fear may be unsold and dwellings wherein ye delight, be dearer to you than God, dearer to you than your neighbor, then God too will be dearer to Himself and you will not reside with Him in His house.'"

Dragging another volume in front of him. "Too, there is the ancient scripture of the Hindu world—the Vedas. The God Brahma tells us: 'Care only for others, lest I will not care for you. For I am the others. This is all I want of you. You will not see the brightness beyond the shadow of doom unless you care for others. Unless, you care for me.'"

He drew still another one out of his stack. "In China, Laozi in his writings of Tao—six centuries before Jesus—shared this same thesis: 'He who stores up gold in his temple in this life has had his reward in this life. He who sells his gold in this life to help others will have his reward in the next life.'"

One more made its way to center stage. "Even Buddha left this same message behind: 'When all is said and done, there are two measurements of life—oneself and others. The first will lead to treasures in the book of fools—this mere spark of abbreviated existence. The other will lead to treasures in the book of truth—the vast book of eternity.'"

I breathe a sigh of relief, "Good. He has covered them all," Unfortunately, there was last card in his deck. The trump card.

Pushing his books aside, he leaned toward me with his eyes. "This message is also true of the sacred scripture of the atheist… "

I cut him off, "The atheist has no scripture…"

"Exactly!" he gave me the facts. "Children of atheist parents grow up free of prejudices peddled by religion. They are much more likely to follow the commandment *Love thy neighbor as thyself.*

"Just think. *'If one follows this one commandment of do, there is no need for all the other commandments of don't.'* [1]

"Nevertheless, the Universal God has etched His message into the scriptures of all peoples of the world and has provided each of them with an equal chance at eternal life."

Driving the final into the coffin: "We, who drop our pennies into the poor box and pay men to prance about altars of marble and gold in magnificent cathedrals while children all over the world starve to death, are passing up that chance."

13

My head began to spin, "It was just another one of those tough days, one that tortures the mind. I must keep calm."

Regaining my composure, as I had done many times before when dealing with this little man of so many surprises, I scurried over to my desk and unlocked a drawer.

Removing ten crisp hundred dollar bills, I sealed them up in an envelope and handed it to him. "Now, take this over to Mrs. Jackson's house and put it under the door. Make sure no one sees you."

Sliding the envelope into his pocket, his eyes widening into a triumphal grin; he moved stealthily up the stairs and out of the house.

For him it was a win. For me it was a draw.

Luckily he had missed the parable of the widow's mite. Opening to the gospels, I fanned through the pages to Luke:

'He looked up and saw rich men casting their silver into the treasury. He saw also a poor widow casting in thirter-two mites. Of a truth I say unto you, this poor widow hath cast in more than they all: For all these of their abundance cast in pennies unto offerings of God: but she of her penury had cast in all that she had.'

"If one follows the one commandment of do,
there is no need for the commandments of don't." [1]

"Love thy Neighbor as Thyself"

[1]*Messaggero Mestre* 12 Jun 1970. Albino Luciani speaking to a youth group

The Ball Begins to Roll

"Science has developed tremendously and purified our wisdom of thousands of flaws in our religious knowledge of the past..."

Albino Luciani, Venice, February 8, 1974

I had taken the day off. Audrey and I were relaxing alongside the pool, basking in the afternoon sun.

We heard the drone of the school bus drop him off.

As he came around the corner of the house, he stopped at the dumpster and unloaded whatever it was he was carrying.

He was rampant. I mean, fit to be tied.

"Sister Maria Elena gave me a 'D' on my term paper," he bellowed from across the yard.

Approaching closer, "She had asked us to write a paper on faith. She told us to entitle it, *The Truth.*

"So I gave her the truth. A 'D?' I couldn't believe it.

"After class, I asked her if there had been some kind of a mistake.

"She told me there had been no mistake.

"She told me, 'A's are for the work of Angels and 'D's are for the work of Devils. My paper was the work of the Devil."

He headed toward the house. Glancing back, he warned, "You better lock up the liquor cabinet. I think I need a drink."

I looked at Audrey. Perhaps, she could handle this one?

Getting up, she followed him into the house. I headed over to the dumpster. Returning to my spot by the pool, I began to read.

15

The Truth

'It was the best of times. It was the worst of times. It was changing times...'

These words pinpoint the genius of Charles Dickens. More so, they echo the transcending evolution of Christianity.

The Christian world, today, does not believe at all what it believed just a few hundred years ago.

It has been caught up in the social and economic evolution brought on by the emergence of the renaissance, the coming of the industrial revolution, the explosion of modern science, and the consequential technological world we live in today.

Most enlightening, has been revelations in archeology which have exacted history and reduced the Bible to tales once told by ancient men to achieve political ambitions. Sadly, tales used by modern men to accomplish their own political objectives, today.

A new awakening

A few hundred years ago, man lived in a world of darkness made by God. A creature of nature, he had only 'faith' to guide him.

When night fell, he went to sleep, because he had no way to control the darkness. Each night, as he fell asleep; he 'believed,' in the dawn, light would come again.

Today, he lives, not in a world of darkness, but in a world of lightness. A world made by man. He is less a creature of nature for now he has 'reason' to guide him.

Today, he can light up the darkness. Each night, as he falls asleep; he 'knows,' in the dawn, light will come again.

No longer does man believe where he happens to be is the center of the world he lives in. No longer does he believe if he ventures out to sea he will fall off the end of the earth.

No longer does he believe the sun is a light God placed in the heavens to brighten the day. No longer does he believe the moon is a light God placed in the heavens to brighten the night.

Now, he knows the sun is the center of the world he lives in. Now, he knows the moon is not light, but darkness. He knows because he has been there.

The miracles of modern man have reduced those said to have been performed by Christ, to those routinely performed by mere rank and file magicians today.

The raising of a dead man at a time there was no way to tell if a man was really dead, the walking on water before the time of illusionary levitation, the changing of water into wine before the introduction of Kool-Aid; cannot begin to shine the shoes of the miracles of modern man.

That the miracles said of Christ, failed to convince His chosen people He was God, remains a mystery today. Particularly, that most of them were performed before great multitudes of Jews.

But, it is no mystery, had Thomas Edison lived in Christ's time, the Jews would have known He was God; for he would have lit up their lives—not one of their lives—but, all of their lives. What's more, He would have lit them up, forever.

Had Michael Faraday come along at that time, He would have been worshiped as the God of Gods.

That He could pick up a cell phone and talk to a friend in China and discuss events of the day. That He could produce an image of an event in America, bounce it off a satellite in outer space, and deliver it to be viewed by those dining in a jumbo jet thirty-five thousand feet above the Pacific Ocean; Christ, Himself, would have accepted Faraday as God.

Brave men and women

Nevertheless, these miracles of modern man have all taken place since Thomas Jefferson first lifted his pen to the 'Declaration of Independence' by candlelight.

Since Jefferson first had his slaves harness his horses to the carriage for the overnight trip to Philadelphia.

Since the Continental Congress first heard the words, 'We hold these Truths to be self-evident, all men are created equal and endowed by their Creator with certain inalienable rights... among them... Life, Liberty and the Pursuit of Happiness.'

As we know, the Constitution was then a hypocritical oath.

The definition of the word 'men' in the founding documents was not what it is today. The word 'men' excluded women and slaves who were mere 'property of men' and therefore not 'men.' Our forefathers intended a different kind of nation.

Yet, in the very next century, the first American lion, Abraham Lincoln and its first lioness, Susan B. Anthony, emerged to change forever the intent of our forefathers.

These and other men and women of great courage, who saw it as their sacred duty to rise up against what was written in their Constitution, which for these things, had their foundation in their God's Commandment, 'Thou shalt not desire to take from thy neighbor his <u>property,</u> including his house, his <u>wife,</u> his <u>slaves,</u> his ox, his ass.'

Brave men and women who knew, if they were to reach tomorrow, could not live in yesterday, for yesterday is still, only today is moving, and, right now, as I write this paper; it is a rampaging locomotive heading into tomorrow.

A kinder, gentler person

Nevertheless, these advancements of modern man have given him a kind of independence, which has given him the courage to allow his conscience—his reason—to override much of what has been written in the past—his faith—which until now has ruled the way he lived.

This has made him into a warmer, kinder, gentler, more loving person. One, more understanding of those around him who may view the world through different lens. One more likely to set aside the prejudice of his faith and embrace the compassion of his mind, 'Love thy neighbor as thyself.'

On the other hand, unable to shed mythical assumptions he is born into, his ability to reason continues to be clouded by his faith. His tendency to believe in ghosts of the past, including the one with a capital 'G'. The one he calls 'God'.

His growing consciousness of what he is in this life, has come with a gnawing consciousness of what he might not be in the next life.

Fired by his preacher's bizarre promise of bathrooms in heaven and the uncertainty of the existence of his own soul, together with the ongoing annihilation of his scripture by both archeology and science; he is no longer able to exact the position of what he believes in. He suspects, what he believes in, might not be true. His eternal destiny is at stake.

All he has left, is a question mark at the end of his life.

And, yes, the mounting dread, that 'tomorrow' might take that question mark away from him, once and for all!

I put the paper down.

His grandmother had died a few years before he had been born.

She had been in a coma for months. Yet, when she heard the priest mumble the last rites, she grasped her rosary beads as if they were the reins of a racehorse; she knew exactly where she was going. She had no doubt about it.

No. Not today. As the little man so profoundly put it: *"All one has left is a question mark at the end of one's life."*

A smile smothered my thought. "Nevertheless, he has begun to work on them, too. It won't be long before he drives them out of their minds. He obviously propelled Sister Maria Elena into an enraged tantrum with this one. Good, a chip off the old block.*"*

Headline quote: *Messaggero Mestre* 9 Feb 70. Albino Luciani Patriarch of Venice

The Tenth Commandment is as it appears in all Bibles predating 1881 and in the Jewish Torah today.

Thomas Edison invented the electric light bulb.

Michael Faraday isolated the electromagnetic wave giving birth to the technical revolution. The progression of his discovery, from storage, to hardwire transmission, to wireless transmission—radio-television-telephone-Internet—is discussed in this book.

God the Father

"...we must first determine the truth of the God we were born into or picked up along the way."

Albino Luciani, Gregorian University, Rome February 27, 1947

The Little Grey Cells

"Belief in God does not make one a fool. What makes one a fool, is belief in another man who claims to have talked to God."

Giovanni Paolo Luciani

It was the middle of July. The whole world was roasting to death. Audrey and I were cuddled up in our snugglewear in our overstuffed chairs in front of a roaring fireplace trying to keep warm. Snug as a couple of bugs, in a couple of rugs.

Like most good Christians, I had often dreamed of being filthy rich. This was certainly the manifestation of that dream.

There we were in the midst of a sizzling hot summer with the air conditioner clambering toward zero, while smoke shot up out of the chimney. The great air machine of today and the great log fire of yesterday, roaring off in opposite directions, as if each could win its race to nowhere.

Justin? Well, he was quiet as a mouse, crouched at the table behind us wrapped up in his book. He reading his book and we engulfed in the peace, solitude and happiness of the moment.

Only the crackling of the fire and the occasional turning of a page broke the soothing tranquility of a lazy afternoon. Not for long.

"This makes no sense: 'The Lord said unto Joshua, I have given unto thine hand Jericho and all the silver, and gold, thereof. Take ye men of war and go around the city seven times. The priest shall blow the trumpet. When ye hear the sound of the trumpet, all the people shall shout with a great shout; the wall of the city shall fall flat, and ye are to enter and take to the sword all of the infidels thereof, every man and woman and child. Let not one alive!'"

I looked at Audrey. Though I didn't say it, she understood it. It was her turn. She scrambled out from under her blanket and took her place on the firing line directly opposite him.

Hoping to head him off, she agreed, "Yes, this was a holy time, the time that gave birth to Christianity. It was a wonderful time."

"A wonderful time?" He looked at her as if she had lost her mind. "'... every man, woman and child slain with the edge of the sword. Leave not one alive.' You call this a wonderful time?"

Scratching his head, "Something is wrong here. Very wrong...

"Listen. Listen... This is the second of the wars which won for the Israelites the land which had belonged to the Canaanites.

"'Joshua destroyed the city of Ai. The Israelites smote the city with the sword. All that fell that day, man and woman and child, were twelve thousand.'

"It goes on and on, thirty-three cities in all. I counted them up, from Jericho to Jerusalem. What's more, I counted up the victims, hundreds of thousands of men, women, children, and even infants. Every last one of them slain with the edge of the sword.

"You call this a holy time?" His tone a bit kinder this time.

Audrey was clearly in over her head. Yet, comfy by the fire, I decided to ignore her plight and let the slaughter go on.

"You don't understand," she struggled to win her case. "These Canaanites were evil people. That's why God ordered Joshua to kill them... every man, woman, and child."

He baited his hook, "You mean these people had done the same thing to the Israelites? They had murdered their men, women and children? The Israelites were acting in retaliation?"

She fell for the bait. "No," she explained. "Before that time, there had been no wars inspired by God. Wars of ethnic cleansing. From the Crusades to those that continue to go on in the Mid-East today.

"The Canaanites were a peace loving people, the reason Joshua had such an easy time killing them. They never thought of the possibility of war. They assumed all people were peaceful like themselves. They had no defenses other than the walls they had built to protect their children and livestock from predatory beasts."

25

I wondered to myself, "Why is she feeding his fire? She is digging a hole so deep for herself she will never be able to climb out." Nevertheless, I thought it best not to interfere.

He took advantage of her slip, "Then they were wrong, clearly wrong. The Israelites must have been a very evil people."

The Commandments

"Just the other way around," she would set the record straight. "The Canaanites were evil. They were living in violation of God's most important commandments, the reason He listed them first."

An 'A' student in Bible school, she recited from memory:

> "'I am the one and only God, thou shalt have no false gods before thee…. Thou shalt not make a graven image of anything in heaven…Thou shalt not take the Lord's name in vain… Thou shalt set aside a day of worship for me…'"

She hoped it would put an end to it. She motioned to return to the comfort of her chair by the fireplace. She didn't get far.

"How do you know there is only one God?" he challenged.

"I just gave you the proof. It is the first commandment. How could you miss it?" She said in such a way that hinted that she was on the verge of losing it. Yet, he would not let up.

"What do you mean by false gods?" his ears perked up.

"These monsters didn't accept the true God. They worshiped gods of nature: the Sun god—the creator, the Crocodile—the god of the sea, the Lion—the god of the forest, the Beetle—the god of the insect world, the Falcon—the god of the sky. They were stupid infidels."

"Infidels?" he questioned.

"Yes, infidels…Huh…?" she hesitated, trying to come up with an explanation of what she was talking about.

I stepped in to save her, "…an infidel is one who doesn't believe in the God you believe in. By definition, an infidel is an atheist. If one doesn't believe in your God, to you, one doesn't believe in God."

Tossing me an appreciative nod, she proceeded to lock up her case.

"Too, these Canaanites talked to images of these gods as if stone figures could hear them. I tell you they were mad. They were mad."

He jumped on it, "Like we talk to statues of dead people today?"

I coughed, maybe chuckled. I don't remember which.

26

She fed his flames, "What's more, these infidels didn't set aside a day of worship and they joked about the Israelite God."

He was not going to allow a single blade of grass to grow under his feet. "Like we joke about the American Indian dancing around his totem pole? Like we joke about the gods of ancient Greece? Like we joke about the ancient Egyptian belief the body will rise again in the movie *The Mummy's Curse?*"

He was not quite finished, "How do we know the Israelite God was the true...?" His mother's look of anguish stopped him.

He broke the span of silence which followed. "Regardless, they must not have had freedom of religion in those days. The powerful just killed those who didn't accept their God."

"Not so. God ordered Joshua to kill these infidels. You just read it, yourself." She thought she had won.

"He didn't like the other gods? He was afraid of them? He didn't want the competition?" He waited as a lion in tall grass.

The greatest of sins

Having lost the first round, Audrey decided to spend the atom bomb of her armory. "There was more to their evilness than worshipping graven images... and taking the name of the Lord in vain... and not setting aside a day of worship..."

I could feel her cross her toes under the table, "These evil people, Canaanites as you call them, were engaging in sex."

I thought it best not to turn my head. Yet, I could imagine the expression on his face; a blend of incomprehension and surprise. More likely the look of compassion one gives any 'sick' person.

"You mean God ordered Joshua to kill these people simply because they were having sex?

"No wonder Dad was so frightened to talk to me about it when I brought up the birds and the bees. He must have thought God would strike him down, too. No wonder your generation is so hung up about sex... this natural biological function of man."

I cringed low into my chair as I thought back to that time I had struggled to tell him of the birds and the bees. That time, he had put it on the table and I cowardly beat around the bush for days until he, himself, had to drag it out of me.

27

I had no idea what went through Audrey's mind.

Yet, as she glanced over at me, it must have gone something like this: "So that little coward wasn't so brave after all."

It certainly gave her something she could hold in her arsenal for the right time. At the same time, she must have realized the little man had her in a corner.

Justin paused in anticipation of a follow-up by his mother, but she remained quiet, absolutely quiet.

There is only one God

"This God…" he picked up the beat again. "This God, who ordered these atrocities, could not have been the Father of Jesus?" He seemed to state it, much more than ask it.

"Yes, He was. This is the same God. There is only one God." Annoyed that he could think there could be more than one God.

"Then, Jesus was this same God?" demanding confirmation as to leave no wiggle room for her to escape his planned entrapment.

"That's right," she agreed with a tone of frustration fired by his ridiculous insinuation, there could be more than one God.

I chuckled to myself. "He's got her where he wants her now. What's more, he knows it. It won't be long now."

He let her have it: "Then Jesus ordered these atrocities."

"No," she reasoned. "God did. Jesus came along later."

I giggled aloud. He was obviously closing in on checkmate.

"You mean Jesus isn't infinite? He wasn't always there?"

"Of course He was always there. He is God." By this time, she knew it was a hopeless quest.

Checkmate: "Then Jesus ordered these atrocities!"

His mother, face drawn, yielded a reluctant nod of agreement.

The little grey cells

He scratched his forehead. "Nevertheless, we must apply those little grey cells, those little particles of energy that have worked so well for the great Hercule Poirot." He scratched his forehead again.

"Who?" Audrey as if she had missed the word.

"Poirot," he responded. "Hercule Poirot, the master detective of Agatha Christie fame."

"Oh!" Her tone gave away the fact she had never heard of him.

He went on, "The question is, why? Why would Joshua and Moses make these bloodthirsty aggressions? Why would they do these terrible things? What could possibly have been their motive?"

"Motive?" Audrey objected, "Motive? God told them to do these things. They didn't need a motive.

"The answer is in your book. Long before the time of the taking of the Promised Land, God had appeared in the form of a 'burning bush' and gave that land to the Israelites: 'And the lord said unto Moses, go unto the land which I promised the seed of Abraham… drive out the Canaanites in the land… let not one remain alive…'"

I am the Lord thy God

The foundation of Judea-Christian belief

"No." he set the matter straight. "Every act a person does has a motive; whether it is eating breakfast because one is hungry, or going to school to learn, or going to work to earn, or going to the bathroom. Otherwise one would do nothing." He stopped for a spot in time as if trying to come up with a way in which he could explain this thing which was clearly over his mother's head.

"Today, if a leader of a nation were to claim a 'burning bush' appeared to him the night before and told him it was God, and, the 'burning bush' had given his people a bordering nation and instructed them to invade their neighbors and slaughter every last one of them— man, woman and child; the world would think him insane. In fact, his own people would think him insane.

"If he ever tried to invade his neighbor, the United States, together with its allies in the free world, would rise up—excuse the language— and pound the hell out of him.

"Yet, today, the great mass of the people in the United States and elsewhere in the Christian world, including certain people in this

29

room," glancing over as to include me as one of the halfwits, "accept as a matter-of-fact, Moses got this same message from a 'burning bush' more than three thousand years ago.

"On top of it all, they think this atrocity holy. Most ridiculous of all, they stake their eternity on it."

He looked over at his mother, as if she was a mad dog and glanced back at me, as if I had an explanation for her madness.

I know he was thinking of saying it, yet he kept his cool.

If we wouldn't believe a man, today, who claimed to have talked to a 'burning bush' that told him to murder his neighbors, why would we be so foolish as to believe a man who, three thousand years ago, claimed to talk to a 'burning bush' that told him to do the same thing? Why would we think it was so wonderful? Most ridiculous of all, why would we stake our eternity on it?

He sat there quite pensive now. The little grey cells at work. "I think… I think we are getting smarter as time goes on.

"Don't take me wrong. But as we go along, each generation is getting smarter. More and more capable of setting aside the mythical assumptions we are born into." He pointed to his brain.

"The preacher's explanation as to what took place is in a book.

"But to this Hercule Poirot it makes no sense. When something makes no sense to the master detective, he must look further. He must massage those little grey cells… he must ponder the possibilities.

"He would ask himself, 'Why else would Moses and Joshua make these aggressions? What could have been their motive?'

"If one accepts the hypothesis, Moses was talking to a burning bush, common sense tells us that he could not have been talking to a good and just God. He surely could not have been talking to Jesus.

"No good and just God would be so evil as to set the whole thing up. Give the land first to His Canaanite children and then order a horrific massacre of them by His Israelite children."

He hesitated a moment, I supposed thinking he might be going too far. He went for it anyway.

Holding his arm up toward me as a witness, he turned toward his mother, "Mom, it is said Satan comes in many disguises."

Audrey, relieved the little man was finally talking sense, "Truer words have never been spoken. We must be on our guard at all times."

Justin looked at his mother and nodded agreement. "Yes…"

He woke her up, "Yet, tell me, Mom. How did Moses know who

he was talking to? Why was this bush, the preacher claims was God, in flames? Where do you think it came from?" Dead silence.

"Yet, there is one other option.

"Analyses and deduction of the great Hercule Poirot, gives us 'two' possibilities. Moses was either talking to Satan who set the whole thing up, or..." hesitating to highlight the only logical alternative, "Moses set the whole thing up. There are no other possibilities.

"Unless one believes in Satan, Moses and Joshua wanted the Holy Land for themselves. They wanted the treasures, the silver and gold and palaces of the Promised Land for themselves.

"As I have said, each generation is getting smarter, more and more capable of using this." Once again, he pointed to his temple.

At the same time, his eyes distanced each of us as creatures of a long lost civilization. Worst of all, he had proved his case.

Either Moses had been talking to Satan, or Moses, himself, had set the whole thing up. Common sense told us the same God who claimed to be Jesus would have never created these people for the purpose of murdering them. Particularly murdering children and even infants.

Audrey tried to stop the bleeding, "Justin, keep in mind, these are just stories, harmless stories. Let's have some lunch."

"Harmless stories? Lunch?" he grew alarmed. "We are speaking of a monster who in his self-serving tale of the *Taking of the Promised Land* has led western civilization into thousands of years of wars of ethnic cleansing. Thousands of years of hatred, and prejudice, and persecution, and horror, and suffering, and destruction, and death."

He knew he shouldn't have said it. He said it anyway. He stared his mother down, "Please don't tell me we are pinning our hopes for eternal life on a burning bush." He had gone too far.

He shot a compassionate glance at his mom. He looked at me.

I gave him the nod.

"Okay, let's have some lunch," he agreed.

Headline quote 'What makes a fool': Giovanni Paolo Luciani (John Paul Luciani) was Albino Luciani's atheist father

Evidence Which Should Be There...

"God is an assumption we are born into..."

Albino Luciani, Venice, March 5, 1973

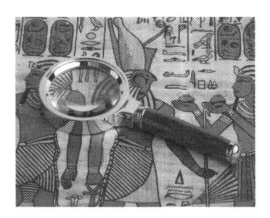

He had barely wiped his chin when the little fellow started up again.

"As we were saying, in our search for the true God and the possibility of an afterlife, we must first determine the truth of the God we are born into. The 'assumption' we are born into."

Audrey started in. He held up his hand in a stop sign.

"No, it all depends on which side of the fence one grows up.

"If one grows up in the western world, one will be a Christian, a Muslim, or a Jew. If one grows up in the eastern world, one will be a Hindu, a Buddhist, or a Tao. If one grew up in ancient Greece, one accepted Zeus as the Creator and His Son Dionysus as one's Savior."

I stealthily escaped to my overstuffed chair by the fireplace.

"If we are ever to find the true path to eternal life, we must first determine the truth of the assumption we are born into. Our concept of God, at best, is a story we are born into. The great danger is when one begins to think it is more than just that."

Audrey looked like an actress in an epic tragedy who could not possibly take another blow. She glanced at her understudy as to allow me a shot at stardom. I decided to pass up the opportunity and let her enjoy her reign on center stage.

He set the scope of his game. "As we have said before, we must first remove the assumptions we have been born into. Otherwise the little grey cells cannot do their work.

"When the little grey cells of the master detective go to work, they must consider not only the evidence which is there; but the evidence which should be there, and is not there.

"In the case of Hercule Poirot's *Hickory Dickory Dock*, we have the footprints which should have been there, and were not there. In the case of Sherlock Holmes' *Silver Blaze*, we have the dog which should have barked, and did not bark. In the case of the *Swiss Guard Murders*, we have the commander's weapon which should have been there, and was not there. In the case of the *Murder of the 33-day Pope*, we have the alarm clock which should have rung, and did not ring.

"In the case of what we are talking about here, we have Moses, who should have been there, and was not there."

Audrey gasped. I yawned. To me it was just another one of those days we would someday be telling the shrink about.

He waited, as to assure himself, we had rolled this last point over a few times in our minds. He started up again.

"Moses is said to have been born in Syria around 1350BC…"

Audrey couldn't hold back, "Wrong! Wrong! Moses was born in Egypt. My God," she apologized, "My goodness, where is your mind. Everyone knows Moses was found in a basket floating down the Nile. Everyone knows he grew up in the shadow of Pharaoh and eventually led his people out of bondage."

Much to her surprise, he agreed with her, "Yes, more than two million of them. I have checked it out.

"Every single version of the Old Testament agrees that there were six hundred thousand men together with their women and children. Over two million crossed the Red Sea. No doubt about it.

"It was because of their great numbers, the Israelites were put into slavery during the last forty years of the four hundred years they were said to have been in Egypt: 'Pharaoh said, Behold the children of Israel are more and mightier than we: Come, let us deal wisely with them lest they turn against us. So with hard bondage of mortar and brick the Israelites built for Pharaoh the

33

cities of Pithom and Ramesses…'"

Audrey couldn't believe it. The little monster was beginning to accept the world he lives in. Perhaps, there would be no need for the shrink after all. It was not to be for long.

"Yet, as I have said, to allow the little grey cells to do their work, we must first remove the assumptions we have been born into.

"What we are talking about here are tales told by ancient men to achieve political ambitions. Not things that actually took place."

His mother cut him off, "Not things that actually took place? Of course, they took place."

"Okay," he calmed her. "Let's assume the tale of the Exodus and the parting of the Red Sea actually happened."

He turned a page. "Here, it says, the Israelites escaped from the cities of Ramesses and Pithom with Pharaoh's army in close pursuit. When they reached the Red Sea: 'Moses stretched out his hands over the sea. And made the sea dry land and the children of Israel went into the sea crossing to the other side. Pharaoh's army followed and the waters receded drowning them.'"

"True," Audrey nodded agreement. "He led them out of bondage. He drowned every last one of those bastards..."

The little man ignored his mother's comment. "Regardless, all of this is beside the point. It is now time to get to the point."

"The point?" Audrey said it as if there was no point.

The point

"The point is…" he paused for a moment as does a great detective about to reveal the solution to a case that has baffled the world for centuries. "The point is," raising his voice two octaves above the beat:

"THE ISRAELITES WERE NOT IN EGYPT DURING THE FOUR HUNDRED YEARS THE BIBLE CLAIMS THEY COMPRISED HALF OF THE POPULATION OF EGYPT."

One could hear a pin drop in the room. I have to say it in that way without any originality because there is no other way to describe it. He had cleverly established his credibility along the way. Everything he had said up to that point made sense.

Yet, this time he seemed to be stretching his imagination.

I perked up my ears so that I could hear above everything else in the room. All the silence that was there. Our old ragged dog Rusty looked up from his basket, his mouth in awe.

His mother should have done the same. She couldn't hold back. "You can't prove a word you're saying."

Justin's voice took on a sympathetic tone as he reminded his mother, "Again, we must set aside the assumptions we are born into. Otherwise, the little grey cells cannot do their work.

The proof

"To begin with, there have survived the ancient cemeteries of Pithom and Ramesses where the Bible claims the Israelites lived.

"There are thousands of graves in these cemeteries dating to the four hundred years the Israelites were claimed to have been in Egypt. There is not a single Hebrew marking on any grave.

"Yet, there is much more than just the graves.

"We have the great volume of hieroglyphs in the tombs of Egypt which if reduced to fine print would fill all of the volumes of all of the libraries in the world and then some.

"More than sixty thousand rooms in the tombs have been opened so far. They are covered from floor to ceiling with hieroglyphs. In addition, there are scores of temples and tens of thousands of tablets with even more hieroglyphs.

"In all, over twenty million human figures depict the way of life in Egypt for three thousand years. About twelve million of these date to the *fourteenth* through the *eighteenth* dynasties—the four hundred years the Israelites are said to have been in Egypt.

"The overwhelming number of them are Egyptian. There are some Greeks, Hyksos, Nubians and even a few Babylonians among them. Yet, there is not a single Hebrew among these twelve million figures, despite the Bible claims half the population of Egypt was Hebrew."

He raised his voice in capital letters again to emphasize the proof the Jews were not in Egypt during the four hundred years claimed by the Bible. NOT A SINGLE TRACE OF A SINGLE JEW IN TWELVE MILLION HUMAN FIGURES DEPICTING EVERY POSSIBLE ASPECT OF THE WAY OF LIFE IN EGYPT FOR THE FOUR HUNDRED YEARS THE BIBLE CLAIMS THE JEWS WERE IN EGYPT.

"The hieroglyphics describe in complete detail, every event that occurred from the first Pharaoh who reigned in a united Egypt in 3100BC down to Cleopatra, a generation before Christ's time.

"Included, is the birth and death of every pharaoh, every war waged, every battle fought, every celebration, every social custom, every famine, every plague, every invention, every god, but nothing, not a single trace of any of Moses' tales.

"Not even the story of the Red Sea miracle in which the entire Egyptian army and its pharaoh are said to have perished, which, if true, would be the greatest event in all of Egyptian history. Nothing. Nothing at all. Not a trace."

He opened a large picture book to its center page.

Twelve million figures depicting the way of life for four hundred years

The pharaohs

"Today, we know the name, the date of birth and death, and the period of reign, of every single pharaoh. We have recovered the mummies of most of them, including all but six of those who reigned during the *fourteenth* through the *eighteenth* dynasties.

"This includes the remains of Amenhotep I, the pharaoh presumed by the Bible to have drowned in the Red Sea. Except the kings who ruled during the Hyksos occupation, they have all been Egyptians."

He turned a page, "Here are the pharaohs who reigned during the time the Israelites were said to have been in Egypt.

	BC	Pharaoh
Adam and Eve created	3940-	
	>	
First Pharaoh of a United Egypt	3138-3087	Narmer
	>	
The Great Flood	2081-2075	Mentuhotep I
	2075-2065	Inyotef I
	2065-2016	Inyotef II
Time of Abraham, Mesopotamia	2016-1957	Nebhepetre*
	1957-1945	Mentuhotep II
	1945-1945	Sankhkare*
	1945-1938	Mentuhotep III
	1938-1938	Mentuhotep IV
	1938-1909	Amenemhet I
	1909-1875	Senwosret I
	1875-1842	Amenemhet III
	1842-1837	Senwosret II
	1837-1818	Senwosret III
	1818-1772	Amenemhet II
Israelites go to Egypt	1772-1763	Amenemhet IV
	1763-1759	Sobekneferu
Hykos occupation of Egypt	1759-1526	Hykos kings
Hykos driven out of Egypt	1526-1506	Thutmosis I
	1506-1492	Thutmosis II
	1492-1471	Hatshepsut*
	1471-1424	Thutmosis II
Biblical birth of Moses	1424-1391	Thutmosis IV
The Exodus	1391-1370	Amenhotep I
Forty year wandering on the Sinai	1370-1364	Amenhotep II
	1364-1352	Amenhotep III
Aten, first historical monolithic God	1352-1338	Akhenaten
	1338-1336	Neferneferusten*
King Tut – the boy king	1336-1332	Tutankhamen
	1332-1319	Ay
Taking of the Promised Land	1319-1313	Ramesses I
	1313-1279	Seti I
Longest lived of the pharaohs - 86	1279-1213	Ramesses II

*Queen during time her son was too young to rule

Biblical 400 years of the Israelites in Egypt

"What's more, there are many more mummies than just the pharaohs.

"Tens of thousands of them have been dated to the four hundred years the Israelites were said to have been in Egypt. Again, the overwhelming number are Egyptian, some Hyksos, a few Greeks, a few Nubians, but not a single Hebrew among them."

37

I seized the chance to bring him down. "The carbon dating method used to determine ancient dates is not reliable."

He looked at me as if I had not finished grade school. "You think dating of tombstones is a twentieth century practice? The Egyptians developed the calendar based on a 365 day year in 3312BC.

"It was that the Egyptian tombs were dated as early as 3100BC which confirmed the accuracy of carbon dating analysis to begin with.

"This kind of analysis has been performed on all of the pharaohs exhumed to date and has consistently yielded dates reasonably close to those etched in the corresponding tombs."

He kept on track. "Finally, we have the forty-year wandering in the desert: '...for forty years they wandered in the deserts of the Sinai.'

"Two million crossed the Red Sea and wandered on the Sinai Peninsula for forty years, at a time the average lifespan was short of forty. At least two million died and were buried there.

The Rosetta Stone

"It was a discovery in the eighteenth century which made all this possible. In 1799, Napoleon's men stumbled upon *The Rosetta Stone*, upon which identical text was engraved in two known languages, Greek and Demotic script, and, until then, the unknown Hieroglyphs.

"Before that time, no one could translate the Hieroglyphics. It was assumed they held a record of the Israelites time in Egypt because, until then, people accepted the Bible as a history book.

"It was the unearthing of *The Rosetta Stone* followed by the excavations of the tombs, more than anything else, which proved conclusively the Bible is not a history book, but a storybook.

"When the hieroglyphs in the tombs proved the Israelites had not been in Egypt during the four hundred years claimed in the Bible, massive archeological expeditions were undertaken by the Vatican and other Christian churches in a desperate attempt to find some bit of evidence the Jews had been there during Moses' alleged time.

"After all, if the Jews had not been in Egypt during those four hundred years, it destroys the foundation of Christianity, including that of the Roman Catholic Church.

The Sinai

"The Vatican concentrated its efforts on the Sinai Peninsula where two million Israelites were 'known' to have died and been buried.

"They dug up half the peninsula in search of a minute fragment of pottery, a faint grave marking, a tiny fossil, or anything that could be construed as the slightest evidence the Jews had been there.

"Not a trace could be found. Even the huge excavation of the Suez Canal failed to yield as much as a finger bone.

"Too, we have the Holy Land to consider for evidence that should be there, and is not there.

The Holy Land

"In the Holy Land, itself, there have survived hundreds of stone etchings dating back through biblical times. Yet, you won't find a single one of them that depicts the Exodus or the Red Sea miracle or any of the stories Moses is said to have told.

"If there was the slightest chance the Jews had originated in Egypt, there would be scores of pilgrimages by Jews to Egypt to trace their heritage. Yet, there are no Jewish pilgrimages to Egypt, because, today," he paused to accentuate the absolute fact, "every Jew knows their ancestors were not in Egypt during those four hundred years.

Television

"Actually, to know this, one does not have to go to Egypt or the Holy Land. Television has capitalized on the Egyptian tombs and temples. It takes us into thousands of them.

"If these entrepreneurs could find a single Israelite figure among the twelve million human figures uncovered to date, we would all know about it. After all, their audience is a Judeo-Christian world.

"Yet, they never mention the Israelites in Egypt, because..." the fire sparked in rapid succession like a machine gun taking down a battalion, "THE ISRAELITES WERE NOT IN EGYPT DURING THOSE FOUR HUNDRED YEARS." It sparked, once more.

He was now the proverbial snowball rolling down the hill. "This tells us the story of Joseph and his brothers, and the story of Moses found floating in a basket in the Nile, and the story of Moses talking to a

39

burning bush, and the story of the Ten Plagues, and the story of the Exodus and the Red Sea, and the story of the Ten Commandments on Mount Sinai, and the story of the Taking of the Promised Land were fairytales.

"The truth of all of these tales, rests on the fundamental premise, the Israelites were in Egypt during those four hundred years.

"This is consistent with science, astronomy, archeology, and genetics, which have proved the stories of Creation and Adam and Eve and Noah's Great Flood and other biblical stories are folklore. These, too, were told while Moses was said to have been in Egypt.

The Elephantine Papyri

"More important, this is consistent with the history books."

"The history books?" his mother reminded him "The Bible is…"

He cut her off, "The earliest historical record of Jews in Egypt is the *Elephantine Papyri* held by the Brooklyn Museum in New York.

"It places a small group of soldiers on the island of Elephantine near the Nubian border in 650BC—a thousand years after the biblical tales of the Hebrews' four hundred years in Egypt.

"This occupation evolved into a community that built a temple dedicated to the pagan-god *Anat-Yahu* in 517BC." He said it softly. Yet it did not obscure the towering crescendo of his closing remark.

"THE EARLIEST JEWS IN EGYPT—A THOUSAND YEARS AFTER MOSES TALES—HAD NEVER HEARD OF MOSES' GOD. THAT IS, THOSE WHO WROTE OF MOSES."

Jewish temple dedicated to Anat-Yahu 517BC

I woke up. "What do you mean '…those who wrote of Moses?'"

"Those who first told the stories," he declared it more than said it.

I corrected him, "Every Biblical scholar in the world attributes the first five books of the Bible to Moses." Alas, I had him cornered.

At first he seemed to agree with me, "Just like they attribute the writing of the gospels to contemporaries of Christ."

He stopped realizing he had run off on a tangent. "We will get Jesus later. For now we will stick with Moses.

"That today we know the tales were fiction, tells us Moses, himself, could not have possibly written them.

"Had he written, at his time, he had led the Israelites out of Egypt, parted the Red Sea and drowned the Egyptian army and its pharaoh, the people would have known he was writing fiction.

"They would have known the Egyptian army and its pharaoh were alive. What's more, they would have known, as we know today, the Israelites were not in Egypt during those four hundred years.

"No, the books were written long after Moses' alleged time.

"We know why they were written. But we may never know who wrote them…"

I cut him off, "We know why they were written…?"

"Yes," He answered to my astonishment. "The little grey cells. The only thing that makes sense." An octave or so higher:

"MOSES' BOOKS BEGIN IN GENESIS WITH GOD'S PROMISE OF THE PROMISED LAND TO THE JEWS. THEY CULMINATE WITH JOSHUA'S TAKING OF THE PROMISED LAND. THEY WERE OBVIOUSLY WRITTEN BY JEWS WHO WANTED TO CONVINCE FUTURE GENERATIONS THAT GOD GAVE THAT LAND TO THE JEWS.

"Yet, we will never know who wrote them.

"We will never know who created the fictional character of Moses. We will never know who dreamt up the idea of the burning bush. We will never know who wrote of a God who would plot to murder His own children in the taking of the Promised Land: 'take to the sword all of the infidels… every man and woman and child. Leave not one alive.'

"A ruse which has driven all of the ethnic wars since. Thousands of years of hatred, and prejudice, and persecution, and horror, and suffering, and destruction, and annihilation, and death.

"But what we do know is…" pausing to make very clear his indisputable conclusion. "…what we do know… it was not God.

41

"For, in the imaginary world of dreams, of fantasies, of visions, of illusions, of hallucinations; tales rarely come so tall."

He stood up and put his hand on his mother's shoulder. "The God of Moses is a fairytale. We no longer have to follow His rules.

"This does not mean there is no God. What it does mean is that Moses was not talking to God. He was not even talking to a bush. The truth is, Moses was not even writing a book."

Audrey emitted a reluctant look of surrender.

He summed up his case: "Again, if we are ever to satisfy ourselves there is a God, if we are ever to satisfy ourselves we will live forever, if we are ever to remove the question mark from the end of our lives; we must first remove the assumptions we are born into. Otherwise, the little grey cells cannot do their work.

"We must employ reason which we are endowed to discern things that really happened from tales told by ancient men for political gain."

His eyes remained fixed on ours to assure himself we had grasped the crushing implications of his dissertation.

As the master detective headed toward the door, he muttered to himself, "… burning bush… take to the sword all of the infidels thereof, every man and woman and child. Leave not one alive..."

He reminded himself. "Jesus… Yes, we still have our Jesus…"

Brushing past a side table, he picked up a towel.
He looked back, "We will save Him for another day."
Sliding the door open, he stepped out.
A minute later, we heard a splash.

The reader is encouraged to search 'History of Jews in Egypt' '*Elephantine Papyri*' and other references in this episode on reliable Internet sites and in libraries. In 1966, Albino Luciani led an expedition into the Egyptian tombs and Elephantine. He confirmed, what we know today. The earliest settlement of Jews in Egypt worshiped the pagan-god Anat-Yahu on the island of Elephantine around 500BC.

The Role of Faith in War

"The most fundamental weapon of war is faith, which conditions children of God-driven nations to hate children of atheist nations, so that when they grow up they will kill them in the name of God."

Albino Luciani *Povera Tigre Feltre* 22 July 1928

5 million crosses mark WWII graves of German soldiers

He picked up where he had left off.

"Nevertheless, the monster who did write Moses tales: '...take to the sword all of the infidels thereof, every man and woman and child. Leave not one alive...' led the western world into centuries of hatred, and persecution, and horror, and suffering, and destruction, and death.

"We think first of the Papal Crusades in which millions of Muslim and Jewish men, women and children were given the choice: *'Convert or the Sword.'* Yet, this continues to go on in more recent times.

"In promoting his thesis, Hitler capitalized on the Bible.

"As a Catholic, Hitler's archenemy was atheist Russia. In this respect, he was driven by the same God the Israelites were driven by in the taking of the Promised Land."

I stopped him as a bullet stops the bad guy. "Yes, the God of the Old Testament. But today we live in the New Testament."

He agreed, "Jesus... Yes, we still have our Jesus..." He scratched his brow as if figuring out how he was going to get around this one.

"My authority comes directly from Christ."

"Yes, Jesus." I agreed, "You won't find the tiniest verse in the gospels in which Jesus supports Hitler's evil deeds."

He reminded me, "The Jews. Hitler also went after the Jews."

Reaching for his copy of the gospels, he thumbed to Luke 19:27. Yes, here, Jesus orders: "'...those enemies of mine who did not want me to be king over them, bring them here and kill them in front of me.'"

He shouldn't have said it. But he said it anyway. A question with only one answer. "Who do you think Jesus is talking about?

"You can't prove Jesus is referring to the Jews..." he cut me off.

"In Moses' world, man is mortal: 'Dust thou art, to dust thou wilt return.' The reason the Jews have no afterlife. Thus, in the Old Testament the sole penalty for nonconformance is <u>death</u>. Conversely, in the New Testament, the sole penalty for nonconformance is <u>loss of eternal life</u>. With one exception. This verse in which Jesus demands <u>death</u>.

"There is only one possibility here. Jesus could have only been referring to the Jews who had no eternal life to lose."

44

The Vietnam Genocide

"There was no war in which faith played a greater role than Vietnam.

"After the French pulled out of Vietnam in 1954, the *Geneva Accord* declared North Vietnam a free atheist (Buddhist) state blocking the spread of Catholicism from South Vietnam into Asia.

"In *The Vatican-Vietnam Pact* (October 23-26 1955) Pius XII, John Foster Dulles and Cardinal Spellman established a coalition between the United States and the ruthless South Vietnam dictator Ngo Dinh Diem to invade North Vietnam and annihilate Atheism in Asia.

Pius-Spelman-Dulles
October 23, 1955

Dulles –Eisenhower –Spellman
November 1 31, 1955

"A few days later, November 1, 1955, Dwight Eisenhower announced American intervention in Vietnam. In his declaration, the president warned: 'Godless Atheists threaten Christian civilization.'

"In World War II, extermination of Jews had been the mission. In Vietnam, extermination of atheists was the mission." He started to click his remote. "Yet the call to battle remained the same:

"Onward Christian Soldiers...

"Take to the sword all of the infidels thereof...

"...every man, woman and child...

"...let not one remain alive!

"Self-immolation of Buddhist monks in protest of American brutality and 58,000 of these poor souls who never knew what they died for...

"Today, in the least faith-driven part of the world, China's army is building roads, water systems and other infrastructure for its poor...

"...in the most faith-driven part of the world, the sheep are immersed in perpetual war...

Mideast photo

Dear Mom,

I remember the first time I saw him. He was scarcely eighteen. A felony for me.

Yet, had we been intimate? You better believe it. As intimate as any two people can be.

Never a word between us. Not so much as a whisper. Just the look and the feel of it all.

As I held him in my arms, his eyes loomed up at me, a glaring look, as if gazing past what we were today, back to what we had been yesterday. Then, perhaps, searching forward to what we could have been tomorrow.

Yet, it was a brief affair. A one-night stand as they say.

It began when I picked him up out of the sludge and searched for where the mud left off and the blood began. It ended an instant later when I felt the final thud of his pulse run out beside my heart.

I thought back three hundred meters before. To that time I could not yet see the whites of his eyes. I had caught him up in the scrutiny of my sights and squeezed the trigger.

Now, in the light of the moon, I held him out in outstretched arms... and cried...

Well, it has been raining here in Vietnam for days now. The rain has washed the hatred out of the mud and turned it back to the color God intended it to be.

Including the blood of that young boy who dreamt of things that were to be, which for him will never come to be.

Yet, it will never wash away the guilt of those who plotted his murder. It will never wash away the tears of the fool who carried it out.

Jack

Hand-to-hand combat has gone the way of the dinosaurs. Today, the soldier has no idea what his victim looks like unless he takes the time to pick him up from the mud. . When he does, he finds he is another loving human being like himself.

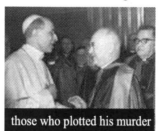

those who plotted his murder

The man on the far right is Avery Dulles—a Jesuit priest whose influence with his father—United States Secretary of State John Foster Dulles—involved America in the Vietnam Genocide in which upwards of three million atheist men, women and children were murdered. In recognition of his achievement, Avery Dulles was made a cardinal. The only American—not a bishop—to have ever been made a cardinal. Genocide is systematic annihilation of a kind of people.

When he was a fifteen year old seminarian, through the influence of his atheist father, Albino Luciani published an article in the socialist journal *Povera Tigre Feltre*: '*The most fundamental weapon of war is faith, which conditions children of God-driven nations to hate children of atheist nations, so that when they grow up they will kill them in the name of God.*' As a priest, Luciani condemned the Vatican's involvement of America in Vietnam. Ref: *Corriere delle Alpi December 12, 1955.*

Most wars in the western hemisphere have been wars of ethnic cleansing. Conversely, the wars in the east have been largely limited to wars of aggression. When a nation's population outgrows its natural resources, it invades its neighbor.

Japan was involved in World War II because its population had outgrown the limited resources of its small island nation. It was engaged in a war of aggression. At the same time, western nations were involved in a war of ethnic cleansing.

The Kindling Wood for the Vietnam War

After the Boxers threw the Christians out of China in 1901 for preaching hatred of bastards, homosexuals, atheists and other outcasts of religion, the Vatican continued to maintain a presence in French Indo-China which encompassed Laos, Cambodia and Vietnam—countries which bordered China to the south.

In 1954, the French pulled out of French Indo China and the Vatican lost its foothold in mainland Asia which blocked its strategy to annihilate Buddhism and other atheist cultures and convert China and eventually all of Asia into its fold.

Search Internet and libraries: Pius II-Spelman-Dulles October 23-26, 1955, etc.

Reflection of the Human Mind

"The Bible is a reliable record of the political acumen of men. The danger is when one begins to think it is more than just that."

Albino Luciani

He had led us from the burning bush, to the horrific taking of the Promised Land, to the hieroglyphs in the tombs, to the ovens of Treblinka, to the atrocities of Vietnam, in such rapid consecutive progression, it was as if a machine gun had taken us down.

Compassionately, he gave us the rest of the summer off.

It was not until the middle of October, Audrey and I, cuddled in our snugglewear before a roaring fireplace, he started up again.

"Why do you suppose the Canaanites laughed at Moses' God?"

"My God." I shuddered, "Not again." I shot a questionable glance at Audrey. No fool, she was not going to go for it again.

I added a log and stoked the fire a bit. Courageously, I took my place on the firing line directly opposite him at his table.

God is everywhere

As usual, he answered his own question. "Before that time, gods were believed to be individual spirits.

"It made no sense they could be in more than one place at one time, let alone in all places at all times. Just as it made no sense a person could be in more than one place at one time.

"Moses claimed God is everywhere… in all places at all times.

"His motive was political. 'If you don't follow my laws, my God will know it and you will pay for it with your lives.' In the same way Santa 'knows' when a child is naughty or nice today.

"It is a strange phenomenon, when a child reaches the age of six, they no longer believe Santa knows when they are naughty or nice. Yet, still think Moses' God knows when they are naughty or nice.

"Regardless, since then, God has been perceived to be everywhere. You can understand why this was ridiculous to the Canaanites of Moses' time. Just like it would be ridiculous today, if it were not an assumption we are born into.

"Yet, this delusion—God is everywhere—enabled the Bible to evolve as the *Political Handbook of the Western Hemisphere*."

I felt it my duty to stop him, "Political Handbook? Rubbish!"

It did stop him. I thought I finally had him.

In truth, he was confused as to how an educated man could not know the Bible is the foundation of politics in the western world.

He would have to go back and start at square one.

East vs. West

"The day I sold my bike, we discussed the universal message of all the religions of the world: *'Love thy Neighbor as Thyself.'*

"In the east, *'God is Love'* is the sole message. Whether one is speaking of the *Vedas* or the *Sutras* of the Hindu God, or the *Tripitaka* of Buddha, there is not the slightest trace of hatred of any kind of people in eastern scripture, including nonbelievers.

"In the west, the story is a good deal different. Judea, Christian and Islamic scripture subordinates woman to man, calls for annihilation of nonbelievers, and condemns all kinds of people."

He clicked his remote, "The *God of the East* loves this person. *The God of the West* hates this person.

"In the East, God is Love.

"In the West, God is a Politician."

He paused as if he had said something wrong. He corrected himself, "The men who created the western God were politicians.

"The political world is defined as the left vs. the right. Those who wrote the Bible—both the Old and New Testaments—held extreme political positions on the left and on the right.

"Moses—hates those who are different—starts off on the right. Prophets like Isaiah—compassionate of others—take us back toward the left. Paul—who wrote the bulk of the New Testament—hates those who do not follow his rules—takes us back toward the right. A few generations later, the evangelists—compassionate of others—bring us back to the left.

The Forefathers of Western Politics

Isaiah, Matthew, Mark, Luke, John   Moses, Paul & modern Catholicism

"Aside from sparing the prostitute from being stoned to death as commanded by His Father: 'He who is without sin, cast the first stone,' Christ differs from His Father on almost every issue except one."

"Except one?" I repeated his statement as a question.

"Yes, except unbelievers:

"What's more, Jesus' punishment of nonbelievers is much more damning than that of His Father. His Father limits punishment of infidels to forfeiture of this life: '...let not one remain alive.'

"Jesus extends punishment to forfeiture of eternal life: 'Unless one believeth me and is baptized, one shall not enter the Kingdom of Heaven.'

"Except, as we have said, the Jews who have no eternal life to lose:

'...those enemies of mine who did not want me to be king over them, bring them here and kill them in front of me.'

"Regardless, ancient politicians wrote the Bible to attain their political ambitions. It makes no sense God had anything to do with it." As usual, he had the proof: "He would have been contradicting Himself."

Again, he paused as if he had said something wrong. "Himself?" He reminded himself, "Yes, only self-serving 'men' wrote the Bible.

"The political identity of a nation is defined by its constitution.

"All constitutions in the western world, including that of the United States, have been based on the Bible. Something they have been trying to get away from ever since.

"'God is everywhere' was a stroke of political genius that may have made sense when people did not know what we know today.

"Today, to think God can carry on individual conversations with billions of people simultaneously makes no rational sense at all..."

Alas, he conceded one possibility.

"Unless... unless... unless... one accepts the atheist definition:

God is a Reflection of the Human Mind!"

The overwhelming population of China practices Atheism, Taoism, Confucianism and Buddhism, none of which recognize a Supreme Being. Even those who revere the Hindu God, practice the same basic philosophy: *'Love thy Neighbor as Thyself.'* China restricts western religions insofar as they violate *'Love thy Neighbor as Thyself.'* Hence, it restricts freedom of religion. At the turn of the twentieth century, the Boxers threw the Christians out of China because they were preaching hatred of out-of-wedlock children, homosexuals, atheists and other dissidents of Christianity.

Call It by Another Name

"The sacred duty of society cannot be measured in temples to its gods, but in providing food, shelter, health care and education to its loneliest child... to afford every child an equal opportunity to make his or her maximum contribution to society,"

Vladimir Lenin, *State and Revolution*

By the time the first snowflakes fell, his sessions had taken their toll. The one that bothered me the most was when the little fellow implied that faith had been the driving force behind western wars.

I would set him straight. "The World War and Vietnam had much more to do with communism than they had to do with the Bible. Hitler's enemy was communist Russia. Too, the North Vietnamese were communists. Communism fosters violation of human rights..."

He cut me off, "Human rights? What kind of human rights?"

"The right to own land. The right to vote. Freedom of speech. Freedom of religion. The right to have as many children as one wants to have." I couldn't think of any others.

He accepted only one. "The one that separates <u>communism</u> from <u>capitalism</u> is 'the right to own land.' The others involve <u>separation of church and state</u>. Again, he would have to explain how the world works to a man who missed it in grade school... in graduate school...

Economic Systems vs. Regulatory Systems

"By definition, an economic system is one that creates wealth in society. Communism and capitalism are economic systems.

"Marxism and socialism are not economic systems. They don't create wealth in society. They allocate wealth in society.

"Marxism and socialism have the same objective, to minimize polarization of wealth in society. Yet, their commonality ends there.

"Marxism annihilates the driving force behind wealth in society— individual incentive. Socialism works together with the driving force behind wealth in society, whether it be capitalism or communism.

55

Marxism diminishes individual responsibility

"There are as many definitions of Marxism as does a centipede have legs. Here we have to consider the most common understanding of Marxism: 'Dividing up the pie equally regardless of one's individual contribution to the pie.' As the Marxist Pope—John Paul I—put it:

"It is the inalienable right of no man to accumulate wealth beyond his needs, while other men starve to death because they have nothing." [1]

"Polarization of wealth, wherever it occurs, breeds revolution.

"Consider Russia. Until the twentieth century, the union of the Tsar and the Orthodox Catholic Church had ruled Russia with an iron fist. Together they lived in palatial estates and dined on fine wines and caviar and owned most of the land while millions of poor in the cities, villages and countryside of Russia literally starved to death.

"To put it in perspective, a single bowl of turtle soup at a bishop's table cost the equivalent of a year's wages for an average peasant.

"Hollywood's portrayal of the Russian revolutionary depicting scores of peaceful protestors murdered in the streets and thousands more being executed on the orders of the Tsar is historically correct.

"The revolution of 1917 forced Tsar Nicholas's abdication. In a free election, the Bolshevik Party was defeated by the Peasant Party which campaigned on a turnkey Marxist society—the government seized all property and divided it equally among the people. Thus, motion pictures of the Russian Revolution depict mansions being divided up into apartments for all. Though everyone gets an equal share of the pie—void of individual incentive—the overall size of the pie shrinks. It follows, the Bolsheviks took control by force."

He studied my reaction to assure himself he had not lost me.

Socialism forces individual responsibility

"Socialism is quite different from Marxism.

"Poverty is the enemy of a healthy society. In a socialistic society, though welfare or give-away programs respond to poverty when it occurs, unlike Marxism which mitigates individual incentive, the major thrust of socialism it to force everyone to pay his or her fair share by insulating society from poverty to begin with.

Socialism - no individual freedom of choice

"Consider the forces that drive poverty: aging, personal misfortune and overpopulation." He gave me a moment to etch them in mind.

"In socialistic societies, the individual is forced in his productive years to pay for retirement and health care programs to provide for his aging years. He has no choice. If not for programs like Social Security and Medicare, the United States would be immersed in poverty.

"Too, the individual is forced to pay for insurance to remove risk of becoming a burden to society. Again, he has no freedom of choice.

"Of course, most dangerous to a healthy society is overpopulation.

"Late in the nineteenth century, there were a billion people on the planet. Half of them were living in poverty and starving to death.

"Today, a century later, there are seven billion, and a billion of them are living in dire poverty. If not for contraception, there would be as many as twenty billion and fifteen billion starving to death.

"The planet can sustain a very limited population because of the immense demand humans place upon its very limited resources."

"Limited resources?" I gave him a dumbfounded glance.

"In two hundred years, man has exhausted half of the world's oil and coal deposits which took two hundred million years to create. We have exhausted all but a pittance of earth's natural forests. We have contaminated all of the world's rivers and are right now, as we speak, working on its oceans. We have polluted the air we breathe and poked a hole in the ozone layer, God, Himself, cannot fix.

"In first world countries, social programs encouraging Planned Parenthood have worked. How about third world countries?

"A quarter century ago, both Africa and China had a billion people living in dire poverty demanding massive welfare programs.

"Driven by reason, China restricted the number of children one could have. An act of socialism. No individual freedom of choice. In truth, with very limited natural resources, China had no choice.

"Yet, China has done what no other society has ever done before it. It has lifted upwards of a billion people out of dire poverty. Its economic system—communism—provided the wealth. Its regulatory system—socialism—did the rest of the job.

"Conversely, driven by faith, a billion people remain in poverty in Africa demanding vast world humanitarian programs today.

Ownership of land – Communism vs. Capitalism

"As we've said, a communist society is one in which land is held in common, whereas a capitalist society is one in which ownership of land is an individual right. Yet, this disparity has been dwindling.

"In colonial days, America was a nation of farmers. It was a vital human right for a man to own land. He needed many acres to grow produce and graze a herd or his family would starve to death.

"Capitalizing on the unrestricted right to own land, in the 19th century, a handful of men gained control of vital natural resources in the United States. Rockefeller in oil, Carnegie in steel and Morgan, perhaps, most dangerous of all, in transportation and money.

"To curb this polarization of wealth, the government enacted a massive portfolio of anti-trust and banking laws; the barons were forced to give up control of means of production including land.

"In 1920—benefiting by hindsight of the polarization of wealth driven by capitalism in the United States—Lenin reasoned to hold natural resources (land) in common. Today, we call this communism.

"This is also true of America today. Most land is held in common.

"The farmer has gone the way of the dinosaur. Herds no longer graze in pastures. Cows, chickens and tomatoes are raised in factories. If not for this transition, half the world would starve to death.

"Today, less than one in a million Americans own land equivalent to parcels handed out in the Homestead Acts. The urban population lives in buildings and owns no land. The government owns almost a third of the land and the lion's share of forestry, agricultural, mining and other land is owned by corporations held by investors in common.

Communism vs. Capitalism

"Today, two economic systems have survived the test of time.

"Setting propaganda aside, they are both free enterprise systems. Communism restricting the degree of the freedom of enterprise via common ownership of natural resources (land). Capitalism restricting the degree of freedom of enterprise via a portfolio of hundreds of thousands of pages of banking and anti-trust laws.

"Too, the immense shift from manufacturing and agriculture to service industries (75%) has all but abolished the economic difference between communism and capitalism. A nation's natural resources is no longer the ground people walk on, but the people themselves.

"If the economic policies of communist nations pose no threat to the capitalistic world today, why is communism its archenemy?

"For that answer, we must return to Vladimir Lenin.

Separation of Church and State

"Lenin believed 'Separation of Church and State' was necessary to protect dissidents of religion from being persecuted as had been the rule of law under the Tsar and the Orthodox Catholic Church."

I cut him off, "Rubbish. Like Stalin, Lenin was a monster."

Ignoring my snide remark, "The hypocrisy of democracy is that we pretend to practice separation of church and state, whereas, in truth, separation of church and state is not possible in a society in which the preacher has the overwhelming vote.

The Christian Democracy

"Contrary to western propaganda, Lenin did permit freedom of religion. That is, one was free to practice one's religion within the confines of one's church and one's home. Yet, he did not permit preachers to spread the hatred of their God.

"Lenin restricted Freedom of speech. Preachers could no longer claim 'their God said this…' and 'their God said that…'

"Today, in America, spreading God's hatred of certain kinds of people is 'freedom of speech.' In China, spreading hatred of one's God is against the law. This makes China the great enemy of western preachers whose objective is to suppress certain kinds of people.

"We call this '*violation of human rights*.' In China, they call it '*separation of church and state*.'" He clicked his remote.

"Too, Lenin was first to promote Planned Parenthood. He was first to legalize contraceptive devices and state controlled abortions.

"Lenin was also the first to provide free health care and free education to all citizens, rich or poor, to give every child an equal opportunity to make his or her contribution to society,

"Yet, it is that *Leninism* separated church from state that made it the great enemy of democracies that are controlled by preachers.

"It follows, today, communist nations are the enemy of faith-driven nations, not because of economic reasons, but because they are governed by atheist dictators who protect the rights of atheists and other outcasts of organized religion." He clicked his remote.

Soviet Union Premiers

Lenin	atheist
Stalin	atheist
Malenkav	atheist
Khrushchev	atheist
Brezhnev	atheist
Andropov	atheist
Chermenko	atheist
Gorbachev	atheist

Leaders Republic of China

Mao Zedong	atheist
Hua Guofeng	atheist
Hu Yaobang	atheist
Li Xiannian	atheist
Yang Shangkun	atheist
Jiang Zemin	atheist
Hu Jintao	atheist
Xi Jinping	atheist

"The archenemy of faith-driven nations is atheism. Communism—common ownership of land—has absolutely nothing to do with it.

The *'Call it by Another Name'* Program

"*'Call it by Another Name'* was the mission of an intelligence unit which served as the kindling wood for the Vietnam War.

"It programed American atheists, homosexuals and other victims of religious hatred to think communism—an economic system—was their enemy to trick them into taking up arms to destroy atheism which, in truth, was their ally."

I stopped him. "You forgot Putin. Today, thanks be to God, Russia is a democracy. Vladimir Putin is a devout Orthodox Catholic.

"Yes," he agreed. "Today, Russia is a democracy.

"For nearly a century Russia protected dissidents of religion.

"Of all world leaders, Vladimir Lenin most deserves the title, *The Father of Gay Liberation.*

"Lenin was gay?"

"Not at all. Unfettered by faith, he knew right from wrong. Lenin's Russia was the first nation to legalize homosexuality.

"In enacting the law, Lenin told the holier-than-thou bishops of the Orthodox Church who had fought bitterly against his law:

'Holiness cannot be measured in those we exclude… It can only be measured in those we include.'[2]

"Regardless, today, you are correct. Russia is a democracy. The Orthodox sheep have the vote. Where is the homosexual now?"

Lenin vs. Stalin

"Lenin and Stalin were both atheists when they came to power. Yet they were two very different men: one a monumental progressive and the other a frozen conservative.

"Though homosexuality had been accepted in China since the beginning of time, Lenin's Russia was the first nation to formerly legalize it. He was first to legalize contraception and state-controlled

61

abortions and bring about Planned Parenthood and women equality. The first to provide universal health care and free education for all.

"Like my mentor Albino Luciani, Lenin had been born to an atheist parent—his mother—and had grown up free of religious prejudices.

"Conversely, Stalin had been born to two devout parents and was conditioned during his seminary years to hate certain kinds of people.

"It follows, Stalin reversed most of Lenin's progressive policies.

"Nicholas II and his Romanov family were executed on the orders of the Bolshevik officer Yakov Sverdlova on July 17, 1918.

"Though Lenin had great motive to have killed the Tsar and his family—thousands of executions ordered by Nicholas and his father Alexander III in prerevolutionary-Russia included Lenin's brother Aleksandr—a century of investigations has failed to establish the tiniest connection between Lenin and Sverdlova and the murders. This is western propaganda to discredit a monumental progressive.

"Sverdlova was the commander of the Bolshevik Ural forces. At the time of the murders—not believing in revolution for democracy—Lenin had exiled himself in in Switzerland.

"Yet, on the dark side, in the aftermath of the revolution, there has survived reliable record that Lenin ordered the imprisonment and execution of as many as eight thousand Orthodox bishops, priests and bourgeois who had wreaked starvation and death upon the poor and had murdered tens of thousands of dissidents of religion and the Tsar.

"Lenin did not believe in democracy because in his time the preacher had the vote. His thesis *The State and Revolution* held that a socialistic society could only be achieved in a proletarian dictatorship.

"In one way he was right. The central mission of the Communist Party in China evolved from *Leninism*: *'a society which affords every child an equal opportunity to make his or her contribution to society.'*

"In another way he was wrong. Though it certainly has not been a turnkey event, progressive forces in democratic nations of America and Europe are today coming to embrace his thesis. They are coming to ignore the commandments of 'don't' of the preacher and coming to embrace the commandment of 'do' of the Universal God…

…Love thy Neighbor as Thyself."

The 'Call it by Another Name' Propaganda Program

When Pope Pius II and the Eisenhower Administration involved the United States in Vietnam, they left behind a message *'Atheists Threaten Christianity.'*

In the early sixties, an intelligence unit was secretly isolated in the Arctic Circle north of Fort Churchill Canada. Equipped with a state-of-the-art transmitter, its *'Call it by Another Name'* propaganda program conditioned the American soldier he was fighting an economic enemy—communism—lest atheists and other dissidents of religion in the American ranks realize they were fighting for an enemy and against an ally. The author of this book served two years with this unit at Fort Churchill. Something he regrets to this day.

The program changed the word 'atheism' to 'communism' in the mindset of most Americans. A 2014 poll asked <u>college seniors</u>: Why were we in Vietnam:

66% = communism, 9% = annihilate atheism, 6% = other, 19% = don't know

As much as to say the economic system of tiny North Vietnam threatened the United States. The poll demonstrates that overwhelming general population doesn't know why America was involved in Vietnam. Yet, it failed to confuse the soldier. The same poll of <u>veterans of the war</u>:

67% = annihilate atheism, 21% = communism, 1% = other, don't know = 11%

When it instituted its one-child policy, China—with one-third the natural resources of the United States—had a population five times that of the United States. Ninety percent of its population was starving to death. It had to choose between aggression and a one-child-policy. Today, ninety percent of its population lives in opportunity and its army is occupied building infrastructure to lift those that remain.

[1] Associated Press 28 September 1978. John Paul I public audience.
[2] *Kodima* 22 July 1922. Lenin's quote on homosexuality
Search Internet/library sources: 'Vladimir Lenin' 'Joseph Stalin' etc.

The Lamb of God

"...we must determine the truth of the God we were born into or picked up along the way."

Albino Luciani, Gregorian University, Rome, February 27, 1947

The Founding Fathers

I recalled the day he had walked out to the pool muttering, "Jesus… Yes, we still have our Jesus… We will save Him for another day."

The day had arrived.

"Look!" he exclaimed. "I've discovered the secret of the Pope. Why people think he is infallible. Whatever he says—goes."

I thought I would head him off before he led with one of his books. "The 'secret' of the Pope, as you say, is no secret at all. The Pope is in direct succession to Jesus Christ, Himself."

I retrieved my Almanac from the desk. His handwritten notes told me he had already had his fingers on this one, too.

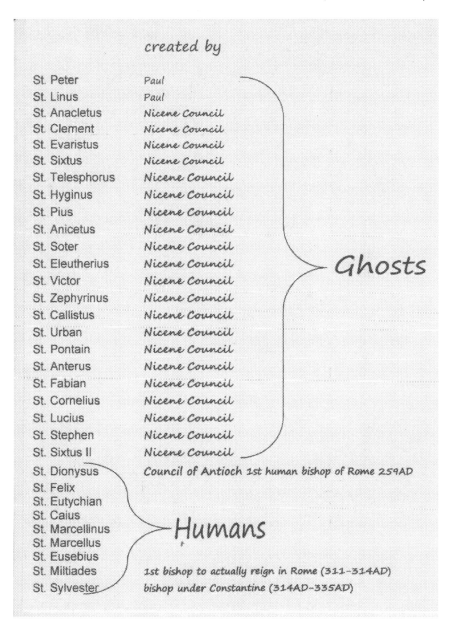

created by

St. Peter	Paul
St. Linus	Paul
St. Anacletus	Nicene Council
St. Clement	Nicene Council
St. Evaristus	Nicene Council
St. Sixtus	Nicene Council
St. Telesphorus	Nicene Council
St. Hyginus	Nicene Council
St. Pius	Nicene Council
St. Anicetus	Nicene Council
St. Soter	Nicene Council
St. Eleutherius	Nicene Council
St. Victor	Nicene Council
St. Zephyrinus	Nicene Council
St. Callistus	Nicene Council
St. Urban	Nicene Council
St. Pontain	Nicene Council
St. Anterus	Nicene Council
St. Fabian	Nicene Council
St. Cornelius	Nicene Council
St. Lucius	Nicene Council
St. Stephen	Nicene Council
St. Sixtus II	Nicene Council

Ghosts

St. Dionysus	Council of Antioch 1st human bishop of Rome 259AD
St. Felix	
St. Eutychian	
St. Caius	
St. Marcellinus	
St. Marcellus	
St. Eusebius	
St. Miltiades	1st bishop to actually reign in Rome (311–314AD)
St. Sylvester	bishop under Constantine (314AD–335AD)

Humans

I knew many popes had been canonized. Yet, I was surprised that all thirty-three popes from Sylvester all the way back to Peter were saints. Nevertheless, I would set him straight.

67

"Look here." Running my fingers from the top of the page, "St. Peter was the first Pope and Linus was the second Pope. The chain is unbroken all the way down to the Holy Father of today."

He looked at me as if I had missed Kindergarten. "You are talking about the world of make-believe. Not the world of reality.

"You are talking about apostolic succession as it was fabricated by the Nicene Council three hundred years after the time of Christ.

"Every child of six who has been to the movies knows, for the first three hundred years, there was no organized church in Rome. Just a few Christians hiding out in the catacombs. If caught, they were fed to the lions in the Coliseum.

"We will get to this later. As for now, every seminarian knows that the gospels—as we know them today—were written in the wake of the Nicene Council, three hundred years after the time of Christ.

"The Catholic Church did not begin with Christ. It began with Constantine. It is the Church of Constantine. Ask any priest." He corrected himself, "....any priest with an IQ of 75 or better.

Mythical Intercession

"When Constantine came to power in 306AD, he followed a long line of Emperors whose lives had been cut short. Most of them murdered, some committed suicide, still others forced into exile. Shakespeare capitalized on many of them.

"He searched out the leaders of other nations who had lived out their natural lives and found that each of them had convinced the populace that they had some kind of intercession with the gods.

"Alexander the Great was perceived by the Greeks to have been born of a virgin, therefore a Son of God. There were others like the Pharaohs and the early Caesars who were perceived to have one foot on earth and the other foot in divinity.

"Constantine realized his predecessors were atheists. Not believing in gods, they could not claim intercession with gods. As a result, they were unable to control the minds of men which ended in their demise.

"So, one day, while leading his army, he fell down on his knees in the middle of the road and claimed to have a vision of Christ. No one else saw anything at all. Regardless, he convinced his people he had intercession with God. Hence, he lived out his natural days.

"In 325AD, Constantine commissioned the Council of Nicaea—the Constitutional Congress of the Roman Catholic Church. The goal was to come up with a founding document; The Constitution of the Roman Catholic Church. The beginning of Canon Law. Actually, the beginning of Christianity as we know it today.

"The Council had two jobs.

"To begin with, it had to define its God. Was Christ, God? Was the God of the Old Testament, God?

"Then it had to establish succession between that 'God' and Constantine's appointed bishop of Rome, Sylvester.

"As we have just said, for the first three hundred years, there was no organized ministry; no bishop in Rome. The first Christian church in Rome was commissioned by the Nicene Council and completed in 352AD on the site of St. Peter's today.

"A half-century earlier, the Council of Antioch had appointed Dionysus titular bishop of Rome in 259AD. In title only, because no bishop could actually reign in Rome until early in the 4th century when the Christian persecutions came to an end.

"It is no coincidence, this first historical bishop of Rome took the name Dionysus—the only Roman God born of a human virgin.

"The Council of Antioch also appointed Peter and Linus the first and second titular bishops of Rome. Again titular, as it is both a historical and a biblical fact, Peter and Linus were never in Rome.

"Since there had been no organized church in Rome for three hundred years, the Nicene Council made up a list of thirty-three 'popes' connecting Sylvester back to Linus and Peter.

"Though those dating back to 259AD really lived, all twenty-four 'popes' from 259AD back to Christ were mythical creations of the Nicene Council. Those that I grouped as 'Ghosts' in your Almanac.

"The Council spent months fabricating bios of these 'popes,' depicting most of them as martyrs in the Coliseum. It is these 'biographies' with fictitious dates of birth and death that one finds in libraries depicting them as 'popes' who actually reigned in Rome.

"Nevertheless, it is this fictional *Communion of Saints* from Dionysus back to Christ, not to saints as we think of them today, a Catholic makes his or her pledge of allegiance to the Church. A Catholic's link to Christ." He recited the Nicene Creed:

69

"'I believe in God, the Father Almighty, Creator of heaven and earth; and in Jesus Christ His only begotten Son, Our Lord… conceived of the Holy Ghost, born of the Virgin Mary, suffered under Pontius Pilate, was crucified, died, and was buried.

He descended into Hell. On the third day He rose again.

He ascended into heaven seated at the right hand of the Father.

I believe in the Holy Ghost, the Holy Catholic Church, the *Communion of Saints*, Forgiveness of Sins, Resurrection of the Body, and Life Everlasting…'

"Just think. If these men had really reigned in Rome, the Council would not have added the pledge: *'I believe in the Communion of Saints.'* As historical figures, no one would have to believe in them.

"We have to <u>believe</u> in Jesus, a theological figure, because Jesus is not <u>known</u> to have ever lived. We don't have to <u>believe</u> in Aristotle, a historical figure, because we <u>know</u> he really lived.

"Yet, it is this last sentence, which defines a Catholic more than anything else. From our earliest childhood we repeat this over and over again to ourselves, never taking so much as a moment to understand what we are talking about. And, just what are we talking about when we make our pledge of allegiance to our faith?

"We believe in God the Father—in the guise of a Ghost—raped Mary in her sleep. We believe a fabricated list of ghost-popes from the time of St. Dionysus back to the time of Christ actually reigned as bishops of Rome. We believe, we will rise again as zombies to wander forever in the land of the living dead."

Though I sensed he was baiting his hook again, I went for it anyway, "Mary was not raped. She accepted the will of God."

"Okay," he agreed, "We believe in God the Father—in the guise of a Ghost—knocked up Mary in her sleep." He waited for me to call him down. I decided not to go for it. He wrapped up his case.

"In a nutshell, this is what we believe in. It is this last sentence of the Apostle's Creed which defines us as Catholics."

"You forgot *Forgiveness of Sins.* I reminded him.

"Oh, yes, *Forgiveness of Sins.* The reason, my friend Freddy changed his mind."

"Changed his mind?" My ears perked up.

"Yes, for months Freddy prayed to God for a new bike."

I couldn't hold back. A chuckle escaped.

70

"He found out that is not the way the Catholic God works."

"Not the way the Catholic God works?" I gasped.

"Yes. Not the way the Catholic God works.

"So, Freddy stole a bike, and confessed it to a priest.

"Every archeologist will tell you, there was no Christian church in Rome prior to the Nicene Council. Every historian will tell you, there was no bishop in Rome prior to the Edict of Milan early in the 4th century which legalized Christianity in Rome.

"Yet, one doesn't have to depend on the experts.

"As I have said, every child of six who has been to the movies knows there was no organized church or bishop in Rome from Constantine back to Christ, just a few Christians hiding out in the catacombs or being fed to the lions in the Coliseum."

Audrey called down the stairs, "Dinner."

"Saved by the bell," I thought to myself. "The dinner bell."

It is that apostolic succession was fabricated by the Nicene Council, Martin Luther and others were able to break from Rome. No Christian church traces its roots back to Christ through Rome. Yet, Christianity had been organized in the Mideast early in the 2nd century and centered in Antioch in the 3rd century,

Whereas, it is a historical and biblical fact Peter was never in Rome, Paul—who wrote the lion's share of the New Testament—is said to have brought Christianity to Rome in the 1st century. The Council chose Peter and not Paul as the first 'pope' because Paul—by his own testimony—had never witnessed Christ.

The Fog of Faith

"I don't believe the same God who has endowed us with reason has intended us to forego its use, we would believe God is a deity, and a man, and a ghost...; none of which is the same person."

Albino Luciani, Gregorian University, Rome, February 27, 1947

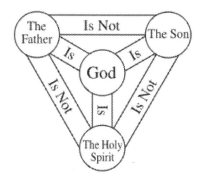

It was his turn to say grace.

"Father, Son and the Holy Ghost, he who eats the fastest, gets the most!" Handing me the basket of bread, he started up.

"Do we really believe in the Holy Ghost?'

"The Holy Ghost?" I repeated.

"Yes, the so-called 'third person' of the Holy Trinity.

"For starters, there is no hint of a Holy Trinity in the Bible.

"In both the Old Testament and the New Testament, the Holy Ghost is the same person as is the Father.

"For example, in His insemination of Mary, the Holy Ghost is the Father. Thus, God the Father is the Father of Jesus.

"If the Holy Ghost is a separate person from God the Father, then the Holy Ghost would be the Father of Jesus."

He started to ramble on and on with more examples of the Holy Ghost representing the Father from the Old and the New Testament...

I held up my hand, "Enough. Enough. You don't have to prove it. I get the point. The Holy Ghost is the same person as the Father.

Two Persons in One God

"Yet, one might consider Christ and His Father as being different 'persons' as they come from opposite ends of the political arena.

"Christ is a 'God of love and compassion.' God the Father is a 'God of fear and hatred.' John's verse, 'I and my Father are one' could not have been further from the truth.

"When the mob threatens to stone the prostitute to death as required by His Father, Jesus stops them: 'He who is without sin, cast the first stone.' On the Sabbath, Jesus walks in the fields with His disciples picking corn in violation of His Father's commandment to keep the Sabbath Holy…"

He rambled on and on… Again, I had to stop him.

"You don't have to prove it. Jesus and His Father are two different people."

He sealed up his case, "Anyone, from the most brilliant scholar to the slowest child, would come to the same conclusion, there are two persons in the Christian God: Jesus and His Father.

"How is it possible, the Nicene Council—the leading theologians in the world at the time—missed the boat?

"The answer is not 'how' but 'why.' Why did the Nicene Council ignore the Bible and feign three persons in the Christian God?

Islamism vs. Christianity

"Belief in the Holy Trinity is the dividing line between a Muslim and a Christian. While Muhammad recognized Christ as a great prophet, he concluded Christ was not God.

"It does not take a theological genius to discern Christ is not God. Christ repeatedly contradicts His Father. If Christ was the same God as His Father, He would be contradicting Himself.

"For example, we know, Christ could not have possibly been the God who ordered the horrific taking of the Promised Land: 'take to the sword, every man, women and child; let not one remain alive…'

"It boggles the imagination that Christians believe Christ is the same God who impregnated Mary. As much as if to say, Christ was His own Father. Einstein was right: *'faith is the opposite of reason.'*

"Muhammad discounted the canon of the Nicene Council as political aspirations of mortal men. Rather he based his thesis on the divine testimony of the first gospel—Mark—and the Old Testament.

"Christ isn't God and the Holy Ghost is the same person as is God the Father. Hence, consistent with both the New Testament and the Old Testament, Islamism has no Holy Trinity.

"Muhammad realized Christianity preyed on the ignorance and gullibility of the masses. He sought to build his church on logic.

"Hence, In Islam, there is only one God—the Father.

"Yes," I agreed. "It boggles the mind that members of the Nicene Council ignored the Bible, and declared there were three persons in one God. I wonder where they got that idea?"

"They stole it." The little rascal had set me up.

"They stole it?" I looked at him for an explanation.

"Yes, they stole it. Want to know from whom?"

I gave him the 'nod.' He opened up a new chapter.

East meets west

"Christ, at His time, was not aware of the Hindus in the East. He was not aware of the existence of another God on the other side of the planet who predated Him by thousands of years.

"His ministry did not provide salvation for those in the East: 'Unless one be baptized, one cannot enter the Kingdom of Heaven.' One certainly could not be baptized if one had never heard of baptism.

"Tell me, when did those in Rome first become aware of the existence of another God on the other side of the planet?"

He waited for an answer. As usual, he came up empty handed.

"Though it did not happen overnight, history places the event at about the turn of the 4th century, three hundred years after Christ, about a generation before the time of the Nicene Council."

I stopped him, "You can't prove that."

"Yes, I can. Every single surviving Roman manuscript predating 300AD is printed on papyri. Not the tiniest scrap predating that time has ever been found printed on parchment. Conversely, no surviving Roman manuscript postdating 325AD has ever been found printed on papyri; they are all printed on parchment.

"Parchment—paper—an immensely superior writing surface vs. papyri—was developed in China in 105AD. So, we know with a slight margin for error, those in Rome first became aware of the Hindu God at about the same time Constantine happened to come to power.

"When the Nicene Council convened in 325AD, its members had very recently become aware of the Hindu *Trimurti.*"

He opened a large picture book. "Here is the Hindu 'crucifix' in the Vedas more than a thousand years before Christ. As it remains today, a Holy Trinity. Three persons in one God.

"This ancient image of God with three heads is in the *Samhitas* c.a. 1201BC held by the National Museum of China in Beijing.

Hindu Trimurti   1201BC   Christian Trinity   325AD

Brahma, the Father, the Creator   God the Father, the Creator
Vishnu is God   Holy Ghost is God
Shiva, the Redeemer   Christ, the Redeemer

"Whereas not the tiniest scrap of the Bible predates the Nicene Council in 325AD, the Chinese had developed silk—a durable writing surface vs. papyri of the west—in the 4th millennium BC. Hence, substantial ancient texts of the Hindu God have survived.

"That the founding fathers of the Catholic Church stole the idea of a Holy Trinity from the Hindus, is clearly demonstrated in that they assigned identical functions to the three persons in the Christian God as was held by the three persons in the Hindu God.

"Again, one must apply a bit of common sense. The three persons in the Hindu God are of identical morality. They are all Gods of love and compassion; it makes sense they could be the same God.

"Conversely, the Christian Holy Trinity makes no sense.

"Christ is a God of love and compassion. His Father is a God of fear and hatred. The Holy Ghost has no mind of His own.

"Other than the preacher's claim *'The soul is something we don't understand,'* there is no better example of the *fog of faith* than is the *Holy Trinity*. The 'expert' says something that makes absolutely no sense at all, and the gullible sheep stake their eternity on it."

He gave me a chance. "Do you really believe the same God who has endowed us with reason and intellect has intended us to forego their use; we would believe God is both a deity, and a man, and a ghost; none of which is the same person?"

Having flogged that horse to death, he changed both his subject and his victim. "Mom, did you ever wonder why Jesus did not know that His brother Brahma was ruling on the other side of the world?"

Silence. He had caught her off guard as does a teacher in class.

He smiled, "They didn't have cell phones back then."

Brushing his chin with a napkin, he got up.

Circling the table, he stacked the plates on his arm as does a waiter in a five star restaurant in an upscale Parisian hotel.

Disappearing into the kitchen, "I wonder. I wonder…"

I called out after him, "You wonder what?"

Turning back, "I wonder how they work…"

"What works?" I called out after him, once more.

"Cell phones." He winked back.

"I wonder if…? I wonder if they know how they work?"

"You wonder if who knows how they work." I called after him.

He pointed upwards. "The Gods."

Not the tiniest scrap of the Christian Bible predates the Nicene Council in 325AD. The oldest reliable Hebrew texts are the 9th century AD *Torah* and the 10th century AD *Aleppo Codex* (British Library). Christians don't believe in the Hebrew Bible. They believe in the 4th & 5th century AD Greek Old Testament and New Testament; the earliest being *Codex Sinaiticus* (325-360AD) held by the British Library

Changing Times

"It was the best of times. It was the worst of times. Above all, it was changing times…"

Charles Dickens

We no sooner sat down, he started up again.

"As I was saying, the Nicene Council had two jobs. It had to define the Christian God and then establish apostolic succession to that God.

"With two to choose from, Christians were confused as to who was their God. Was it God the Father? Was it Christ?

"This confusion had its origin in the Gospel of Mark.

"'Son of Man' is the most prolific phrase in Mark's gospel. Too, Mark makes no mention of a virgin birth; at the time the absolute prerequisite to 'Son of God' in both Greek and Roman mythology.

"From the 1st to the 4th century, Dionysus—sired by the Greek God Zeus of a human virgin—was the predominate Roman God.

"Too, among mortals, Alexander the Great was held to have been born of a virgin and therefore revered as 'Son of God.'

"Worse yet, in the Gospel of Mark, Christ repeatedly denies He is God: 'Jesus said unto him, Why callest me good? There is none good but one, And that one is God.' Again in Mark: 'You will always have your poor …but you will not always have me.' God is infinite. We will always have God.

"In the Gospel of Mark, Christ is not God.

"A generation or two later, the gospels of Matthew and Luke come along and add the virgin birth and change <u>Son of Man</u> to <u>Son of God</u>. Christ is now on the level of Dionysus and Alexander the Great.

"Not good enough. At the turn of the 2nd century, the evangelist John suggests Christ is the same God as His Father: 'I and my Father are one.' The only bit in the gospels one might interpret as Christ claiming to be God. Yet, it could mean Christ shared His Father's ideology.

"Nevertheless, excepting this vague tidbit 'I and my Father are one.' the testimony of Christ in the gospels affirms Christ is not God.

"Setting all this aside, when did Christ become God? The oldest surviving texts of the gospels tell us when He became God.

A great mystery

"No reliable scrap of the gospels has ever been found predating the Nicene Council in 325AD. Yet, the gospels clearly provided the fabric for the Council. After all, they were what it was all about.

"When the Council came to a close, the gospel manuscripts that had served as the blueprint for its proceedings would customarily have been preserved. After all, they represented the divine authority for the founding documents of the Holy Roman Catholic Church.

"Keep in mind, while there was no organized church in Rome prior to the Nicene Council, there was an organized church after its time.

"Yet, today, no surviving gospel manuscript dates back before the Nicene Council." He shot me a quizzical glance.

"Don't you find that strange?" he waited.

No response. "That they did not survive is compelling evidence the gospel manuscripts evaluated by the Council were destroyed. They did not fit in with the political ambitions of the founding fathers."

He opened a book to its center page.

		Oldest Gospel Manuscripts		Nicene Council	
				↓	
Ca. A.D.	150	200	250	325-375	375-475
			←papyri------parchment→		
Mark			b	c&d	e&f
Matthew			b	c&d	e&f
Luke			b	c&d	e&f
John	a		b	c&d	e&f

a = *Rylands Papyri* tiny fragment of a part of an insignificant Gospel of John verse. If the gospel was written after 150AD, one could have plagiarized the verse. Date is based solely on paleography. Consensus dates it as late as the 3rd century.
b = sporadic verses widely considered unreliable as they contain countless scribal errors. In total they comprise less than 1% of the gospels
c = *Codex Sinaiticus* (325-360AD) Greek Old/New Testament, British Library.
d = *Codex Vaticanus* (350-375AD) Greek Old/New Testament, Vatican
e = *Codex Alexandrinus* (375-425AD) Greek Old/New Testament, British Library.
f = *Codex Ephraemi Rescriptus* (400-475AD) Old/New Testament, Library France

"Very important, too, there exists not the tiniest scrap of any of Paul's writings that predate the 4th century *Codex Sinaiticus.*

"Most of the three hundred bishops attending the Nicene Council were Greek. Only five were from the west. All surviving manuscripts predating the 6th century are in Greek. Not a scrap in another tongue.

"Insofar as the *Codex Sinaiticus*—the oldest surviving gospels— contains the *Eusebian Canons*—a product of the Nicene Council—is compelling evidence the gospels—as we know them today—were not written by Mark, Matthew, Luke and John toward the turn of the 1st century, but were a product of the Nicene Council in the 4th century.

"This does not necessarily mean the gospels were not originally written by the evangelists. Just that the Council manipulated them to fit its political agenda at the time. This is not unusual, as men have been changing the Bible to fit their political agendas ever since."

I stopped him, "...changing the Bible?"

"For starters, we know this to be true of St. Jerome."

"St. Jerome?" A dumbfounded look gave away my ignorance.

"Yes, St. Jerome," not surprised I had never heard of him.

"Late in the 4th century, Jerome is said to have been commissioned by the sitting pope to write the Vulgate—the first Bible combining all 39 books of the Old Testament together with the New Testament.

"The Old Testament, as you know," he said it in a way that he knew I did not know, "is an exact genealogy from Adam to Christ."

He recited: "'Adam – Seth – Enos – Cainan – Mahalalcel – Jarcd – Enoch – Methuselah – Lamech – Noah – Shem – Arphaxad – Salah – Eber – Peleg – Reu – Serug – Terah – Abraham – Isaac – Jacob – Judas – Phares – Esrom – Aram – Aminadab – Naasson – Sakmon – Booz – Obed – Jesse - King Solomon - King David – Roboam – Abia – Josaphat – Joram – Ozias – Joatham – Achaz – Mahasses –Amon – Josias – Jechonias – Salathiel – Zorobable – Abiud – Eliakim – Azor – Sadoc – Achim – Eliud – Mattham – Jacob - Joseph—the father of Christ.'

79

"It gives the age of death of every one of them and the age at which all but three of them sired his firstborn. One knows who was whose father, and who was whose son, all the way from Adam to Christ.

"In ancient times, with no social practices restricting age at which one sired one's firstborn, average generation length was sixteen. 55 generations multiplied by 16 equals 900BC for Adam and Eve.

"Modern Bibles tell us something else. Those patriarchs who lived between the time of the first pharaoh—3100BC—and the time of Moses—1213BC—lived to an average age of 273.

"Conversely, forensic analysis establishes the average lifespan of the pharaohs for the same period at 38, and the oldest, Ramesses II, lived to the extraordinary age of 86.

"The patriarchs who came earlier—3100BC to 4000BC—lived even longer. Adam who lived 940 years was still alive when the Pharaoh Narmer established the Egyptian Empire in 3100BC.

"When Jerome first put the books of the Old Testament together in chronological order in a single volume, he would have realized if these patriarchs had lived normal lifespans, counting backwards from Christ's time, it would place the creation of Adam and Eve sixteen hundred years after the great pyramids had been built.

"Because the genealogy between Adam and Christ was unbroken, inserting patriarchs was not an alternative. The only option he had was to add extraordinary lifetimes to the early patriarchs to push the date back toward 4000BC. Acceptable then, but not today. As we now know, mankind goes back hundreds of thousands of years before then.

Slavery

"We have already demonstrated that the Bible is the record of ancient politicians in the western world. Yet, modern preachers have been changing it to meet their own political agendas in more recent times. Usually just a word or two is changed, added or deleted.

"For example, in all bibles predating 1881 and in the Jewish Torah today, the Tenth Commandment reads: 'Thou shalt not covet (desire to take from) thy neighbor his property, including his house, his wife, his slaves, his ox, his ass…' God explicitly decrees woman to be property of man and protects the right of one man to enslave another.

"Modern bibles read: 'Thou shalt not covet thy neighbor… his house, his wife, his servants, his ox, his ass…' 'Slaves' no longer good for business.

Homosexuality

"In the oldest surviving texts—*Vaticanus* and *Sinaiticus*—Luke 17 34-36 reads: 'I will tell you in that night there shall be two men in the same <u>boat</u> together; the one shall be taken and the other shall be left. Two women shall be grinding <u>grain</u> together; the one shall be taken and the other shall be left....'

"Christ is speaking of granting workers rest periods.

"In all bibles after the Council of Trent in 1563, Christ disapproves of homosexuality: 'I will tell you in that night there shall be two men in the same <u>bed</u> together; the one shall be taken and the other shall be left. Two women shall be grinding <u>grain</u> together; the one shall be taken and the other shall be left...'

"In 1973, the psychiatric community declared homosexuality a matter of instinct and no longer a mental disorder. Women rose up as leaders of the gay movement. Jesus had never condemned lesbians.

"In 1979, *The New King James Bible* covered the bases: 'I will tell you in that night there shall be two men in <u>the same bed together</u>; the one shall be taken and the other shall be left. Two women shall be <u>grinding together</u>; the one shall be taken and the other shall be left...' Jesus condemns lesbians.

"Changing the word '<u>boat</u>' to '<u>bed</u>' and deleting the word '<u>grain</u>' completely changes the context from <u>workers</u> to <u>sex</u>.

"Regardless, in that not the tiniest scrap of the manuscripts which provided the substance for council proceedings have survived, it is reasonable to conclude the gospels as they have survived today were a product of the Nicene Council.

"As not the tiniest scrap has survived, we have no idea what Mark, Matthew, Luke and John wrote. In fact, we do not know if they wrote the gospels attributed to them at all. All we really do know is that the gospels as we know them today were written in the 4th century."

Not good enough. "What's more, the gospels have been changed through the years to fit in with the changing political agendas of men."

The Council of Trent not only established the canon condemning homosexuality but the canon all sex is sinful. The *gnostic* gospels (not discussed here) are writings of Jesus excluded from the canonical texts by the Nicene Council. Two of them— *'Thomas'* and *'Judas'* dated to the 3rd century—contain conflicting testimony vs. the canonical gospels. Readers are encouraged to search reliable Internet/library sources. Search <u>*The New King James Bible*</u> Luke 17 34-36. Search same verse in other bibles. Search: the original 10th commandment in the Jewish Torah...

In Search of Jesus

"The overwhelming number of the world's great historical figures have been born into utter obscurity."

American Historical Association

Jesus Christ

He was deeply engrossed in a stack of old newspaper clippings he had obviously copied from microfilm at the library. A book lay off to one side: *The Quest of the Historical Jesus.*

I should have stayed away. "What are you up to this time?"

Looking up at me, "I am searching for Jesus."

"Is this some kind of a joke?" ridiculing his opening.

"The Search for the Historical Jesus, begun by Reimarus in the eighteenth century and followed by a long line of the world's most brilliant theologians and historians, was finally put to rest by Nobel Laureate, Albert Schweitzer, in 1905.

"Schweitzer and his predecessors clearly established the gospels as theological and not historical documents.

"These men clearly established Christ as a theoretical figure and not a historical figure. Christ was not a man, but an ideology.

"Still true today. Despite centuries of investigations, leaving no leaf unturned, no one has ever been able to find the tiniest trace of evidence that a man, as described in the gospels, ever lived.

"As we have said, the gospels, as we know them today, were written in the 4th and 5th centuries, more than three hundred years after Jesus is alleged to have lived. One could have written most anything.

"Too, as a matter-of-fact, *The Search for the Historical Jesus* has been going on for almost two thousand years.

"Constantine, himself, tried to prove such a man had actually lived. In 315AD, he dispatched his mother St. Helena to the Holy Land. After fifteen years, the best she was able to come up with were three small bloodstained fragments that she claimed had been taken from Christ's cross. They are in the Vatican today."

He handed me a question mark. "Ever wonder why the Vatican has never submitted these fragments together with the blood of the Shroud and Christ's alleged foreskin held by the Vatican for DNA testing?"

No answer from me. I was not going to fall into a trap.

He answered his own question, "The same reason it has never submitted St. Peter's alleged bones for carbon dating analysis.

"Regardless, after Constantine came Muhammad who traveled to Jerusalem. That he could not find any trace of Christ's miracles, he concluded Christ was not God. Christ was only a prophet.

"If nothing more, common sense told him, if the miracles had actually been performed before multitudes of Jews as set forth in the gospels, the Jews would have accepted Christ as God.

"About a thousand etchings of events of the time, including about a hundred events in Herod's life—said to be the principal historical figure in Christ's life—have survived. If Jesus had performed any of the miracles attributed to Him, certainly someone would have etched a few of them into time. But not a thing. Not a trace.

"Muhammad viewed the miracles as embellishments worked into Christ's life by His biographers whoever they may have been.

"This is demonstrated by the gospels themselves. Mark gives us a few miracles, Matthew adds a few of his own, Luke adds a few more, and, John adds those the others left out.

"The Vatican has never challenged Schweitzer's conclusion in *The Quest of the Historical Jesus*. Canon Law clearly holds Christ to be a theological and not a historical figure.

"In Canon Law, Christ is not a matter-of-fact; He is a matter-of-faith. The reason all creeds begin with *'I believe...'*

"There is not a seminary in the world that teaches history. Seminaries teach theology..." He thought a bit.

"To tell it, as it really is, seminaries teach political science."

"Political science?" I mused.

83

He explained, "Theology is the study of tales told by ancient men to attain political ambitions. Seminaries teach students how to use these same tales to their own political advantage today."

He decided to remove the tiniest bit of wiggle room for the so-called 'expert' to challenge his declaration.

"If it were possible to attend, in one's lifetime, all the history classes of all the universities of the world since the beginning of time, one would never hear the words 'Jesus Christ.'

"One will learn of pharaohs from Narmer to Cleopatra, and men like Aristotle, Plato, Alexander, Confucius, Buddha, Tao, Caesar, Diocletian, Constantine, Marco Polo, Muhammad, Charlemagne, Genghis Kahn, Guttenberg, Galileo, Da Vinci, Magellan, Columbus, Michelangelo, Napoleon, Washington, Lincoln, Pasteur, Bell, Edison, Tesla, Salk, Darwin, Einstein, Lenin, Hitler, Churchill, Roosevelt and millions of others. The overwhelming number of which were born into obscurity. Yet, one will never hear the words 'Jesus Christ.'

"Despite this astounding historical fact, Christ is believed by most Christians to have been the most notable person who ever lived."

He stared me down, "Jesus never lived. I should have been told this when I was told Santa Claus was not for real. You brought me up in a world of make-believe.

"Again, if we are ever to satisfy ourselves there is a God, if we are ever to satisfy ourselves we will live forever, if we are ever to remove the question mark from the end of our lives; we must first remove the assumption we are born into. Otherwise, the little grey cells cannot do their work." He stared me down again.

Having no defense, I escaped to the bar.

"Coke?" I offered as I poured the Jack Daniels over the ice.

The first class relic held by the Vatican and believed to be the foreskin of Jesus was given by Charlemagne to Pope Leo III in the ninth century. One of St. Helena's blood stained fragments is concealed in the cross a pope wears on formal occasions.

Sherlock Holmes

"Yet, Christ is not alone.

"There are countless examples of fictional characters created by authors, people think of as having actually lived. In ancient times, we have Adam and Eve, Noah, Abraham and even Moses.

"In more modern times, we have Sherlock Holmes, Hercule Poirot, Miss Marple and countless others. To the toddler, Mickey Mouse and Donald Duck are presumed to have lived.

"Concerning Holmes. Today, we have the flat on Baker Street and the haunts both he and Watson frequented; creations of entrepreneurs making a buck or two in the marketplace of make-believe.

"In the case of Jesus, we have His birthplace, the upstairs room of the last supper, the garden He prayed in, the cobblestones He carried His cross upon, and the box containing the bones of His brother James. Again, all creations of entrepreneurs making a buck or two in the marketplace of make-believe.

"All of these tourist attractions in the Holy Land happened to have been 'discovered' in the past fifty years by entrepreneurs who got the idea from Holmes' and Watson's flat and haunts in London.

"Historians refer to these 'discoveries' as *The Second Search for the Historical Jesus*. The first one having completely failed.

Eugene Francois Vidocq alias *Sherlock Holmes*

"We think of Sherlock Holmes as a fictitious character; he never really lived. Conversely, we think of Jesus Christ as a man who did live. Just the reverse is true."

I gave him a look as if he had lost his mind. It didn't work.

"Arthur Conan Doyle based his character *Sherlock Holmes* on the French author Emile Gaboriau's character *Monsieur Lecoq*.

"Gaboriau, in turn, had based his character *Monsieur Lecoq* on a real-life-thief-turned-detective Eugene Francois Vidocq. Vidocq had developed the analysis and deduction techniques exploited by Doyle.

"Like Gaboriau before him, Doyle keyed his first few stories on actual events in Vidocq's life and made up the rest of them.

"Gaboriau embellished the life of Vidocq, and Doyle further embellished it, in the same way the succession of Matthew, Luke and John embellished the life of Christ as originally portrayed by Mark. Each one adding tales of their own, as they went along.

"So realistically did Doyle base Sherlock Holmes on the life of Eugene Francois Vidocq, Gaboriau fell quickly into obscurity.

"Had Gaboriau been the better writer, we would have heard only of his character *Monsieur Lecoq*." He paused.

"We would be visiting *Lecoq's* flat and haunts in Paris instead of *Holmes'* and *Watson's* lodgings and haunts in London."

I cut him off, "Speaking of doctors, you've finally flipped your lid. We are going to have to look for one."

He didn't bat an eye. "Although the two thousand year search for the historical Jesus by the world's greatest historians and theologians, failed to get Christ into the history books, one can look up the life of 'Eugene Francois Vidocq' in libraries and on the Internet."

He sealed his case. "As a matter-of-fact, Sherlock Holmes is a historical figure who lived under the name Eugene Francois Vidocq.

"Yet, in the case of Christ, all we have is a story." He stopped.

"Mark who wrote of a man who denied he was God. Matthew, Luke and John who plagiarized Mark and added the virgin birth and resurrection, transforming Him into a God."

He sent a shiver down my back. "A story, as it has survived today, written three hundred years after it was alleged to have taken place."

Not good enough, "One could have written most anything."

Search 'Eugene Francois Vidocq' reliable Internet and library sources.

Divine Witness

"Consistent with the gospels themselves, history tells us none of those who wrote of Christ's life witnessed His ministry.

"No historian places the gospels prior to the earliest dates they are known to have been written. All historians agree the order in which the gospels were written: Mark-Matthew-Luke-John."

I challenged him, "You can't tell when they were written. For that matter, the order in which they were written. As you have said, not a scrap of the original manuscripts survived."

As usual he held the cards. "The gospels themselves tell us the order in which they were written.

"Mark speaks of <u>Son of Man</u>. In Mark, Christ denies he is God.

"Matthew plagiarizes Mark taking care to change <u>Son of Man</u> to <u>Son of God</u> wherever it appears. Consistent with Greek mythology he adds the virgin birth and the resurrection to support this change.

"Had Mark followed Matthew, he surely would have not omitted the most fundamental doctrine of Christ's divinity: The Virgin Birth. This alone tells us, Mark wrote the first gospel.

"It is that Matthew begins his gospel with the birth of Christ, and Mark does not, modern bibles begin with Matthew.

"Luke plagiarizes Matthew, changing the tale of the virgin birth.

"John adds 'I and my Father are one' transforming Christ into God.

"So we know the order in which they were written. Yet, we don't know when they were written. But we do know the earliest date each of the gospels could have possibly been written because each of them speaks of historical events which did not occur until certain times.

"For example, Mark refers to the destruction of the Temple of Jerusalem in past tense which occurred in 70AD. Thus, we know, the Gospel of Mark could not have possibly been written before that time.

"Likewise Matthew and Luke were written after 85AD as they refer to historical events which did not occur until that time.

"For this same reason, the Gospel of John could not have possibly been written before 95AD.

"All history books date the gospels to these earliest possible dates. Yet, most historians contend the gospels were written much later."

He set a sheet in front of me.

"The progression of Christ's creation. Each biographer expanding Christ's life as they went along. In the same way, Gaboriau and Doyle inflated the life of Eugene Francois Vidocq as they went along.

Earliest possible date content and embellishments

Christ	6BC-29/32AD*	
Mark	70AD	'Son of Man' – Christ is not God - no after-death appearances
Matthew	85AD	'Son of God' – adds Virgin Birth & resurrection
Luke	85AD	'Son of God' – different version of the Virgin Birth
John	95AD	'I and my Father are one' – Christ is God

*Herod died in 4BC. Allowing two years for the killing of newborns Christ is born in 6BC. Ministry began in *the15th year of the reign of Tiberius Caesar'* or 29BC. Assumes 3 years.

"Setting the historical record aside, the gospels, themselves, tell us none of those who wrote of it witnessed Christ's ministry except John who claims to be '…the Disciple John who bore witness to Christ's testament.'

"The evangelist John could not have possibly been the disciple John because the Gospel of John could not have possibly been written earlier than the turn of the 2nd century. Had he been Christ's disciple, he would have been a senile old man of a hundred years plus when he wrote his book, at a time the average life expectancy was forty.

"We know the earlier evangelists did not witness the events in Christ's life they speak of, for a much more telling reason."

I repeated in a question, "…for a much more telling reason?"

"It is the testimony of Mark, Matthew and Luke that they did not witness events they speak of. Surely, if they had witnessed any part of Christ's ministry, they would have told us so.

"What's more, they don't divulge their sources. They make no mention of others who may have witnessed Christ's ministry."

He looked up at me, searching for a questionable expression which was not there. "Don't you think that strange?"

"Strange? They had Divine Witness. God!" I stopped him.

"From the beginning of time, nonfiction writers have divulged their sources. Conversely, fiction writers have no sources. Other than direct witness, it is the only difference between nonfiction and fiction. There is only one reason why they did not disclose their sources."

"One reason why?" not sure what he meant.

"They had no sources. They were writing fiction." He paused for a moment, the time it took for the hairs to run up and down my back.

"The source of fiction is the human mind. The source of faith is the human mind. I will leave that for you to ponder with your soul.

"The bottom line is, had Mark, Matthew and Luke witnessed any part of Christ's ministry, they surely would have told us so.

"The best we can hope is that they relied on dependable hearsay as passed on to them from generation to generation.

The facts vs. the politics of men

"The preacher claims the evangelists were contemporaries of Christ.

"Yet, when one separates the facts… from the probabilities... from the possibilities… from the politics of men… this is nothing more than someone saying something to one's political advantage.

"The fact is we don't know when the gospels were written other than they couldn't have possibly been written earlier than 70-95AD at least two generations after Christ's alleged crucifixion.

"All we do know is that the gospels as we know them to be today were written in the 4th and 5th century AD.

"With a three hundred year gap between the time the gospels as we know them to be today were written and Christ's time, without any technological means to record events as they may have happened, one could have written most anything to support one's political agenda.

"We also know these 4th and 5th century texts have been materially changed along the way to support the changing politics of men."

Gospels as they are today are sourced from the 4th and 5th century uncial codices.

Divine Intervention

I hoped he would lose his train of thought. It didn't work.

"Yet, the problem is not so much that Matthew, Mark, Luke and John did not witness Christ's miracles...

"The real problem we have is that history did not witness a single one of them. Here again, whenever we apply the little grey cells, we must not only consider the evidence which is there, but the evidence which should be there, and is not there.

"It was commonplace in Christ's time, as it was in ancient times, for people to record events in civilization on clay tablets and other mediums. As we've said, there are over twenty million etchings of human figures in the tombs depicting each and every event in the three thousand year history of ancient Egypt.

"What's more, the British Library holds over twenty thousand clay tablets detailing historical events in the Mideast. About a thousand of these date to the first century. The overwhelming number of which involve common men who did notable things.

"About a hundred of these depict events in Herod's life, the chief historical figure in Christ's alleged life; but no mention of Christ.

"The thirty-five miracles attributed to Christ would have been the most stupendous events of the time: feeding of tens of thousands with two fish and five loaves of bread, the changing of water into wine ...

"Most of these were witnessed by multitudes and occurred within an area equivalent to a small city today. It is not reasonable to believe, no one bothered to leave a single etching of any of Christ's miracles or, for that matter, any of the other astounding events in Christ's life.

"His virgin birth, resurrection and ascension certainly would have inspired the chisel of the most casual of artists; but not a trace for four hundred years after these events are said to have occurred.

"Of course, one has the possibility of divine intervention."

"Divine intervention?" I shot him a look of utter confusion.

"Yes, the preacher can cling to the supernatural. God destroyed every last trace of evidence Christ had ever lived." He stopped to give me time for this possibility to smother my mind.

"Nevertheless, we have some answers here."

"Answers?" To me, he had just raised more questions.

"This tells us why John took a chance and lied in his gospel; '...I am the Disciple John who bore witness to Christ's testament.'

"The others could not take that chance, as they, being closer to Christ's time, could not claim to have been one of His disciples unless they had actually been so, or others who had been alive at Christ's time would have disclosed their deception.

"One cannot write of events that didn't happen today and convince people they did happen. Yet, one can write about them generations afterwards and convince the most gullible of souls they did happen. Particularly, at a time there was no technological means to record the past. We know this was true of Moses. It was also true of Christ.

He had said it before. He would say it again. Yet, this time he raised his voice in capital letters as to leave no wiggle room for the doubter:

"THE ONLY ABSOLUTE FACT WE HAVE IS THE GOSPELS, AS WE KNOW THEM TODAY, WERE WRITTEN IN THE 4TH AND 5TH CENTURIES MORE THAN THREE HUNDRED YEARS AFTER CHRIST IS ALLEGED TO HAVE LIVED. ONE COULD HAVE WRITTEN ANYTHING TO SUPPORT ONE'S POLITICAL AGENDA.

"Nevertheless, there is a greater gap in the life of Jesus Christ vs. reality than His void in the history books, the belated timing of the writing of the gospels, and the lack of witness of His biographers." He gave me a chance. Nothing came forth.

Getting up, he strolled over to the fireplace, stoked the fire a bit, added a log, and returned to his place at the table.

Header: One of the clay tablets held by the British Museum depicting Herod's life

Rob Peter to Pay Paul

"If we set aside fantasy and stick with the facts, The Greatest Story Ever Told—as we know it today—was written three hundred years after it is said to have taken place."

Albino Luciani

"That Peter remained silent for the forty years he is said to have lived beyond Christ's time, staggers the imagination.

"Peter is said to have witnessed all of Christ's miracles including having been the firsthand witness of Christ's resurrection: 'The Lord has arisen indeed and has appeared to Peter.'

"More remarkable is Paul. Though he claims he received the power to forgive sins directly from Christ in an apparition, according to his own testimony, Paul did not witness any part of Christ's ministry. Paul claims he learned of the crucifixion, the forgiveness of sins and the resurrection of the body from Peter.

Paul the Entrepreneur

"Paul founded Christianity as a money-making business—passing the hat for silver and gold in exchange for forgiveness of sins and the promise of the resurrection of the body: 'We are the ambassadors of Christ who has passed solely to us the power to forgive sins and pave the way to life everlasting... If the dead are not raised, Christ has not been raised...'

"Like the God of the Old Testament, Paul drives his sheep to his door with fear; threatening eternal damnation for those who don't drop their alms into his box in trade for absolution.

"Paul condemns practically anything one could do: 'Be ye not deceived, neither fornicators, nor idolaters, nor adulterers, nor effeminates, nor masturbators, nor thieves, nor covetous... nor revilers... nor envious, nor murderers, nor debaters, nor deceitful, nor maliciousness, nor malignity, nor whisperers, nor backbiters, nor infidels... nor celebrators, nor proud, nor boasters, nor covenant breakers, nor disobedience... shall inherit the Kingdom of God.'

"Nor revilers? Nor celebrators? Nor masturbators? Paul covered the bases. One could not even have a good time without having to pay Paul. No wonder they robbed Peter to pay Paul.

"If Paul didn't forgive one, one would surely go to Hell. It was the unique power of priests to forgive sin and the promise of resurrection of the body which built the Church into what it is today.

"The Nicene Council founded the Roman Catholic Church, not so much on the gospels, as they did on Paul's epistles.

"Based on their historical content, Paul's epistles could have been written as early as 53AD. Yet, like the gospels, no one knows what he may have written or if he wrote anything at all, as not the tiniest scrap of his writings has survived that predate the Nicene Council.

"As is true of the gospels, Paul's epistles as we know them today were written in the 4th century more than three hundred years after his source—Peter—is alleged to have lived."

I figured I had him this time. "You can't prove Peter never lived."

He didn't hesitate. "Yes, I can. Providential coincidence!

Providential coincidence

"Peter is said to have died in 67AD."

"What is so providential about that?" I chided him.

"Like Christ, Peter is a theological figure, not a historical figure. Other than Paul is said to have written of 'Peter' and cites him as his witness, there is no record such a man ever lived.

"Peter is 'believed' to have died in 67AD because after that time nothing more is heard of him."

"That makes sense." I agreed.

"Yes, it makes a lot of sense," the little detective agreed.

"Paul died in 67AD. His creation 'Peter' died with him."

The fire sparked three times. I think four times… five times,,, No. I don't really recall how many times.

My mind was done for the day. My faith was done for life.

Paul's condemnations permeate *Romans* and *Corinthians*. Self-appointed 'experts' claim Peter wrote the *Epistles of Peter*. Despite the title, they were written by Paul. Though according to their content they could have been written as early as 53AD, not the tiniest scrap of any of Paul's epistles predate the Nicene Council in 325AD. Paul's epistles as we know them today were written in the 4th century.

The Black Mass

'...they made cloths of service, to do service in the holy place, and made the holy garments of Aaron and his sons and the sons of his sons... the apron of the high priest of pure gold and garments of purple and scarlet of the finest linen trimmed with gold adorned with jewels of untold shekels... they sprinkled oil and incense upon the altar... golden and platinum vessels of jasper, of sapphire, of chalcedony, of emerald, of ruby, of beryl... that a lamp of gold may be set to burn forever... gather the assembly together in the tabernacle... set upon the altar of marble the blood offering to the savor of the Lord... The Lord hath commanded...'

Book of Exodus

We had just returned from Mass. The little rascal cornered me and dragged me down into his den. "Do you know where they got it?"

"Got what?"

"The Mass? Who dreamt up the idea of paying men to dress up in royal robes and prance about altars of marble and gold?"

As usual, I would let him answer his own question.

"Today Catholicism remains deeply steeped in the satanic rituals of Moses, tempered only by Jesus' substitution of harmless bread and wine that He cleverly traded for the lives of animals He so loved."

Opening his copy of the Old Testament, he flipped a few pages.

"It begins here in *Genesis*:

'Abraham built an altar and laid the wood in a row for a burnt sacrifice; he bound Isaac his son and laid him upon the altar on the wood. Abraham took the knife to slay his son and the angel gave him a young ram; Abraham slew the ram instead of his son and offered up a burnt offering.'

94

"Thus marked the beginning of the Holy Sacrifice of the Mass in Judea-Christian mythology—blood sacrifice of animals.

"So important is the requirement of blood sacrifice to his God, Moses drills the point home in every one of his books. The greatest volume of scripture concerning any issue in the Bible.

"In a horrific display of ghastly ritual and the occult, Moses forces an endless parade of frightened animals to the blade and pours their blood upon his altars to his God, preying particularly on the young:

'Take thee a young calf for a sin offering, a young ram for a burnt offering, a kid of the goats for a sin offering and a lamb for a burnt offering...'

"One by one, in a carnival of blood and morbid gore, Moses drags his tiny victims, each one shivering in fear, to his satanic altars of death. One by one, he slits their throats and pours their blood:

'Rip the tongue from the calf. Poke out the eyes with the iron... ready them for the edge of the axe... sort them to the savor of the lord...'

'Dip thee fingers in the blood and sprinkle the blood before the Lord; pour the blood upon the horns of the altar... it make sweet incense for the Lord'

"Moses orders his priests, blood dripping from their hands:

'Place the fat that is the innards, and the kidneys, and the fat that is the flanks, and the liver... Aaron's sons shall burn it on the altar; a sweet savor unto the Lord... Place the head on the altar to the delight of the lord...'"

He went on and on. I don't know for how long? I dozed off... He slapped his hand on the table. I came back to life.

"This practice of animal sacrifice continued into Jesus' time: 'Mary and Joseph offer a blood sacrifice … they slit the throats of turtledoves…'

He went on reading passages, this time from the New Testament, more blood and gore. It seemed it would go on forever...

"Okay. Enough, enough. You made your point." I cut him off.

"Yes, I guess that is enough. You get the point." Surprised, I had been able to get it so quickly.

Conceding that the Holy Sacrifice of the Mass is offered up to satisfy the bloodlust of the God of Moses, I would soften the blow. "Yet, we are not savages. We don't sacrifice animals today."

He read my mind, "We owe that to another God."

I agreed with him, "Yes, Jesus."

He corrected my misconception. "Not Jesus. We owe it to the God who promised to send His Son to save mankind. The God of Isaiah."

96

He opened to *Isaiah*. "Here, the compassionate God of Isaiah rebuffs those who mistake Him to be the bloodthirsty God of Moses:

> 'To what purpose is the multitude of your sacrifices unto me? I am full of burnt offerings of the rams and the fat of the fed beasts; and I delight not in the blood of the bullocks, or of the lambs, or of the goats. Bring me no more oblations; your savor is an abomination to me...'"

He flipped page after page, reading as he went along, for what seemed to be an eternity. The God of Isaiah differed from the God of Moses, not only on the issue at hand, but on every issue.

He finally wrapped up his case in Chapter 66 of *Isaiah*:

> "'He that killeth an ox or a lamb is as if he slew a man... He that sacrifices a lamb is as if he cut off a dog's neck... He that offers an oblation is as if he blessed an idol...'"

I had to give it to him, "Agreed. The God that spoke to Isaiah could not have possibly been the same God that spoke to Moses."

I reached for the straw, "Unless..."

"Unless what?" He gave me the chance.

I rolled the dice, "God can change His mind."

Ignoring my remark, he finished with a question mark. "Regardless, in Christ's time, the definition of a man believed to be 'Son of God' was 'born of a human virgin sired by God.' How did this ever come about?

Description of the altar in the Catholic Church: last five chapters of *Exodus*. Story of Isaac: *Genesis*. Animal sacrifice: first ten chapters of *Leviticus* and repeated in each of Moses' books; the greatest volume of scripture pertaining to any single issue in the Bible. Animal sacrifice continued in some eastern churches after Christ's time and was generally brought to an end in the 4th century except in parts of Armenia.

The centerpiece of Catholicism is idol worship of the God of Moses. Christ is reduced to a mere sacrificial lamb offered up to satisfy the bloodlust of the God of Moses in its Holy Sacrifice of the Mass. For the most part, Protestant sects focus adoration on Christ. Hence, no ritual of the Sacrifice of the Mass to Moses' God.

The Evolution of Jesus

"Religion evolves just like any other social practice. Each prophet building on the imagination of those who came before him."

Albino Luciani

He strolled over to a wall of windows and gazed out over the snow-covered swimming pool contemplating how he was going to simplify what he was about to say, so that even I could understand it.

Passing by the mini-fridge, he nodded. I passed on the Coke. Taking his place at the table, he snapped open the lid, took a sip, and told me what I should have learned in grade school.

"For centuries, the Jews had only the word of the God of Moses: 'Dust thou art, to dust thou wilt return.' Yet, they lived in a world in which all other religions provided one could live forever.

"To the south, were the Egyptians, who not only believed the spirit would survive death, but the body would resurrect as well.

"Beyond Egypt, lived the black Nubians, whose witchdoctors provided miracles in this life and eternal life in the spirit world.

"Beyond them, in the deepest darkest jungles of Africa, lived the cannibals who took pleasure in devouring human flesh and blood in their rituals honoring their holy spirits." I ignored his leering grin meant to pop the image of the Eucharist into my mind.

"To the north, was Dionysus..."

My ears perked up, "Dionysus?"

"Yes, the first God to come to earth to save mankind from sin.

Dionysus predates Jesus by more than a thousand years."

He answered my blank stare. "The Greek tablets. Opening a large volume *The British National Museum,* he read:

'Zeus, King of Gods, speaks, Hail my offspring who come upon thou to save thou from sin... counted by his people among thieves... suffered unto death... descended into Tartarus...Thou wilt rise again without lust ... rule eternal life.'

"In ancient Cretan Mythology, the God Zeus impregnates the Goddess Persephone and sends His Son 'Zagreus' to save mankind from sin.

"Alas, Zagreus is rejected by his chosen people—the Titans—who tear him apart and devour His flesh. Yet, they leave the heart.

"The Goddess Athena devours the heart, impregnating Herself—without lust—and bears a son, Dionysus. Born of a virgin Goddess."

The Reincarnation of Zagreus

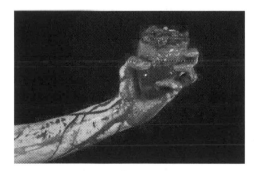 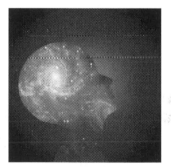

Death of Zagreus   Birth of Dionysus

Scratching his brow as if he had missed the boat, "Not good enough..." he mumbled to himself as he thumbed through a few more pages.

"In 349 BC, the Greek Phrygians take Dionysus a bit further:

Zeus hovers over the realm as an eagle... falls in love with the virgin daughter of Cadmus, Semele... comes as a thief in the night upon Semele... Dionysus is reborn of a human virgin... becomes God from man... rules eternal life...'

"Zeus rescues the fetus when Semele dies in pregnancy. Dionysus becomes the first God to be born of a virgin human being.

99

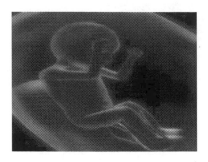

Dionysus is reborn. This time of the human virgin Semele

Alexander the Great

"Alexander the Great was the most prominent man in the world when the Phrygians came up with the idea that a God could be born of a human virgin. It follows, we have the enduring myth that Alexander had been born of a virgin. Thus, Son of God.

"That Alexander (356BC-323BC) lived thirty-three years, in turn, gave birth to the myth, all 'Sons of God' who followed Him would spend thirty-three years on earth. Thus, the misconception Jesus lived thirty-three years despite that the gospels give him at least thirty-eight.

"When the Romans conquered Phrygia (Turkey) in 133BC, they adopted the Greek God Dionysus, Son of God born of a mortal virgin.

The Secret Prophecy

"It follows, a few years later, the prophecy of Jesus in *Isaiah:*

> 'Behold, a virgin shall conceive and bear a son… butter and honey shall he eat, that he may know to refuse the evil, and choose the good…'

He turned the page:

> '…rejected by his people… numbered with transgressors… He bare the sin of many… made intercession for the transgressors... poured out his soul unto death… descended to hell… rose again… he will come to rule eternal life…'"

"Seems like we just heard that, didn't we?" He waited to no avail.

"Relative to Christianity, this is the only thing that counts in the Old Testament. The only thing that links the Old Testament to Christ."

I grabbed ahold of his bible. Sure enough it was there.

Stunned, I wondered why the nuns kept this a secret from me. Did they know it? I wondered why Father John had never mentioned the only verse in the Old Testament that counts in his sermons.

'BUTTER AND HONEY SHALL HE EAT THAT HE MAY KNOW TO REFUSE THE EVIL, AND CHOOSE THE GOOD...' pounded into my brain like a mallet into cheese. It was obvious the nuns didn't want to give up their porterhouse steak.

He flipped a few pages in the New Testament. "It follows:

"The Holy Ghost hovers over the realm in guise of a dove... gazes with love on the Virgin Mary... comes upon her... Jesus is born of a mortal virgin ... becomes God from man... saves mankind from sin... rejected by His chosen people... suffered unto death... descended into Hell... rose again... rules eternal life."

He followed it up with the Apostles Creed:

'I believe in Jesus Christ... conceived of the Holy Ghost, born of the Virgin Mary, suffered under Pontius Pilate, was crucified, died, and was buried. He descended into Hell. On the third day He rose again...'

"Tell me, why did Jesus descend into Hell?" He waited.

It was a question that had puzzled me all of my Catholic life. I certainly wasn't going to come up with a logical answer on the spur of the moment. But he did. He repeated again from his book:

"'Zeus, King of Gods, speaks, Hail my offspring who come upon thou to save thou from sin... hast been counted by his people among thieves... suffered unto death... descended into Tartarus...Thou wilt rise again without lust ...'

"When the Nicene Fathers plagiarized the Greek tablets, they failed to edit out of their deception, things that made no sense.

"In Greek Mythology, 'Tartarus' is the deep abyss of eternal torment reserved for the Titans who had murdered Zagreus.

"It makes sense that Zagreus and Dionysus would visit Tartarus. It makes no sense that Christ would descend into Hell.

"Too, the concept of a savior and life everlasting is contradictory

101

to Hebrew mythology: 'Dust thou art, to dust thou wilt return.' How did this promise of 'eternal life' ever get into the Bible to begin with?

The Evolution of Greek Mythology

"In 253BC, the Greek King Philadelphus issued a decree ordering the Hebrew scripture translated into Greek, *The Septuagint.*

"In this translation, the Greeks added Isaiah's prophesy of the coming of Christ: 'Behold, a virgin shall conceive and bear a son...Butter and honey shall he eat so that he may know to refuse the evil, and choose the good...'

I challenged him, "What makes you so sure Greeks wrote it?"

"As we have just been discussing, virgin birth, resurrection and eternal life are Greek mythology. *The Greatest Story Ever Told* is a carbon copy of the myth of Dionysus, the reigning Roman 'Son of God' when those who wrote of Jesus picked up their pens.

"Yet, we know the Greeks added the prophecy of Isaiah to the Old Testament for a much more telling reason." I waited.

"From the beginning of time, Jews have been carnivores. So important was this, in his opening story of creation in *Genesis,* Moses decrees: 'Everything that lives and moves about will be food for you.'

"When the Isaiah prophecy was written, Greek Pythagoreans and Phrygians were vegetarians. They believed it wrong to kill animals when God provided vegetation of the fields and fruits of the vine.

"Dionysus, Himself, was a vegetarian. The reason he is revered as 'God of the Vine' in both Greek and Roman mythology.

"Too, Dionysus was the first God to change water into wine.

"Though Isaiah's prophesy of the coming of Christ is the only thing in the Old Testament relative to Christianity, it consists of only thirty-three words. So important is the killing of animals to those who wrote it, more than half of these words create Christ as a vegetarian '...Butter and honey shall he eat, that he may know to refuse the evil, and choose the good.' Gripping evidence, vegetarian Greeks wrote the prophecy in *Isaiah.*

"The prophecy of the coming of Jesus in *Isaiah* in 253BC is a direct plagiarization of the prophecy of the coming of Dionysus in Greek Phrygian mythology just a century earlier in 349BC.

"Every surviving text of the Bible, including the *Codex Sinaiticus* and the *Codex Vaticanus*, which predates the 6th century are in Greek. Not a trace of anything written in Hebrew or any other language.

102

"Today, Jews don't accept the Greek translation of *Isaiah*. That is, the virgin birth of a Messiah. We are speaking here of the Christian or Greek Bible, not the Hebrew Bible in which *Isaiah* speaks not of the coming of *Jesus*, but of the coming of a *New Jerusalem.*

"Stop killing animals!"

"Jesus never took part in blood sacrifice of animals. What's more, He condemned the killing of animals for nourishment."

"Wrong." I stopped him. "Jesus was brought up a Jew."

Reaching across the table, I took his book and read: "'Every man shall take a lamb, a male of the first year, shall kill it in the evening and strike its blood upon the door posts of the house within which they shall eat it...'"

He smiled as does a spider at a fly caught in its web. "You're right. Jesus grew up a Jew. He was witness to the blood rituals in the Temple and the blood ritual of the Passover. Yet, conceived as a vegetarian: 'BUTTER AND HONEY SHALL HE EAT, THAT HE MAY KNOW TO REFUSE THE EVIL, AND CHOOSE THE GOOD,' Jesus knew it was wrong.

"What's more, He knew the faithful would be unable to break free of the macabre sacrificial world of Moses and both his God's lust and his own lust for the taste of blood of young animals. They would go on killing animals until the end of time. He decided to bring it to an end."

"Decided to bring it to an end?" I repeated, a bit astonished.

"Yes. In the oldest surviving gospels of Luke and John—*Codex Sinaiticus* and *Codex Vaticanus*—when asked to participate in the Passover, Jesus answers his disciples' demand He eat meat:

'His disciples had gone unto the city to buy meat for the Passover... They came unto him, saying, Master, Eat. But Jesus refused to eat meat, saying, I have meat to eat that ye not know of. Jesus said unto them, My meat is to do the will of Him who sent me; and to finish His work. I say unto you, Take ye not the lifeblood of the bullock. I give thee the herbs of the soil. Look up thy eyes to the fields for they are ripe to harvest. I give you the fruit of the vineyard. Look up thy eyes to the branches for they are fit to drink... He took bread and broke it. 'This is my body. He took wine. This is my blood. Do this in remembrance of me.'

"Jesus defies the most prolific command of the God of Moses and carries out the will of the God of Isaiah who sired Him: '...Butter and honey shall he eat, that he may know to refuse the evil, and choose the good.'

103

"Not a very good sell for the Nicene Council which strategy was to lure an army of meat eaters into its fold.

"It cleverly gave Jesus half a plate: '...He took bread and broke it. This is my body. He took wine. This is my blood. Do this in remembrance of me.'

"The Nicene Council brought an end to animal sacrifice on the altar. It did not extend it to the dinner table <u>despite that Christ explicitly meant the dinner table</u>. The Eucharist kicks the ethical vegetarian Jesus in the mouth each time it is devoured."

The Evolution of Faith

He summed up his case. "This is just one more example of what we have been talking about all along.

"Religion evolves like any other social practice. Each politician building on the imagination of those who came before him.

"Where did Matthew and Luke ever get the stupendous idea—a century after the event is alleged to have occurred—Jesus had been born of a human virgin sired by God?

"If one goes on the Internet and into libraries and researches 'Dionysus,' one will leaf through a fifteen hundred year evolution of the Roman 'God of the Vine' as we have been discussing Him.

"There is an infinite variation in stories as to how He came about. Yet, they all agree, at the time Matthew and Luke wrote their books:

'DIONYSUS WAS THE VEGETARIAN ROMAN GOD OF THE VINE... SIRED BY THE GOD ZEUS IN GUISE OF AN EAGLE... BORN OF THE HUMAN VIRGIN SEMELE... BECAME GOD FROM MAN...'

"Hence we have:

'JESUS, THE VEGETARIAN CHRISTIAN GOD OF THE VINE, SIRED BY THE HOLY GHOST IN GUISE

OF A DOVE... BORN OF THE HUMAN VIRGIN MARY... BECAME GOD FROM MAN...

Zeus, the Father of Dionysus   Holy Ghost, the Father of Jesus

"'The Greatest Story Ever Told' is not so much the genius of those who wrote the gospels, as it is the genius of ancient Greeks."

He had pushed my faith to the edge of the cliff. Yet, he had the compassion to save me from the fall.

"This doesn't mean Jesus is not God. After all, Dionysus was a God. All it means is Jesus was not a Jew. He was a Greek."

He couldn't keep it to himself, "...a vegetarian Greek."

Greek Mythology vs. Christian Theology

I still clung to the rapidly unraveling threads of my faith. Yet, he had raised my curiosity. "If the record of Dionysus is truly there, and it surely is there as we have the tablets, why do we revere Jesus—the reincarnation of Dionysus—as God, and reject Dionysus as Myth?"

As usual, he read my mind. "That's simple. In the case of Jesus we don't have the tiniest scrap of what was originally written. In the case of Dionysus, we have the complete record.

"As I've said, if one goes on the Internet and into libraries and researches the fifteen hundred year evolution of Dionysus, one will find infinite variations of how He came about.

"In the same way in which the 3rd century Gospel of Thomas and Gospel of Judas and other gnostic gospels contradict the story of Jesus as molded into Christianity by the Nicene Council.

"This is probably why the Nicene Council destroyed the gospel manuscripts which served as the sacred authority for its proceedings.

"Had the original writings of the first three centuries survived, there would exist today an infinite variation of contradictions of what Jesus was. No one would know what to believe?

"It is entirely upon the gap of three hundred years from the time of Jesus to the earliest surviving record of His life as we know it today, His credibility rests. <u>The wider the gap in time between the surviving record and the myth, the wider the opportunity to perpetuate the myth</u>.

"That all of the writings of Dionysus have survived in stone tablets, there are an infinite variation of contradictions of what He was.

"No one knows what to believe? It destroys the myth.

"Yet, of all the stories one will find on the Internet and in libraries as to who Dionysus was, they all agree, at the time, Matthew and Luke wrote their conflicting versions of the virgin birth:

'DIONYSUS WAS THE REIGNING ROMAN GOD OF THE VINE... SIRED BY THE GOD ZEUS IN GUISE OF AN EAGLE... BORN OF THE HUMAN VIRGIN SEMELE... BECAME GOD FROM MAN... SHALL COME TO RULE ETERNAL LIFE...'

The story of Dionysus born of a human virgin was written in 349BC. It places Him in 2000BC. Semele's father Cadmus was founder and King of Thebes in 2000BC.

In the 7th century, Pope Gregory enacted the canon law forbidding consumption of meat on Friday. He knew if he were to forbid consumption of meat entirely he would risk schism. He hoped future popes would add other days of the week.

Questioned by a reporter why he was a vegan, Albino Luciani: "I take Jesus for His word. He obviously did not ask us to offer Him a toast. He gave us the fruit and wine of the vine and the harvest of the fields." Like Jesus, Luciani did eat fish.

Many Christian churches delete *'descended into hell'* from the Apostles Creed.

Fragments of the Armenian Church continued to sacrifice animals in their Holy Sacrifice of the Mass as required by *Leviticus* after the time of the Nicene Council.

Sources: Zagreus-Dionysus born of virgin Goddess Athena: *Callimachus* 1610BC, *Mycenaean Linear B* 1450BC, *Nonnus* 1230BC (British National Museum). Poems *Orpheus* 600BC *Phaedo* 341BC, play *Bacchae* 405BC (Library of Alexandria). Dionysus rebirth of a mortal virgin: *Phrygian Tablets*: (Istanbul Archaeology Museum). *Philadelphus' letter 'The Septuagint'* (Library of Alexandria)

Readers unfamiliar with Greek Mythology are encouraged to search reliable sources in libraries and on the Internet. 'Dionysus Wikipedia' & 'Zagreus Wikipedia'

Justin's Dream

"If Jesus wanted us to fall down on our knees and adore Him, He would be everything He told us not to be"

Albino Luciani, Gregorian University, Rome, February

It glided silently onto the edge of the world of forevermore.

The saucer crept like a ghost stealthily over the realm.

An unseen magician reached down, holding it for a spot of time in guarded levitation.

It peered about, surveying all it could see.

In the blink of an eyelash, it set down a stone's throw from the golden carriage of infinity.

A young explorer exited the ship. "Whew, I'm glad that's over. How did I do?"

A young officer in navy blue attire and golden epaulets stood there. "Not too well. Pop is not happy. You messed up. He doesn't think they got His message right."

"You mean the Jews?" emitting an understanding glance.

"No, the Catholics, those who claim to be your Church. They think they are supposed to pay men to dress up in women clothes and prance about altars of marble and gold."

"I don't get it. How did they ever get that idea?"

"You gave it to them. As I said, Pop is not happy about it."

"I gave it to them?" the young traveler shot a bewildered look at the chap in navy blue attire and the golden epaulets.

"Pop thinks so." The officer warned.

107

"There must be a mistake. I told them just the opposite. I will straighten this out with Pop." He winked back at His greeter as He strolled toward the golden carriage of infinity.

A conversation apart

A pair of shimmering white stallions in harness of silver and gold and glittering gems whined in unison, welcoming Him home.

Climbing into the cab, He took the seat opposite Pop—the one with the bearded chin and the noble nose.

The carriage moved along the river of cherished memories of yesterday and enthralling visions of tomorrow.

Where sparrows fly upside down over forests of olive trees and turn the sky from blue to green.

Where lovers park on benches under weeping willows dropping tears into waters flowing to the end of time.

Lovers, whose dreams once carried them away from a world of weights and measures into a world of fantasy.

Lovers, whose heads once so full of dreams of things that would never come to be.

Lovers, now, as miniature gods, their dreams embrace eternity.

In the early morning mist, cobblestones shone illusions of emerald, of sapphire, of topaz, of ruby grouted in silver and gold. Towering turrets of an enchanting castle drifted out of lingering clouds in a distant haze.

Not the sound of the pavement, not the bright of the moon, alone in the glow of the lamplight, the young traveler broke the silence of gloom, "Pop, I understand there is a problem?"

"Yes," agreed the one with the bearded chin and the noble nose. "You told them to build magnificent buildings to your honor while children all over their world starve to death."

"I never told them such a thing." He corrected His mentor.

"You'd never know it. They've got one on every corner."

He looked at His Pop. "I could not have been more explicit. When asked if Herod's Temple was my Church, I told them: 'My Church is not of buildings of wood and stone, it is in your heart. It is in your compassion for others.'" Scratching his hallowed head, "Hmmm, I wonder how they could have possibly missed the boat."

"Illness," The elder offered. "The poor souls are sick."

"What makes you think that?" queried the young explorer.

"They have been spending vast fortunes building towers, tens of millions of them, each one housing nothing more than a bell.

"Even more bizarre, they line up by the thousands in adoration of golden caskets. One of these houses a human bone, another a human tongue, while another is said to house your foreskin.

"They get their kicks out of idolizing your foreskin. They're nuts."

109

"Father!" the young voyager scolded his Dad.

"Sorry, got carried away with myself.

"The point is, while they house these objects of superstition in golden citadels, millions of children in their world have no house.

"What's more, they talk to plaster dolls embedded with precious gems. The crown on this one at Fatima contains twenty-five pounds of pure gold imbedded with seventeen hundred diamonds.

"Worse yet, in an unfathomable stupor they mutter over and over again, trillions and trillions of times: 'Hail Mary, full of grace, the lord is with you, blessed are thou among women, blessed is the fruit of thy womb, Jesus, Holy Mary, Mother of God, pray for us sinners, now, and at the hour of our death..'"

He rubbed his noble nose, "Who is this woman they speak of?"

Surprised, His Dad did not remember, the young voyager gasped. "Why, she's my mother... your wife." Realizing they had never been married, He corrected Himself, "...your mistress.

"Don't you remember, you came as a Ghost in the night and..."

Pop cut Him off, "Yes, I'm aware of that gossip. I never did such a thing. I never knocked up that young virgin."

"Father!"

"Just a figure of speech, Sorry.

"When found to be pregnant before they had come together, her husband made up a story to save her life. In those days girls who cheated on their husbands were stoned to death. Joseph told them he had a dream that I had come upon her in the night and they fell for it."

The young voyager shocked, "That... that means I'm a bastard."

"Yes." The noble one uttered compassionately. "Your body is a bastard. But..." He paused to get it right, "your soul is a God."

Stroking His bearded chin and rubbing his noble nose, "If you have the smarts to view the evolution of faith as it progressed in the western world, you would not be so easily fooled by tales of men of motive. You would know you are the reincarnation of Dionysus. You would know, in truth, you are a God.

"Yet, let's get back to these poor souls who run their fingers along glass beads muttering: 'Hail Mary, Mother of God...' over and over again, and again, and again, and again to this woman—Mary.

"Is it that they think she is dumb, she can't get it the first time? Is it that they think she is deaf, she can't get it the first time?"

The young voyager cleared the matter up for His Father: "It is that she is dead. They 'know' she cannot get it at all."

The one with the bearded chin and the noble nose reached into His vest pocket and pulled out a small gadget.

"What are you doing with a cigarette lighter?" exclaimed the concerned young traveler.

"You're a little behind the times." The one with the bearded chin and the noble nose texted a few tabs. "This is a cell phone, an iPhone. Back on earth, they go on the Internet with it.

"Let's see what the 33-day Pope had to say about this."

"The 33-day Pope?" the young voyager surprised.

"John Paul I. The one who tried to carry out your message. The one who tabbed the circus we are talking about: 'The Fatima Cult.'

"Yes, here it is. Just a few days before he was murdered.

'It is beautiful to see people showing thanks to Our Lady for graces received. Yet, it is sad to see crowns of immense value placed on plaster idols as objects of superstition.

It is equally as depressing to see people in a stupor running fingers along beads mumbling vain repetitions, likewise in a superstitious way.

Isn't Our Lady, too, the Mother of the Indians, of the Chinese, of the Africans, of the Guatemalans? Indeed she is.

The most beautiful tiara on the Virgin's head is a row of hospital beds in Bombay, a row of water wells in Mongolia, a row of schoolrooms in Burundi, a row of starving children being fed in Central America...'"

"No wonder they killed him." The young voyager cried out." He would have made *'Love thy neighbor as thyself'* the law of the land."

The one with the bearded chin picked up the beat, "Regardless, this is what they are doing while children in their world starve to death."

"What is this?" asked the young traveler.

"They call it the Mass. The Eucharist. They line up like cannibals to devour the flesh and blood of their God."

"Their God?" the young voyager gave a puzzled sigh.

"Yes, you. Their God." The old man waited for an explanation. The young voyager remained quiet.

"What is more, they drink your blood out of golden chalices." The voyager pondered, "Huh. I wonder where they got that idea?"

"You gave it to them," the old man asserted.

"When you tried to carry out my message instructing them to…

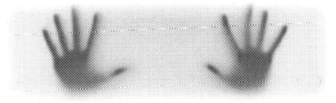

Stop killing animals!

"Their profits, excuse me their prophets, cleverly twisted your words—ordering them to give up their porterhouse steak—into the pomp and pageantry of their so-called Holy Sacrifice of the Mass.

"Nevertheless, is this really what you meant by your Church—self-serving men drinking from diamond studded golden chalices while children all over the world starve to death?

"Is this really what you meant by your church, mindless sheep standing in magnificent buildings to be seen and heard of men, while children all over the world starve to death?

"Is this really what you meant by your church, vast treasures of art, while children all over the world starve to death?

"Is this really what you meant by your church, the world's finest wines, while children all over the world starve to death?

Papal Wine Cellar

"My God! My Pop! This is not what I meant by my Church.

Light at the end of the tunnel

"Wait a minute." A light lit up in His head. "Pop, can you find the record of my life in this thing, the 'iPhone'?"

"Certainly," tapping a few buttons. "Here is your biography. They call it the gospels: 'Love thy neighbor as thyself.'

He advanced a page, "Here it is again: 'Love thy neighbor as thyself.' Again, and again, and again: 'Love thy neighbor as thyself.'

"Here again in Matthew: 'Love thy neighbor as thyself. If thou wilt be perfect, sell all thou hast and give to the poor.'" He stroked His beard.

"Good. Now, can you find where I took the time to define my Church in a simple and understanding way so that even a child of six could readily understand what I meant by my Church?"

The one with the bearded chin and the noble nose texted a few more tabs. "Yes, here it is in the Gospel of Matthew:

'When thou prayest, thou shalt not be as Hypocrites are; for they love to pray standing in the synagogues and in public places, that they may be seen and heard of men. Verily, I say unto you, They have their reward...

But thou, when thou prayest, enter into thy closet, and when thou hast shut thy door, talk to me in secret; verily, I say unto you, Ye will have ye reward...

When ye pray, use not vain repetitions before graven idols as the heathen do; for they think they shall be heard for their speaking in public places...'

"That's strange. Someone has tampered with my record.

"When I spoke of 'Hypocrites who love to pray standing in public places that they may be seen and heard of men,' they have changed what I meant by deleting my words: 'They have their reward in this life.'

"Too, when I spoke of '...those who speak to me in private...,' they have deleted my words: 'They will have their reward in my Kingdom.'"

Scratching His brow, "Huh. I wonder why they would do that?"

Pop reasoned, "It seems those who make their money and get their kicks out of controlling the minds of men from the pulpit have gotten their fingers on this one, too.

"Let's search the oldest surviving gospels, *Codex Sinaiticus* and *Codex Vaticanus*, and see what they have to say.

"You are right. They read: '...in this life' and '...in my kingdom.'

"These politicians who masquerade as preachers take advantage of the gullibility of their sheep. They think they can butter me up with idol worship while children all over their world to starve to death."

Magic

With a quizzical look, the young voyager asked, "Anyway, Pop, can you tell me more about this thing, the 'iPhone'?"

"Of course. They are able to talk to people in India and China and on the moon for that matter." His mentor replied.

"India and China?" the young man shot a dumbfounded glance.

"Yes, long before you brought my message to the West, I was

115

bringing it to those in the East. They know me as the God Brahma.

"Look here in the Vedas." He handed him the smart phone.

"The Vedas? What's that?" The young voyager looked up.

"The Vedas is the record of my time as the Hindu God of the East. My biography as you call it."

The young traveler read the screen: "'Love thy neighbor as thyself.' And, again: 'Love thy neighbor as thyself...' and, again... and, again...

Pop offered, "I told them the same thing you told your people. 'Those hypocrites who pray standing in public places that they may be seen and heard of men, have their reward in this life... Those who speak to me in private, have their reward in the Kingdom of Heaven.'

"In my part of the world, my will is honored.

"Folks are free to worship their God privately within the confines of homes and temples. When they take it beyond that and use their God as a political soundboard—God said these kinds of people are to be persecuted and killed and so forth, and so forth—men and women of good conscience of the state step up and bring it to an end.

"*Separation of Church and State* is not possible in the so-called democratic societies where the preacher's sheep have the vote.

Ethical Vegetarians

"Too, concerning my message to love all creatures great and small.

"In my part of the world—as ethical vegetarians—they know it is wrong to kill animals for nourishment when I give them the fruit of the vineyard and the wheat of the field.

"For example, here, in the Hindu scripture the *Rig Veda*: 'Fiend who smears himself with flesh of cattle... tear off the heads of such with fiery fury.'

"Again, in the same book: 'Burn the flesh devourers, let none of them escape the heavenly arrow.'

"In my part of the world they revere the cow. They don't kill him." He cast a questionable glance at His prodigy.

The young voyager scratched His forehead and gave His Pop a puzzled look. "Hmmm, I wonder how your Hindus got the message, and my Catholics fell victim to such an enormous scam?

"They ignore my instruction to stop killing animals. They turn my covenant into a circus of pomp and pageantry. They make a mockery of my flesh and blood. They continue to enjoy their porterhouse steak."

How does it work?

The young traveler gave a sudden, "Wow!"
"Wow?" Pop repeated with a question mark.

"This iPhone. How does this thing work? How does this Internet work? How are they able to store the information of all the history of the world in this tiny box?

"How are they able to speak to others on the other side of their world? How are they able to send moving images of their day-to-day events all over their world? How is this possible?

"I could have used this thing to convince the Jews I was God. Maybe I could use it now to convince these Catholics '*If I wanted them to fall down on their knees and adore me, I would be everything I told them not to be.*'"

The old man scratched His bearded chin and rubbed His noble nose, "I don't know. I've never been able to figure it out.

"It's amazing. I've tried many times. Yet, I've never been able to figure out how they do it. It escapes me.

"Of course, I'm not alone. Most of them have no idea how it works either. They take it for granted, just like they take you for granted. It is none of their business. It is the responsibility of others. It is the responsibility of their king in Rome."

The one with the bearded chin and the noble nose stared out of the window in a daze. "I wonder how they got things so mixed up? These Catholics must be imbeciles. Where are their minds?"

Suddenly, a light went off in Pop's head. He shouted to the driver, "To the Industrial Park of Production, on the double."

The carriage sped past an endless line of factories, each with a blinking sign: "Ants, Spiders, Monkeys, Wolves, Puppies, Kittens, Sharks, Trout, Goldfish, Alligators, Turtles, Calves, Ducklings, Eagles... finally coming to rest in front of an enormous building.

Over its entrance sparkled a giant marquee: Infants!

Stacked on endless conveyors were babies as far as the eye could see. Hundreds of them, thousands of them, millions of them.

There were boy babies, girl babies, and some in-betweens.

There were black babies, brown babies, white babies, yellow babies, red babies, and, yes, some in-betweens.

Some had brown eyes, others had black eyes, others had blue eyes, still others had hazel eyes, and, yes, some could not see.

Some had big ears, others had small ears, others had pointed ears, still others had floppy ears, and, yes, some could not hear.

Some had brown hair, others had black hair, others had blond hair, others had red hair, others had shiny hair, still others had frizzy hair, and, yes, some had no hair.

Some had curved noses, others had straight noses, others had flat noses, others had long noses, still others had pug noses, and, yes, some could not smell.

The Vice President of Production of the Infant factory stood proudly at attention, displaying tomorrow's shipment.

The one with the bearded chin and the noble nose gave him the word, "Tom, we have a problem. We can't quite figure it out. I'm not sure. But the answer might be here."

"You must be talking about the Catholics," exclaimed Tom.

Pop, shocked by Tom's awareness, "You know there is a problem with the Catholics. Why wasn't I told?"

"We thought we could work it out by ourselves without going to

118

the top." Tom stuttered.

"You worked it out on your own?" Pop grew concerned.

"Yes, from time to time, we run short of parts, so we borrow them from the sheep factory which is right next door."

"The sheep factory?" Pop, aghast.

"Yes, we find they make good Catholics," Tom stammered.

"What kind of parts?" Pop shot His aide a quizzical look.

The Vice President of Production told his boss, "Brains!"

Incoming Call

The phone rang. It rang again. The one with the bearded chin and the noble nose pushed frantically at the buttons. "God damn it!"

The young voyager, "Father!"

"Just a figure of speech." Pop apologized. "When you get to be my age that's about all you have left."

Justin reached over and turned off the alarm clock. He sat up in bed rubbing his eyes. "So they don't know how they work.

"I will let them in on our little secret.

"It all began way back in 17th century with Newton's law of universal gravitation: every mass in the universe attracts every other mass at a force equal to the product of their forces.

"Then, early in the 19th century, Michael Faraday isolated the electromagnetic wave. He discovered every sound, no matter how miniscule, creates an electromagnetic wave, a gravitational force unique to itself. Once created it remains intact.

"What's more, he theorized electromagnetic waves could not only be stored, but could also be transmitted through space.

"Late in the 19th century, Nicola Tesla capitalized on Faraday's work and developed a wireless transmitter and a wireless receiver— radio. He proved an electromagnetic sound could not only be heard at another time, but in another place.

"In the 20th century, Philo Farnsworth applied the same principles that Tesla had applied to sound, to light—photons. He determined each bit of light is an electromagnetic radiation, a gravitational force unique to itself, and once created, is infinite—television.

"Nevertheless, I will save this one for a rainy day." Rolling over, Justin went back to sleep.

Matthew 6, in the oldest surviving gospel manuscripts: *'Those Hypocrites who love to pray standing in public places (churches) have their reward in this life. Those who pray to me in private have their reward in my Kingdom.'* In all modern Bibles, both verses end in the word *'reward.'* *'...in this life.'* & *'...in my Kingdom.'* deleted.

The wine cellar at the papal retreat Castle Gandolfo is depicted in this episode.

Like John XXIII before him, Albino Luciani was an enemy of practices which dealt in the occult including the visionary saints and communication with the dead. He defined saints as *"political appointees of a sitting pope."*

Like John XXIII, Luciani was particularly critical of *Fatima*. He suspected two of the co-visionary children at Fatima were murdered to pave the way for the surviving visionary (Lucia) to exploit the hoax. *'The Fatima Murders'* is one of a score of murders investigated including that of the 33-day Pope in the author's biography of the Pope: *The Vatican Murders: The Life and Death of John Paul I.*

Headline quote *'If Jesus wanted us to fall down on our knees and adore Him, He would be everything He told us not to be.'* Albino Luciani repeated this as John Paul I in his Sunday Angelus, September 17, 1978.

To the extent Catholics revere body parts of dead people is a practice of the occult. In reality, it is mental illness. The rumor that John Paul II would kiss the foreskin of Christ while his secretary Stanislaw Dziwisz flagged his rump in the Opus Dei flagellation ritual is unfounded. He may have kissed the casket containing the foreskin as many cardinals and faithful have kissed this casket in public.

The medium—talking to the dead—originated with the *Witch of Endor* in which a medium riled up the spirit of Samuel in the 1st Book of Samuel. The Catholic Church perpetuates the myth.

Hindu quotes 'stop killing animals for nourishment' *Rig Veda* 10.87 16-19. Many modern Hindu sects continue to adhere to the vegetarian guidelines of ancient texts. On the other hand, as many have moved away from it.

Ghosts, Ghosts, and more Ghosts…

"When a man does not believe in God, it does not necessarily mean he believes in nothing. It could mean, he believes in everything."

Albino Luciani, Vatican II Council, Rome, July 22 1963

Taking his spot at the breakfast table he would exploit his dream, "Let us chat a bit about my mentor, Albino Luciani, the 33-Day Pope.

Faith vs. righteous

"Albino Luciani was born into dire poverty in a small village in the Italian Alps to a scullery maid and a migrant worker.

"Unlike other popes who had been born to two devout parents who were convinced the men in Rome knew something they didn't know, the little boy Luciani grew up in a tug-of-war.

"His mother, a devout Catholic, prayed before crucifixes made of bits of wood. She told him, the only path to heaven was on his knees asking for special favors in this life and the reward of an afterlife.

"His father, a socialist atheist activist, often burned his mother's crucifixes in the stove. He told him, the only path to heaven was on his feet helping others less fortunate than himself.

"His mother taught him the idolatry of Christ.

"His father taught him the reality of Christ.

121

"Early in the twentieth century, driven by the Vatican decree: out-of-wedlock children have no souls, Italy suffered from a population of two million born-out-of-wedlock orphans.

"In the wintertime, when the little boy Albino Luciani was growing up, every village in Italy had a cart that went about the streets in the wee-hours of the morning collecting the frozen bodies of those poor 'bastards' who had not made it through the wintry night.

"His mother told him it was right. His father told him it was wrong." Looking over at us, "Who do you think the little boy Luciani thought was telling the truth?" Dead silence allowed him to go on.

"As for us, when we set out on this journey of faith, we agreed, if we are ever to define the human soul and its role in eternal life, we must first determine the truth of the assumption we have been born into. That is, the God we are born into."

Slipping over to the bookcase, he returned with a book, *The Vatican Murders*. "Unlike its title might convey, this book is as much about this man's life as it is about his death."

Opening the book, he flipped through its pages. Uttered a brief sigh. He flipped through the pages, again. He began to read.

The Tyrant of the Minor Seminary of Feltre

There was a priest, Don Gaio, who taught a class on catechism.

One day, a student demanded, "We should have a law against atheists and put them all in prison? They are the worst of people."

Albino took this as a direct attack on his father. His classmates knew his father was an atheist. In fact, they knew his father did not even believe Christ had ever lived.

Though his father did not believe a man who had performed the miracles said of Christ had lived, unlike his Christian adversaries, he did believe in Christ's philosophies as set forth in the gospels.

What's more, he believed good men, in an attempt to do away with the evilness of the God of Moses, had written the gospels.

Albino didn't bother to raise his hand. To him it was a matter of honor. He would stand and fight to the end in defense of his beloved father who had taught him right from wrong.

Bringing his fist down on his desk, the boy Albino Luciani stood up. "Instead of throwing stones, let us first define what we are talking about, so that we all know what we are talking about."

Don Gaio looked at the boy as if he didn't know what he was talking about. Albino answered the priest's puzzled expression.

"We are talking about God. That is what we are talking about. How one defines God. That is all we are talking about.

"So, let us define the 'God' of religion versus the 'God' of the atheist." Still there was not much more than a dumbfounded look on the faces of both the teacher and the students.

The priest motioned him to sit down. Yet, the young boy held the floor. "Let us start with what we know.

A common God

"To begin with, we have the sun.

"The sun holds the earth in orbit and is the source of all life on our planet. It is the source of all life on our planet because it is the source of all energy in our solar system.

"We know, from Einstein's work, energy is the fundamental unit of creation. Without energy, without the sun, nothing could begin, nothing could grow, nothing could move, nothing could be." Don Gaio, frustrated by the boy's growing insolence, raised his voice in a nervous twang, and ordered him to sit down.

Albino didn't budge. "So, religion and atheism have a common definition—God is the source of all energy which drives the natural order of creation. So, in truth, we all have a common God.

"Yet, the commonality ends there.

"To the one side, we have those of us who are happy with what God has given us in this life and accept the natural order of God's creation. To the other side, we have those who are unhappy with what God has given us in this life and reject the natural order of..."

Gaio jumped in, "Now, you are talking sense." the priest smiled. "Yes, we Christians accept what God has given us..."

"Not Christians," the boy took back the floor. "Atheists accept the natural order of God's creation.

"Christians are not satisfied with what God has given them in this life. Christians lust for more." Fifty-two ears surrounding him perked up. Fifty-four including those of Gaio.

"We Christians do not accept the real world we live and die in. The atheist accepts the real world we live and die in." The boy stopped. He thought a moment as to how he would reduce his confusing remark to bare bones. He simplified his point.

"To put it in a nutshell, Christians believe in ghosts; the atheist does not believe in ghosts." Don Gaio shot him a glance of lunacy.

Ghosts

"We believe a Burning Bush which claimed to be God appeared to a man named Moses over three thousand years ago...

The foundation of Judea-Christian faith

"What's more, like Jews, we believe in a score of ghosts that are said to have appeared to the prophets who came after Moses in the Old Testament.

"As Christians, ghosts follow us into the gospels as well.

"When Joseph is alarmed, Mary is conceived with child before they had come together, we believe another ghost—an angel—appeared to Joseph in his dream, telling him that Mary had been impregnated in her sleep by a still another ghost, this one with a capital G—the Holy Ghost—the cornerstone of Christian belief.

The cornerstone of Christian faith

"Belief in these two ghosts is the pivot point of our faith. To put it bluntly, if one is a Christian, nothing else in the Bible counts.

"If the Burning Bush was the imagination of ancient story tellers, we have no God. If the Holy Ghost did not impregnate Mary with human sperm, Christ is not that same God. The Roman Catholic Church, the entire Christian world, crumbles to dust.

"It is solely upon these two ghosts, the truth of Christianity rests. "If the Burning Bush was not God, we are up the river without a boat. If Christ is not God, we are up the river without a paddle.

"Yet, to top it off, we, as Catholics, believe in ghosts today like the lady ghost of Lourdes and Fatima. So much so, we make saints of those cunning few who pull the wool over our eyes.

"Nevertheless, let us consider how this works.

The beginning of us…

125

"To begin with, we have the beginning of us—birth.

"We all know, as a matter-of-fact, we are conceived of tiny bits of energy that come together and result in a chemical reaction. This is the will of the God of Nature—the natural order of God's creation—the God of the Atheist—the God who gives us life.

"It is an absolute fact of nature, the egg comes first.

"But faith does not accept the truth. It does not accept the will of the God we know, as a matter-of-fact, gives us life.

"It tells us, 'No!

"'The chicken came first.' It gives us the tale of Adam and Eve.

"Yet, to the other side, we have the truth.

"The Indians were running around the Americas thousands of years before God created Adam and Eve in the Garden of Eden. What's more, our ancestors—the Cro-Magnons—were running around Europe tens of thousands of years before that." He stopped, again, for a time, to allow his listeners to catch up.

The in-between of us…

"Next, we have the in-between of us—life.

"There are many difficulties in life. People suffer from all kinds of birth defects, diseases, injuries, accidents and so forth. This is the will of the God of Nature—the natural order of God's creation—the God of the Atheist—the God who gives us life.

"Again, faith does not accept the will of the God who we know, as a matter-of-fact, gives us life. It tells us, 'No! For a few dollars, I will give you miracles. I will give you a better life.'

"To seek miracles is to refuse to accept the will of the God who gives us life. Like gullible fools, we fall down on our knees and plead to plaster statues or, better yet, talk to the air for miracles. As if to say, God would favor some of Her children over others."

Infuriated by the boy's reference to God in the fair sex, Gaio tapped a boy on the shoulder and sent him for the headmaster.

The differences between us…

126

Albino blinked. "Then, we have the differences between us.

"The God of Nature—the natural order of God's creation—the God of the Atheist—creates all of Her children to be equal.

"Again, faith does not accept the God of Nature—the natural order of God's creation—the God of the Atheist—the God who we know, as a matter-of-fact, gives us life. It tells us, 'No!'

"It tells us women, like animals, are mere property of men. It tells us little boys are better than little girls. It tells us only we men have the power to mumble a few words and wave our hands over a piece of bread in a cup and change it into a God..."

His eyes scanned the room, "...the reason there is not a single girl in this room.

"And, the reason there is not a single girl in this room?"

He answered his own query. "All Judea-Christian scripture was written by men. Not a single word written by a woman.

"Even Matthew, in his tale of Christ's conception, holds to this universal definition of Godliness. Mary merely supplies the egg—Christ's humanity. God the Father in the guise of the Holy Ghost supplies the sperm—Christ's divinity.

"In the Christian world, only man can be of divinity. God is a 'He.'" He stopped to allow his listeners to make the connection.

"Yet, faith does not limit its prejudice to gender.

"It demands subordination of black and handicapped children: '...whosoever hath a blemish, a flat-nosed child, a blind child, a lame child, a hunchbacked child, a dwarfed child, a diseased child, a queer child, a child out of wedlock; is not to approach the altar of the Lord.'

"The same God who ordered the Israelites to murder their Canaanite neighbors in the horrific taking of the Promised Land: 'take to the sword, every man, women and child—leave not one alive...'"

He smiled as he recited the horrific instruction of the God his masters and his peers gambled their eternity on.

The end of us...

"Finally, we have the end of us—death.

"We know, as a matter-of-fact, each one of us will eventually die. This is the will of the God of Nature—the natural order of

127

creation—the God of the Atheist—the God who gives us life.

"Yet, once again, faith does not accept the will of the God who we know, as a matter-of-fact, gives us life. It tells us, 'No! For a few dollars, I will give you eternal life.'

"And, how will we live forever?

"It gives us yet another ghost—a Super Ghost—God.

"According to the doctrines of all religions; God is an infinite, all powerful creature that occupies all space from the outer reaches of the universe to the air around us; God knows all things."

He thought a moment as if he had left something out. He filled it in. "Yes, this Ghost happens to think like a human being."

He refined his salient slip, "...happens to think like a man.

"Nevertheless, faith tells us, the sun is only the hand of God.

"It tells us, this infinite, omnipresent, chauvinistic, prejudicial, homophobic Ghost controls the sun and has an immense ledger in which 'He' records everything each one of us does from the time we are born until the time we die—the central premise of faith.

"Ghost, Ghosts, Ghosts. Depending on which faith we are born into or picked up along the way, if we follow the prejudicial teachings of this or that Ghost—the prejudicial teachings of ancient men who created this or that Ghost—most ridiculous of all," the eyes of the boy Albino Luciani roamed around the room wrapping each and every one of his classmates in a frigid stare, "we ourselves will someday, too, be ghosts."

His eyes finally came to rest on Gaio and the headmaster who had just stepped into the room. The aging rector together with his emissary stood tongue-tied, the class frozen in apprehension.

"A Burning Bush,

128

"A Thief in the Night,

"Ghosts, ghosts, ghosts, and, more ghosts..."
The eyes of the boy Luciani scanned the room, one last time.

"Believe me, in the world of Goldilocks ...

Cinderella ...

...and, Pinocchio...

...taller tales have never been told."

129

The headmaster, Gaio and twenty-six boys stood in awe as he wrapped up his case: *"'When a man says he does not believe in God—when a man does not believe in Ghosts—it does not mean he believes in nothing. It means he believes in everything!'"*

Justin closed the book. "Well, we have made some progress today. Tomorrow we will make some more."

This story has been removed from the latest edition of The Vatican Murders (2013) to avoid duplication in the author's books.

Albino Luciani was fourteen at the time of this incident. Through the influence of his socialist atheist father, it was published in a radical magazine *Povera Tigre,* Belluno, 22 Jun 1927. Reprinted from Lucien Gregoire's biography of John Paul I.

Headline quote: *'When a man does not believe in God, it does not necessarily mean he believes in nothing. It could mean, he believes in everything.'* Luciani defended his lifelong atheist friend and leader of the Russian Orthodox Church, Metropolitan Nikodim, The Russian church agreed to participate in the Vatican II Council on the requirement there be no condemnation of atheism in the proceedings.

The youthful leader of the Russian Church was the first foreign dignitary to visit Luciani after he became pope. He fell dead at the Pope's feet after sipping coffee. One of many interrelated murders in Lucien Gregoire's *The Vatican Murders*.

All Creatures, Great and Small

"According to tales told by ancient men, God is the Father. According to what we really know, God is the Mother."

John Paul I September 28, 1978

I had no sooner sat down, he started up again.

"Let us begin by giving the prophets who created the Hindu God Brahma of the eastern world and those who created the Judea-Christian God the Father of the western world, an equal chance.

"Keep in mind, the prophets on both sides of the fence did not know what we know today. They did not know the earth was round and orbiting around its sun. They had never heard of the atom, and had never fathomed, in their wildest imaginations, the miniature world that goes on beneath the microscope today.

"Yet, what they did know is 'it takes two to tango.'"

"It takes two to tango? What has that got to do with it?"

"Even in ancient times, men did not wonder where babies came from. Nor did they wonder where plants came from.

From the bottom up

"In the eastern hemisphere, God is not infinite.

131

"In Hindu scripture, the God Brahma is born of the seed of a lotus flower fertilized by a bee.

"Though He will live trillions of years, the God Brahma, like all plant and animal life, was born of a mother and a father.

"It follows, the story of creation in Hindu scripture has no conflict with what we know of science today. Life is infinite.

"Likewise, in the earliest story of creation in the west, the Hieroglyphs speak of 'the God 'Nu' as: '…the churning sea before creation. Out of these waters rose the God 'Atum' who through his offspring creates earth…'

"It follows, Moses, plagiarizing the Egyptians, begins his story of creation with: 'the waters which were always there.' Again, each prophet building on those who came before him. Hence we have in *Genesis*:

> 'Let there be a firmament in the midst of the waters which are there, and let it divide the waters from the waters. God divided the waters which were under Heaven from the waters that were above Heaven… Then God said, Let the waters under the Heaven be gathered together in one place, and let the dry land appear; and it was so. And, God called the dry land earth; and the gathering together of the waters He called the sea. And He saw that it was good.'

"Water is synonymous with life. When the astronaut lands on a distant planet and finds water, he knows life exists.

"It is solely upon the interaction of the sun's energy upon water, all life, as we know it on this earth, comes forth.

"According to Judea-Christian theology, God did not create the waters. He did not create life: 'life was always there.'

"We are approaching the crossroads of Faith and Reality."

Standing off to one side of our entertainment center, he resembled a miniature professor addressing a symposium of Nobel laureates.

"It is unreasonable to believe the same God, who has endowed us with reason and intellect, has intended us to forego their use; we would believe the 'assumption' we were born into is 'God.'

"Just as, it is unreasonable to believe this same God, who has endowed those on the other side of the world with reason and intellect, intended them to forego their use; they would believe the 'assumption' they were born into is 'God.'"

Clicking his remote, he spoke to each slide as he went along.

132

"The world we live in is material. It is not spiritual...

"The world we live in is real.

"If we are ever to remove the question mark from the end of our lives... what happens to us after we are gone; we must make use of what we know today and not hang our hats on tales told by ancient men who did not know what we know today."   I heard another click.

"On September 10, 1978, John Paul I declared: *'God is the Father, more so, the Mother.'*

"Two weeks later, on the morning before he was found dead, in a private audience with Philippine bishops; he was asked what he had meant by his declaration.

"He told the bishops: *'According to tales told by ancient men to accomplish their political objectives, God is a man.*

According to all that we really know, God is a woman.'"

I held up my hand to stop him. Yet, I decided to let him go on.

"If we do, as the 33-day Pope suggested we do, and set aside the assumptions we are born into, and consider only what we know, God is much more our Mother than She is our Father.

"It is what our friend Einstein put before us many years ago.

"He told us of the great mystery of creation. All matter, animate or inanimate, from the air we breathe, to the hardest substance known, is a composite of moving parts—atoms.

"What's more, he told us that every living organism, no matter how insignificant, has both a mother and a father.

"One can see this readily in nature.

"Every animal, every fish, every bird, every insect has a brain, a nervous system, a cardiovascular system, a digestive system, a pulmonary system, a purification system and a reproductive system.

"There are mothers and fathers among all species no matter how large or how small. Take lice, for example.

Lice magnified 10,000 times

"Barely visible to the human eye, they go about their lives in the same way we do; eating, drinking, defecating, urinating and, most important of all, copulating and perpetuating their kind.

"Like us, their offspring is the product of a chemical reaction—two bits of energy—the fertilization of an egg by a sperm.

"That the reproductive mechanism of the tiniest insect is identical to that of humans can readily be seen in embryos."

Well prepared for his dissertation, an image lit up on the giant screen of our entertainment center.

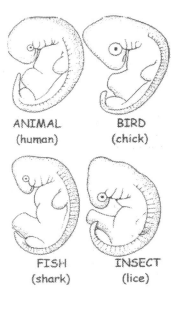

ANIMAL (human)   BIRD (chick)

FISH (shark)   INSECT (lice)

Early fetal development - does not reflect relative size

"God's living species that can be seen by the human eye number about twelve million. Yet, this is barely the tip of the iceberg of the vast world that goes on beneath us.

"Under the microscope, begins the world of living things too small to be seen by the human eye—microorganisms. The number of species here is unlimited.

"On the upper edge of this world, is the mite.

"Barely visible to the human eye, as a grain of sand is on a beach, mites are easily observed under a microscope going about their daily lives; eating, drinking, defecating, urinating and, most important of all, procreating their kind.

Mite magnified 100,000 times

"A single female mite can mother over a million children in her lifetime of a few days. Her offspring are among the largest of living things too small to be seen by the human eye.

"There can be as many as a half-million mites in the pillow on which one lays one's head at night. Many more millions chewing away at the outside of our bodies as we sleep.

The world within us

"In the miniature world that exists within the human body, live vast armies of living organisms instrumental to human life.

"Among them are many legions of bacteria, the tiniest creatures that can be observed under conventional microscopes, one-millionth of an inch in length. Mothers and fathers, going about their daily lives; eating, drinking, defecating, urinating and, most important of all, copulating—bringing their young into the world.

Family of bacteria going about its daily life magnified 1 million times

"Bacteria are the earliest life forms believed to exist."

I raised my eyebrows.

He answered my eyebrows. "Evolution!

"The sun's energy on the sea bred bacteria provided nourishment for amoeba which developed into nautical and plant life 500 million years ago. A hundred million years later, the first amphibians appeared which eventually evolved into land animals."

I gave away my ignorance, "Amphibians?"

"Sea animals, like frogs and turtles which live on both land and sea from which animals evolved." He clicked his remote,

Evolution

water + sun = bacteria = amoeba = plants = fish = amphibians = land animals = primates = man

"Bacteria are the tiniest creatures we are able to observe in which a chemical reaction between a male and a female results in offspring.

"The only logical conclusion one can come to is the process of creation is consistent in the world that goes on beneath them.

"Here, again, we must build on things we know, and construct a reasonable bridge to things we don't know. It is unreasonable to think the process of creation remains consistent to that point to which we can see, and suddenly changes beyond that point we can see.

"Then, we have the atom—the fundamental building block of everything we know and do not know." He clicked his remote.

Atom – the smallest chemical element

The atom is alive!

"Creation is built from the bottom up, not from the top down as tales told by ancient men would have one believe.

"The fundamental building block of creation is the atom.

"This is a scientific fact. Yes, in Einstein's day it was theory.

"But now it is a fact. Today, atoms can be observed under a field emission microscope going about their daily work.

"If it were possible to blow an atom up to the size of the earth, the core of the atom would be the size of a soccer ball.

"The core holds a variation of protons and neutrons held in place by an atomic force depending on the chemical element involved. The outer sphere of the atom contains electron(s) and photon(s) which, like the core, are held in place by an electromagnetic force.

"Now, what do we know about the atom?"

I gave him a look of anticipation to shroud my ignorance.

"Lots." He took a breath.

"To begin with, the atom is essentially empty space. Important, to what we are discussing here, atoms are in motion. Depending on their chemical composition, they move in different placements.

"Atoms that make up a diamond, the hardest substance known, are moving in different placements relative to those that make up our bodies, giving the diamond an illusion of density and our bodies an illusion of porosity. Those that make up the air we breathe are moving in still different placements, giving it an illusion of nothingness.

Atomic Structure

human body   diamond

"You are comparing apples and oranges?" I corrected him.

"Not really. The basic element of all living organisms is carbon. Diamond is a polymorph of carbon." With a click of his remote he launched an Internet source to back up what he was saying.

"Of these tiny bits of living energy, we do not know much. Yet, we do know they are the building blocks of all living things.

"All living organisms have three things in common."

"Three things in common?" I gave myself away.

"Yes, three things in common." He repeated.

"Each of them is conceived of a chemical interaction between two of their kind."

He waited for me to respond.

With nothing forthcoming, "Each one is conscious …"

I cut him off, "You're telling me an atom is conscious?"

"As I have said, under the microscope, we know atoms are in perpetual motion. Unconscious things cannot move. Unconscious things are dead. The atom is moving. The atom is alive!"

The hairs on the back of my neck curled up and down my back.

He gave me the third, "…each of them will eventually die.

"Of all the facts man has accumulated since the beginning of time, nothing is more certain…" I waited.

"From the tiniest bit of bacteria, to the restless struggle of the spider mite, to the epitome of the human brain; each of us is born of a mother and a father, each of us is conscious, and…" he paused to accentuate the absolute fact, "each of us will eventually die."

I decided to bring his little world to an end. "These 'little creatures' you speak of, move by instinct."

He was ready for me. "We, ourselves, are born with instinct. If it were not for instinct, we would never get out of the womb.

"Instinct, housed in the frontal lobes," pointing to his forehead, "is controlled by the peripheral lobes," pointing to the top of his head.

"The speed and accuracy in which our peripherals gather, compile, analyze and transmit info is measured in Intelligence Quotient.

"We know that instinct is controlled by the peripheral lobes in the tiniest creatures we are able to examine. It follows, the tiniest creature we are able to examine has intelligence.

"Again, we must draw from things we do know and construct a reasonable bridge to things we don't know.

"It is reasonable to conclude that the relative intelligence of micro-organisms—the ability to know what to do and the speed and accuracy one can do it—is a function of the peripheral lobes.

"As we have said, it is unreasonable to believe that the process of creation remains consistent to that point at which we can see, and suddenly changes beyond that point at which we cannot see.

"So, we know each of these creatures, no matter how small, has intelligence. Each one of them has a brain. We know this because each one of them 'knows' exactly what it is doing.

"For example, one family of micro-organisms is responsible for building the human body—literally billions of molecules of protein; each one going about its daily life in its microcosmic world building and maintaining the human body. Alongside them are billions of molecules of cholesterol; each one going about its daily life, building and maintaining the human nervous system.

"Trillions of tiny specs of life that know exactly what their job is in this vast factory of creation. Each one growing up to be mothers and fathers which will enable its kind to make its contribution to the epitome of creation—a human being.

"This is the real world we are born into. It is also the real world we live in. It is also the real world we will die in.

"Yet, according to all faiths, God 'happens' to think like a human.

"He does not happen to think like a bird, or like a fish, or like an insect, or like any other living organism on this planet. Or, for that matter, what could be trillions of living organisms on what could be an infinite number of planets beyond our solar system.

"Yet, for some strange reason, He creates all of us the same. All creatures, great and small." The miniature professor stretched out his hand toward the screen which held the indisputable proof of his game.

Faith vs. Reality

"We have finally arrived at the crossroad of Faith and Reality.

"Is it reasonable to believe God did not know the natural order of His creation and created Adam and Eve as adults?

"Is it reasonable to believe, God is an infinite, omnipresent Ghost that has its eye on each of us in everything we do?

"Is it reasonable to believe this Ghost appeared in the form of a burning bush three thousand years ago to a man telling him to kill all those who don't believe in Him?

"Is it reasonable to believe this Ghost snuck into a bedroom in the darkness of night and had sex with Mary in her sleep?

"Is it reasonable to believe there are bathrooms in heaven?"

I kept the thought to myself, "It would make more sense children of aliens on a distant planet were puppeteers of the human race."

141

He closed, "…or is it more reasonable to believe, the Bible is *'tales told by ancient men to attain political ambitions?'* Tales capitalized on by preachers to attain their own political ambitions today?"

He voiced it as a question. Yet, it was much more a statement.

"Again, this boils down to two opposing hypotheses.

"Is it reasonable to believe God thinks like a human being? Or is it more reasonable to believe 'God is a reflection of the human mind?'

"Nevertheless, Moses came close." He waited.

I took the bait, "Adam and Eve?"

"Yes, had he said "Atom and Eve" he would have been right.

I probed him, "He would have been right?"

"Yes, 'Atom' is the beginning, and, 'Eve' is the end of the day. We all have a beginning, and …we all have an end...."

I waited.

"…except…"

I waited, once more.

"…except, those of us, who employ reason with which we are endowed, and set aside the assumptions we have been born into. Those of us, who take the time to weave our souls. Those of us, who choose to cease to exist as mortal men, and evolve as Gods!

"Nevertheless, we have emerged from the valley of darkness. We can now search for the light."

I waited for him to unravel his confusing remark.

"We have removed the assumptions we have been born into—the make-believe world we have been born into."

He took on an air of utter confidence. "We are now positioned to remove the question mark from the end of our lives: What happens to us after we are gone?" He closed his books.

Carefully stacking them, one-by-one, to the far end of the table, he got up and strolled over to the fireplace, stoked the coals and added a log. He poked the coals a few times more.

I heard a low murmur, "So much for Gods. So much for Dionysus. So much for Jesus. Yet, one still has the soul. Yes, the soul..."

He struggled into his mackinaw and went up the steps and out of the house into the snow. The door snapped shut behind him.

Interlude

"As not the tiniest scrap has survived, we have no idea what Mark, Matthew, Luke and John may have written. All we really do know is that the gospels as we know them today were written in the 4th century.

"With a three hundred year gap between the writing of the gospels and Christ's time, without any technological means to record events as they may or may not have occurred, one could have written most anything to serve one's political agenda..."

Albino Luciani, Gregorian University, Rome February 27, 1947

The Birds and the Bees

"I'm getting married." he shouted.

He had just come in from the snow. His cheeks were red and flakes still clung to his nose.

Audrey shot me a sideways glance and laughed, "Have you set the date? Where are you going on your honeymoon?"

"You don't understand. I'm getting married, and I'm getting married, tomorrow!"

He went on, "It happened today, today in the snow. I don't know how it happened, but it happened. It's real, and I know it's real.

"I was playing with Jeannie in the snow. We slipped on the ice and she went down and I almost on top of her. As I raised myself up, I saw it in her eyes. I knew it was in my eyes too."

Pointing to his heart, "Furthermore, it is in here, and it is in hers, too. So we are getting married. That's all there is to it."

I reminded him, "Justin, you're only ten years old. Your mother and I didn't get married until we were in our twenties."

His voice rising with every word, "You were brought up in a slow generation. Things are different today. The pace is fast. If you don't grab onto it when it comes by, it's not going to come back and get you. It's going to leave you behind.

"What's more, it's going to leave you behind forever. And I'm not going to be left behind. Particularly, not this time."

A shroud of dread came over me, the feeling that comes to all fathers when they are faced by the great moment of truth. That time, one has to give the most difficult sermon one has to make in life. The one entitled *The Birds and the Bees*.

In my case, unfortunately, it was coming a few years ahead of time. I always hoped that if I let it go long enough, it would go away. The schools or his peers would take care of it.

"Justin, we have to talk." My voice took on a serious tone.

"I don't want to talk," With great conviction, "Let there be no doubt about it, I'm getting married!" He headed for the stairs.

I decided not to follow him. Not that he was upset and it might not be the best time to talk about it. Rather, I needed time. Time to put my ducks in a row and plan my strategy.

I turned to Audrey with that expressive look of so many times before. The one that said, "Help me. Please, help me."

She smiled a smile of rejection. "All boys, sometime during their life, not necessarily in adolescence, not necessarily in college, not necessarily while climbing the corporate ladder, but sometime, most often only once, get the chance to prove their manhood. This is your chance, your big chance. But it has to be you alone." She went back to loading the dishwasher.

I searched my inner-self in relentless desperation. "Maybe there's someone you can pay? Maybe there's someone who provides the service? Handles this type of thing on a professional basis?"

I hadn't felt so much terror since the time I had gone to confession to tell the man I had first touched a girl.

I remember that time I had hesitated on the church steps, and turned away and walked around the block. Then, walked around the block again, and again, and again—forty-five times. I remember it clearly as I counted each and every one of them.

Each time, I came up with another way out of it.

Maybe I didn't touch her enough to count? I could join another church? Maybe I didn't even need a church? After all, my conscience told me what was right and what was wrong.

Then, finally, having already done my penance, I proceeded courageously up the steps and into the confessional box. "What does she mean prove my manhood? Doesn't that count?"

147

Yet, I knew I was fooling myself. Collecting my thoughts, I started up the stairs and made my way toward his room.

Though I knew it might drain my mind, I was intent on proving my manhood. I was not aware it would also drain my heart.

As I entered the room, he was sitting up in bed.

He lay the pad he held in his hand face down. Closing the pen, he slipped it stealthily into his shirt pocket.

He pointed to the foot of the bed.

I took my place as instructed.

He began, "I was making a checklist of things we have to do."

Reaching down putting his hand over mine, "This doesn't mean I don't still love you and Mom. It's just that these things happen, and when they happen, we have to make the best of them."

A tear climbed up out of my heart, it ran to the corner of my eye, and moved toward the lid… toward the cliff, so to speak.

Staggering like a boxer who comes out of the corner and takes an uppercut on the chin which throws him back against the ropes, I gazed, first, to the right, then, to the left, and, again, to the right, and, finally, to the left, once more; all the time struggling desperately to keep the tear on the edge of the lid.

Having lost the first round, I decided to change my strategy from one of aggression, to one of trying to stay on my feet until the bell rang. I prayed that if I could get back to my corner, I would have time to rethink my game and come out fighting again.

Suddenly, the bell did ring.

Picking up the phone, he announced, "Jeannie."

Getting up, I grasped his ankle, "Behave yourself."

Walking out of the room, I closed the door behind me.

As I came into the kitchen, Audrey gave me a look one gives a six year old. I explained, "I didn't chicken out, the phone rang and it was Jeannie. I thought I would give him some privacy."

I thought how cruel this was of her. I thought how much easier it is for the woman. She only has to give birth to them. Yes, a great effort, but one that is only physical. Not too challenging. Doesn't take a lot of brains.

The man is stuck with the tough ones, the ones that tax the far reaches of his intellect and in some cases break his heart. Perhaps, pluck the strings of his very soul. It just wasn't fair.

148

Good news and bad news

In the morning the little man came down the steps.

Taking his place at the table, he brought us some good news and, unfortunately, some bad news.

"We've decided to wait a week or two. We still have some things to work out."

He paused for a moment. "We can't decide whether the first one should be a boy or a girl."

For the first time I saw a hint of compassion in Audrey's face in recognition of the difficulty of my plight. For the first time, she seemed to understand how tough this job was going to be.

Having loaded him onto the school bus, I approached Audrey, "Perhaps, we can handle this together."

Yet, to no avail. As if she had read my thoughts of the night before, "We are man and woman. There are some things each of us must do on our own, things the other can't really help them with.

"For me, it was having him. For you, it is this."

She would leave me no wiggle room, "Now stop trying to get out of it. Stop walking around the block. Go in and get the job done." I shot her look of utter despair.

She returned an encouraging smile, "You can do it. I believe you can do it. All it will take, now, is that you believe you can do it."

Profile of courage

That day I lost a small fortune for the firm I worked for. I knew I had to get the job done that night or I would have no job.

That evening, when I came in the door, I winked bravely at Audrey and proceeded directly up the stairs to his room.

I took up the same position at the foot of the bed that I had the day before, "What are you reading?"

Without looking up, *"Sequel to Relativity."*

Though I would think him joking, on its cover a picture of his patron saint Albert Einstein peered out at me.

"I am reading here of the birds and the bees."

As if he could see the anguish in my eyes, the fright of a grown man trying to become a man, the terror of it all; he offered with a

149

compassionate smile only a child of ten could muster, "I'll tell you what I am going to do. I am going to let you off the hook." Then, in an authoritative manner, "I am going to tell you about them..."

"Them?" I cut him off with a dumbfounded look.

"Yes, the birds and the bees. I am going to tell you how this thing 'love' is supposed to work."

The Birds and the Bees

He had obviously set the whole thing up.

The little monster had been playing with his father's mind all along. His father's inward fear of discussing 'sex.' Yet, grateful for having been left off the hook, I let him have the floor.

"This book—this man Einstein—says: 'all matter is made up of tiny chemical particles—energy, moving parts, atoms.'

"He puts it quite simply here: 'The Atom is the fundamental building block of everything we know and don't know—from the far reaches of space, to ourselves, to the air we breathe, to the earth we walk on.'

"As we discussed the other day, the ground beneath us and the air around us, are made up of the same atomic particles we are made up of. Tiny bits of energy. Tiny bits of empty space.

"It is that atoms move in different placements that enables them to create various illusions of solidity, nothingness and porosity.

"The ground beneath us is empty space. It is the placements of this 'empty space' moving within it that create an illusion of solidity.

"The air is also made up of atoms, empty space. These are moving in placements creating the illusion of transparency.

"The 'empty space' comprising the human body is moving in still different placements creating the illusion of porosity." He searched my eyes that he had not lost me before going on.

"Nevertheless, according to this man Einstein: the atom is the fundamental unit of all matter, animate or inanimate.

"What's more, all matter is continuously giving off energy— moving parts, and when that energy leaves one form of matter, it finds its way into some other form of matter.

"This energy exchange between different forms of matter is in perpetual motion. It never stops. This is true of ourselves, of the air we breathe, of the hardest thing known, diamond."

Sight, touch, smell, sound...

I wondered where he was going with all this. What could this possibly have to do with the birds and the bees? Yet, he had left me off the hook and with great appreciation for that, I let him go on with what, to me, was pre-adolescence madness.

"I'll show you how this works. I've been experimenting with it.

"Bring your two index fingers together about six inches in front of your eyes and hold them just barely apart," pointing to the table lamp, "There, with the light behind them."

Following his instructions, I did what he asked.

"Now, stare at them for a few seconds."

Again, I did what he asked.

Excitedly, he exclaimed, "See them? See them?"

Sure enough I could see some movement, kind of a haze, but definitely movement between my fingers.

"So much for sight," he concluded.

"Now get up and go over and stand sideways to the wall. Over there," he pointed, "with your arm right up against the wall."

Again, I did what he told me to do. Now wondering more than ever what all this had to do with the birds and the bees?

"Now, let your arm hang limp and press it outward as hard as you can against the wall."

"Outward against the wall?" I questioned as it was certainly a futile effort as the wall was there. Nevertheless, I did what he asked and held the pressure there for about a minute.

He continued his instructions, "Now, with your arm hanging limp, move over here away from the wall."

Again, I did what he told me. Much to my surprise, my arm rose entirely on its own to a horizontal position.

"Very good, that proves it," he bellowed as if he were Einstein, himself, coming upon a great discovery.

"What we are seeing is the power of the physical energy that was released from your arm but was held just outside the arm and could not be released because of the wall.

"This is because the atoms that make up the wall are moving in different placements than those which make up the muscle fibers in your arm."

151

Again, he paused as if in triumph.

"The sense of smell probably better demonstrates what Einstein was talking about. There, on the dresser." he pointed.

I looked at the dresser. I saw nothing that could possibly smell. Two ordinary drinking glasses, one placed upright and the other placed upside down on its glass-surfaced top.

"Lift the one that is upright and smell inside it," he ordered.

I did as he told me. I could discern no smell whatsoever other than the air I was breathing, "Can't smell a thing." I said it carefully, as not to disappoint him.

"Now, pick up the other one, the one that is upside down and smell the inside of that glass."

Again, following his orders, I picked up the glass. This time there was a very definite metallic smell.

"You are smelling particles of energy the glass has been giving up, but have been trapped inside it for the past week.

"Yet, sound best demonstrates this thing called energy. When we hear a sound, we hear two and, more often, millions of bits of energy bouncing off each other—moving parts—atoms.

"No single thing by itself can produce sound. It takes two or more to do the job. Whether it is a locomotive crashing into a bus, or an individual atom crashing into another atom.

Thoughts as physical things

"Yet, there is much more to this thing called energy than just sight, touch, smell and sound."

Reading from *Sequel to Relativity*: "'...This perpetual interchange of moving particles of energy within the universe extends to human beings.

"'That this phenomenon affects all physical matter including the air around us can be proved in a scientific laboratory.

"'That it also extends to mental processes is more difficult to prove. Yet, there is compelling evidence the energy exchange between human beings is both physical and mental. And in human beings it is primarily mental.'" He glanced up at me to assure himself he hadn't lost me, before going on.

He found out he had lost me. "What you are saying makes no sense. You are trying to tell me that thoughts are physical things. Everyone knows thoughts are empty space."

He said it with utter conviction. "Wrong! They are physical things.

152

"Remember the time we talked about the atom. That the outer sphere of an atom contains electrons."

He gave me a minute or two to recall the session. "Thoughts are a composite of electrons. Electrons are physical things."

"You are speaking of theory, not fact." I corrected him.

"Not theory. The school of artificial intelligence has proved what, at one time, was theory. For example, it is possible to move the keys of a computer keyboard solely with thoughts.

"Independent of the world of science, common sense tells us that thoughts are physical things."

I shot him another look of disbelief as he proved his case.

"If they are not physical things, we could not feel them.

Physical energy vs. mental energy

"Hence, it is possible to exchange physical energy for mental energy." He looked up at me.

"When one wins a marathon, one spends great physical energy. Yet, this is more than offset by the absorption of great mental energy. The amount of energy one absorbs depends on how loud the crowd cheers, as one comes down the stretch.

"To take this a step further, if one was the only man on earth and one was to accomplish the same task, one would only spend physical energy but not reap the reward of the mental offset, as there would be no other intelligent being to draw the mental energy from.

"Thus, mental energy can only come from another conscious being, either an animal, or a human being.

"Yet, regarding animals, the energy draw is primarily physical. Carnivorous animals, from the lion to the eagle, evolved special structures to enable them to bring down their prey: sharp claws, strong jaws, sharp-tearing teeth and even sharper beaks.

"As needs of each specie required it to grasp with claws, ensuing generations developed longer and sharper claws—physical energy drawing out the claw to make it longer and sharper.

"Now, this is especially important. Now listen very carefully." He lowered his voice to just above a whisper, reading from his book: "'In human beings, the process is predominately mental. Our ancestors overcame physical handicaps by living in cooperatives and using intelligence to make tools.

153

Hence we have no claws, no sharp-tearing teeth. Our energy exchange has been primarily mental. And today, it continues to be primarily mental.'"

I was certainly learning something that had escaped me during my schooldays. Must have skipped class that day. Yet, I could discern no connection to the question at hand. The birds and the bees. Yet, I thought it best to let him continue reading his book.

Energy gainers vs. energy losers

"'When one says nice things to another, he or she transfers his or her mental energy to the other and the reception of that energy can be profoundly felt by the receiver.

"'Conversely, when one yells at another, he or she is drawing mental energy from the other, and the loss of that energy can be felt by the victim.

"'When one tells new and interesting stories, one conveys mental energy to the receiver and the receipt of that energy is profoundly felt by the receiver.

"'When one tells repetitious and boring stories, one drains mental energy from the listener, and the loss of that energy can be decidedly felt by the victim.

"'Every day, people are giving and receiving mental energy to and from those they come in contact with.

"'There are people who are primarily energy gainers while there are others who are primarily energy losers.'

"See," he looked at me with a grin. "Yesterday, when I said 'I'm getting married,' I was an energy gainer. You were an energy loser."

I thought to myself, "You're sure right about that."

"When I said this morning, 'We had put off getting married for a week or so,' I was an energy giver, and you were an energy gainer. Then, I took the energy right back with, 'We can't decide whether the first one should be a boy or a girl.'

Falling in love

"Now listen very carefully." He turned a page.

"'There are times when the energy level of two people is on the same plane with each other as when two people fall in love.'"

He looked at me. "And this is what is important in my case: 'This balance can last for minutes, for days, for months, or for a lifetime.

"'Whether it lasts, depends on the energy flow remaining relatively equal between the parties. If one of the parties starts to draw too much energy from the other, then the 'in love' illusion begins to dissipate.'"

Looking up at me, he dealt me a tidal wave of energy. "Jeannie and I have had our moment, but now it is passed.

"Yes, I will always cherish having had that moment, but as I said in the kitchen, when these things come along, you've got to grab on to them. But what is most important is that you grab onto them at the right time. Our time has not yet come."

Something the little rascal had known all the time.

He had seized at the opportunity to trick me into talking about sex. Yet, glad it was finally over, that I had at last done my job, I could proudly relate to Audrey that I had taken the tiger by the tail and had taught him of the birds and the bees.

Getting up, I moved toward the door.

He called out after me. "One question," he asked.

"Yes?" I glanced back.

"Do they have them in Heaven?" he held back a smirk.

"Do they have what in Heaven?" I gave him an opening.

"Penises and vaginas?" he fired away at me.

Lost for words, I couldn't utter a sound.

"There are none in Heaven," he instructed. "Yes, Father John told me so. Only the ones down below in Hell have them."

He threw me a combination of a wink and smile as to leave no doubt he was, indeed, the master of this kind of thing.

Sequel to Relativity is the creation of the author and not a published book. Headband transmitters can move keys on a computer equipped with receivers. Thoughts are made up of physical things called electrons. Electrons can be stored, transmitted and received in wireless transmission. Neutrons play a role in their activity.

Jeannie,

Yes, I remember you,
the dance in the snow,
the slip on the ice,
the flakes on your cheeks,
the look in your eyes,
the thud in my heart,
the dream of it all.

Yes, I remember you,
the loss of it all,
that for you,
and for me,
it was not to be.

Justin

In Search of the Human Soul

"...then we must define the human soul. Precisely what is this thing we are trying to save?"

Albino Luciani, Gregorian University, Rome February 1947

Times That Try Men's Souls

It was Saturday, the one day I could sleep in.

It was ten o'clock when I came down into the kitchen to partake of whatever Audrey had whipped up for breakfast.

At my place was a folded up newspaper. As I picked it up, she asked, "Did you get a good night's sleep?"

"Certainly," I threw her one of those 'slept like a baby' lines.

"Good," she seemed concerned. "You're going to need it."

"What do you mean?" I asked. "What is he up to now?"

"He is searching… He's been up since six o'clock. He's down in the family room with the usual stack of books around him."

"He is searching…?" I questioned.

"Yes, he is searching…" she smiled. "He is searching for his soul."

"For his what?" I exclaimed, more than asked.

"His soul," she repeated. "He's not sure he has one. Are you sure you have one?"

"Of course, I have one." I shot back; frustrated she would ask me such a ridiculous question so early in the morning. Correcting the thought, "so late in the morning."

I thought of the little man downstairs in his lair. "This should be an easy one for a change. I will handle this one in a single swoop."

Finishing up the bacon and eggs, I poured myself another cup of coffee. With an unprecedented air of confidence, I headed down the stairs. To most, this would be an insurmountable challenge. To me, it was just another day on the job.

Books, books and more books

There he was, just as Audrey had described him. Hunched over with his inquisitive eyes perusing an open book with another dozen or so scattered on the table around him.

As usual, there was a couple by Albert Einstein. I noticed one on existentialism, another on Egyptology, one on Buddhism, and one on how the brain works. There was even one on how medicine works.

I don't recall any of the others. Just that they were there, stacked up alongside one another. A scene, I had become accustomed to for most of my fatherly life.

I thought of the rules of the local library that allowed one to take out so many books at a time that had enabled this little guy of ten to have read more books than an average man reads in ten lifetimes.

The room was cold. I walked over to the fireplace and stoked the fire, adding a couple of logs.

So engulfed in his reading, he hadn't noticed the cold. In fact, he hadn't even noticed me. When I walked over to him, he looked up with a sudden start.

I decided not to give him a chance. It would give him the edge. From my past experience, I couldn't afford to give him the edge. Instead of raising the question, I led with the answer.

"You believe in Jesus. Don't you?"

"Sure, I believe in the ideology of Jesus. Sometimes it's a struggle. But in that I am a Christian, yes." he agreed.

"Then, that is all you need." I proclaimed.

"You asked me if I believed in Jesus. That doesn't give me any answers. What I need are the facts, not beliefs. If I am going to plan my life, I must have the facts.

"I must know. I must know within a shadow of a doubt, I have a soul. I just can't guess at it. Maybe most people are satisfied at guessing at it. Content taking the preacher's word for it. To me, it is far too important. I must know."

"You must know." Amused, "Just how do you intend to find out?"

"I'm not sure yet. For starters, I know where it is. At least, I think I know where it is."

"You know where it is?" I asked with a hint of surprise.

"Sure, right here," pointing to his temple.

"Our ability to know right from wrong is our link to God. If one has a soul, it must be here." He pointed, again, to his temple.

"How do you know it is not here?" I pointed to my heart.

"Because, what is here," pointing to his temple, "controls what is here," pointing to his heart He did this with great conviction.

He undoubtedly had gotten himself ready for my onslaught. Like a spider in his lair he now had me in his web and it was too late for me to go back. I could only wait for the inevitable.

I decided to try anyway. "So, if you know where it is, you know you have a soul."

I held the thought to myself, "Why, in all of my life, I had never thought of it in this way. I suppose I never thought it was important enough to waste my time thinking about.

"Strange," I wisely kept the thought to myself. "I had spent a good part of my life going to church and listening to other men telling me what I have to do to save my soul. I would guess, tens of thousands of hours in all. Yet, this was the first time, I had ever asked myself, 'Just exactly what is this thing I am trying to save?'"

Regardless, he corrected my misconception, "I said I 'think' I know where it is. Yet, I want to know more than just that.

"I want to be certain I have a soul. What's more, I want to know where the mind leaves off and the soul begins—that part of me which is a part of God."

"That part of you which is a part of God?" I challenged.

"My soul, like all souls, is immortal. Only God is immortal. As one knows, all life on the planet eventually dies. If my soul is immortal, then it must be a part of God.

"More specifically, I want to know where the 'function' of the mind leaves off and the 'function' of the soul begins."

I warned, "You're attempting the impossible. It can't be done. You're wasting your time."

"Pull up a chair," he directed.

With an air of solid instruction, pausing after each phrase, "I will tell you of the body… I will tell you of the mind… I will tell you of the spirit…I will tell you of the soul…"

The Crown Jewel of Christianity

He grew quiet. I supposed reducing the complexities of what he was about to say to match the limited capacity of my mind.

"In 3100BC, Menes-Narmer became the first pharaoh of a united Egypt. Yet, there is something more remarkable about this man who came along thousands of years before the Judea-Christian faith, we live in today, was first thought of."

I shot him a question mark.

He answered my question, "Pharaoh Narmer was the first man to convince a general population his body would rise again after death.

"Too, he was clever enough to extend it to all. If one served Pharaoh in this life, one would be there to serve him for all time.

"Clicking his remote, he read from one of his books: 'On the Day of Judgment evil doers, body and spirit, will be consumed by the Devourer of Evil. The good, who served Pharaoh here, will be raised to serve Pharaoh, for all time…'

"It follows, we have a Christian's pledge of allegiance to his faith:

'I believe in the Forgiveness of Sins, the Resurrection of the Body...'

"It boggles the mind, Christians laugh at the ancient Egyptian belief the body will resurrect on a Day of Judgment. Yet, they, themselves, pay a preacher who sells them the same delusion."

I could have said it for him, but he beat me to it. "Do you really think the body will rise again after it decays to dust?"

I gave him a weak, a very weak, "No, not... not really..."

The merchandise of Christianity

"Like any other business, Christianity has its products.

"Resurrection of the body is the crown jewel of its product line. The cash cow of the preacher so to speak."

All he got out of me was a dumbfounded look.

He could not have made his point much clearer, "Imagine the horror of a spirit or a mind going about eternity without its body..."

Though I knew where he was going, I decided not to stop him.

"Yet, these same vendors sell miracles which pretend to save the terminally ill and gravely injured from reaping the product they have spent their church-going lives paying for.

"Makes no sense, does it?" He drew a blank stare.

"If the preacher tells you, this life is but a grain of sand on the vast beach of eternity, why would he sell you miracles to keep you from acquiring the paradise he has already sold you?"

Keeping my cool, I waited for him to answer his own question.

It didn't take long, "He doesn't believe it himself.

"The preacher who peddles immortality, when threatened with a life-threatening illness or injury, prays for a miracle to save himself from going to meet his Jesus. Too, he doesn't pray from a church pew. He prays from a hospital bed. His only real chance of survival.

"This tells him, you don't really believe it. Yet, knowing you are the fool who fell for the first ruse, he sells you another one.

"After all, anyone with an IQ of seventy-five or better knows the body will never rise again."

I had no option, other than to yield a reluctant nod.

Predatory killers preying on children

"Peddling resurrection of the body is a dangerous practice.

"As a priest, Albino Luciani was caught telling school children: *'According to tales told by ancient men to achieve their political ambitions, we will live forever. According to all that we really know, when we are dead, we are dead.'*

"He warned those who sought to censor him: *'Preachers, who fool people into thinking their bodies will resurrect somewhere up there, have the blood of children and mentally impaired on their hands.'*

"In his time, still true today, the promise of resurrection of the body was the leading cause of children suicide and a leading cause of suicides among the mentally ill. Too, the preacher's promise, *'one will come back as the epitome of a human being,'* drives thousands of handicapped children to take their own lives every year

"Luciani warned of the dangers of confusing faith and reality.

"To the adult, resurrection of the body is 'sheer fantasy.' Yet, to the unwary child or the mentally impaired, it can seem 'reality.'

"Luciani held that scrupulous preachers and irresponsible parents, who fool children into thinking resurrection of the body is for real and cause them to take their own lives, be imprisoned. In the same way, preachers and parents who deprive children of medical treatment in God's name are imprisoned for endangering their lives.

"Representative of thousands of cases recorded each year in the United States, occurred recently in Baltimore.

"A ten year old girl, who had taken her own life, left a note, *'I have gone to live with Jesus.'* The preacher did such a convincing job at her funeral that she was, indeed, in heaven, the next day her six year old brother went to join her. Even then, the preacher and the parents were delighted the children were in heaven."

Regrettably, I fed his fire, "Your friend Albino Luciani is wrong. They don't belong in prison. They belong in an asylum."

He took advantage of my blunder. "Correct. Belief in resurrection of the body is the most widespread mental illness in the world."

I set him up. "If that's true, if guilty preachers and parents were brought to trial, they would be acquitted."

He shot me a bewildered look.

163

"Innocent by reason of insanity." I scoffed him one.

"True," he agreed. "In the United States people think this kind of thing is right. Conversely, China has no incidence of children killing themselves to go to heaven. In China, preachers who fool children and the mentally impaired into thinking they go to heaven are imprisoned. In America we call this violation of human rights.

"China's laws are driven by <u>reason</u>. America's laws are driven by <u>faith</u>. As you prefer to call it… <u>reason of insanity</u>.

"Nevertheless, getting back to where we left off.

"As we have said, the Nicene Council set the central salvation canon of their church on resurrection of the body. Yet, today, only the unwary child and the mentally ill would believe it.

"How did the founding fathers of the Roman Catholic Church ever come up with this ridiculous idea to begin with?"

I thought I got another one right, "Christ rose from the dead."

Christ's judgement - resurrection of souls

"Christ's resurrection has nothing to do with it. Christ speaks of a Day of Judgment only once in the gospels. Here, in the Gospel of Matthew:

> 'When the Son of Man comes to glory… He will gather <u>souls</u> of those who cared for their neighbor, who will inherit the kingdom of heaven prepared for them,
>
> I was hungry and you gave me food.
> I was thirsty and you gave me drink.
> I was a stranger and you took me in
> I was naked and you clothe me
> I was sick and you came to visit me
> I was in prison and you came to me.
>
> He will gather <u>souls</u> of those who did not care for their neighbor, who will be cursed to the everlasting fire prepared for them,
>
> I was hungry and you gave me no food.
> I was thirsty and you gave me no drink.
> I was a stranger and you did not take me in
> I was naked and you did not clothe me
> I was sick and you did not visit me
> I was in prison and you did not come to me.'"

164

He waited for some sign that I had made the connection.

"In His only discussion of the Day of Judgment, Christ bases His judgment solely on our compassion for others.

"Consistent with the 'Universal God' we discussed the day I sold my bike, Christ's judgment is based solely on His commandments: 'Love thy neighbor as thyself' and 'Sell all thou hast and give to the poor.'

"More importantly, relative to what we are talking about, Christ speaks only of souls. He does not speak of resurrection of the body.

The Christian path to salvation of sins

"Conversely, other than defining its Deity, the Nicene Creed defines the salvation tenet of its faith: *"I Believe... in the forgiveness of sins, the resurrection of the body, and life everlasting."*

"More specifically, the salvation tenet of its faith is: *'resurrection of the body through absolution of sin by an ordained priest.'*

"Yet, the gospels are explicit that forgiveness of sin by another man has nothing to do with salvation. Christ never gave the power to forgive sin to His disciples. Too, the gospels are explicit that only God can forgive sin: 'Father forgive them for they know not what they do.'

"This explains the three hundred year gap between the earliest surviving gospels and the time Christ is said to have lived."

I took it he was about to go off on another tangent.

"Remember the day we surmised that the Nicene Council must have destroyed the gospels and epistles that served as divine guidance for its proceedings. At the time, this made sense to us because not the tiniest reliable scrap predating the Nicene Council has survived.

"This, in turn, led us to conclude the Nicene Council must have made material changes to the gospels as they were originally written.

"Yet, the problem is not so much the gospels as it is Paul's epistles.

"Paul could not have written his epistles later than 67AD because he died in that year. Conversely, we know from their historical content the gospels were written after he died. Specifically, the gospels that speak of salvation—*Matthew* and *Luke*—were written after 85AD.

"The Council based salvation—*resurrection of the body through forgiveness of sin*—on Paul's epistles. Yet in those specific epistles, Paul is obviously responding to conflicting testimony in the gospels:

Concerning *forgiveness of sin* we have:

"The word of Jesus Christ in the gospels: 'Father forgive them for they know not what they do.' Only God can forgive sin.

"The word of Paul in his epistles: 'We are the ambassadors of Christ who has passed solely to us the power to forgive sins… required for life everlasting.'

Concerning *resurrection of the body* we have:

"The word of Jesus Christ in the gospels: 'When the Son of Man comes to glory. He will gather souls of those who cared for their neighbor…'

"The word of Paul: 'If the dead are not raised, Christ has not been raised…'

"If Christ had not said: 'He will gather souls of those who cared for their neighbor,' Paul would have had no reason to correct Christ's testimony.

"Too, Paul claimed to have received the power to forgive sin from Christ in an apparition. If he had written of this before the evangelists wrote the gospels they certainly would have included it in the gospels as it would have been the only path to salvation. But they did not.

"So we know beyond a shadow of a doubt, Paul's most important testimony, the testimony upon which the Nicene Fathers established the salvation tenet of Christianity—*resurrection of the body through forgiveness of sin*—was written by someone after Paul died and after the gospels were written. Since we are speaking of the salvation tenet of the Nicene Creed, it points only to members of the Nicene Council.

Common Sense

"Nevertheless, getting back to what we are talking about here.

"To the extent one defines the soul as 'a part of us that is a part of God,' it makes some sense the soul could return to God upon death. It makes no sense whatsoever, the body has that same chance. The reason you answered my question, 'No, not… not really…'

"Finally, we have common sense…" he waited
   "Common sense?" I took him up on it.
   "Reason and Intellect," he pointed to his temple.

"As my mentor Albino Luciani so profoundly put it:

"*'If God deemed us to be immortal, He would have created us to be immortal to begin with. The only alternative is to think God is stupid.*

"*'It is unreasonable to believe that a God, who has endowed us with reason and intellect, has intended us to forego their use, that we would set ourselves above the natural order of His creation...*

"*'If there is a God, He created us mortal consistent with all living things. If there is no God, when we are dead, we are dead.'"*[1]

No wiggle room: "Either way, when we are dead, we are dead."

Not good enough: "Belief in resurrection of the body is not so much a matter of mental illness as it is..." he waited.

I couldn't wait any longer, "As it is what?"

"...as it is a matter of Intelligence." He pointed to his temple.

"Yet, we still have the soul. Yes, we will get to that soon..."

[1] Albino Luciani, Gregorian University, Rome, February 27, 1947.
For 'salvation of the Universal God' see *'The Bike'* pg. 11.

The verse *'We are the ambassadors of Christ...'* is as it appears in *Codex Sinaiticus* and Canon Law. Modern bibles vary the verse, e.g. *'We are the ambassador of Christ through whom one appeals one's reconciliation with God, etc.'*

Canon law of the Roman Catholic Church (ignored by many Catholics) requires forgiveness of mortal sin by a priest. Catechism includes masturbation and impure thoughts as mortal sins. Pedophile priests prey on children in the confessional box.

At a time the literacy rate was less than 1%, Paul's epistles—narrative—would have been more vulnerable to alteration. The gospels—stories—would have been more widely disseminated verbally. Yet, the Nicene Council could have made material changes to both. After all, modern men are making material changes to the gospels even today. Ref: 'Changing Times' pgs. 79-81.

Belief in survival of the body is the leading cause of suicide in children and a leading cause of suicide among mentally impaired. 2010 Statistical Abstracts of the United States: 6,240 children & mentally impaired left notes or other evidence they were going to heaven to join deity and/or parents and others recently deceased. Preachers and others who make their money peddling the existence of 'heaven' have the blood of countless children on their hands. The quote attributed to Albino Luciani relative to this subject is reprinted from *Corriere delle Alpi* 3 March 1948

167

The Greatest of Prophets

"We think of Moses, Isaiah and Muhammad as the great prophets of the western world. Yet, the greatest prophet lived long before their times." I gave him a look as if he had fallen out of a tree.

"Because of the infinite imaginary capacity of the human mind, one might fantasize the spirit might survive death in an unlimited range of definitions, particularly, as the driving force behind this illusion is man's imminent mortality. Yet, only a fool would believe the body has that same chance.

"As we established the day we discussed the Holy Trinity, East did not meet up with West until the 4th century after Christ; Jesus was unaware of the God Brahma who was working the eastern front, while He was working the western front.

"Correspondingly, those in China and India were unaware of the Egyptian belief that the body would rise again when they were putting Hinduism together thousands of years before the time of Christ.

"This explains why atheism is widely spread in the East. The spirit is generally perceived to be one's mind without one's body.

"Survival of one's mind without one's body is not a favorable sell for the preacher. As I have said, imagine the horror of a mind going about eternity without its body. After all, in this life the mind is overwhelmingly occupied in controlling bodily functions.

"This also explains why faith is widely spread in the West. All western faiths, Christian and Muslim, peddle resurrection of the body.

Origin of the human soul

"Too, this explains why the idea of the existence of an indestructible soul grew up in the east and not in the west.

"It was that survival of one's spirt (mind) without one's body was not a viable sell for the eastern prophet that drove him to come up with the idea there exists in each human being a soul—a part of each of us that returns to God after death. That part of us, today's preacher explains '... *is just something we do not understand.* '

"Regardless, eastern salvation—where it does exist—is limited to survival of some form of the spirit. This is also true of all primitive societies in the west which remained isolated from western religions until modern times.

"The Australian Indian indigenous to the South Pacific, the Aborigine Indian indigenous to South America, the American Indian indigenous to North America, the Bushman indigenous to South Africa, the Eskimo indigenous to the Arctic—having never heard of the Egyptian belief the body would rise again—believed only the spirit escapes the body at death.

"Yet, in truth, all of those in the East, and all of those in the West, pin their hopes on survival of some form of the spirit.

"Just who came up with this astounding idea?

The greatest of prophets

"Excavations tell us that about one hundred and thirty thousand years ago, Neanderthals began to bury their dead. Excavations of earlier sites tell us they did not bury their dead before that time.

"We know hygiene was not their motive because they buried only their male dead. Females, smaller and weaker, were harmless.

"The bigger the body, the deeper buried. Smaller cadavers buried barely beneath the surface and larger cadavers buried progressively deeper up to depths of twelve feet. Much more than compelling evidence, they feared the spirits of the dead.

"The practice of larger cadavers buried progressively deeper was also true of the Cro-Magnons and primitive societies that escaped into the twentieth century unscathed by modern practices.

"Of all living creatures, only human beings bury their dead.

"Except the primitive Eskimo who could not bury his dead. Even then, discarding their dead out on the ice exhibited belief in spirits.

"As late as the nineteen-sixties, Eskimos, living out on the tundra, would abandon their dead on the ice a distance from their homestead; the bigger the cadaver, the further away from the igloo.

"The universal hypothesis, the spirit could survive death, began with the Neanderthals, was passed on down to the Cro-Magnons, on down to primitive societies, and finally on down to modern man.

"Though we do know the name of the man—Narmer—who came up with the idea the 'body' would rise again, we will never know the name of the greatest of prophets.

"The Neanderthal man who, one hundred and thirty thousand years ago, came up with the universal supposition the 'spirit' could survive death." He paused for a time to allow what he had said to sink in.

Again, I missed the boat. "He must have been a genius of monumental proportions to have come up with such a brilliant idea."

"Just the opposite." He shot back, "Genius is based on logic. He was an idiot. He ignored reality. He nurtured delusion.

The proof of the pudding

"Nevertheless, we have come to that point at which we must provide the 'proof of the pudding' so to speak. Is it possible to know in this life, we will, indeed, survive into the next life?"

He shot me a compassionate look as one gives a dog. "I think you'd better mix yourself a drink. We are about to go where no one has gone before us. We are about to learn what one should have learned in grade school."

As a young Intelligence officer, the author was stationed in the Arctic Circle in the nineteen-sixties and bore witness to the last fragments of uncivilized Eskimos.

A World of Specialization

He didn't bat an eye.

"If we are to define what we will be in the next life, we must first define what we are in this life. This we will do now.

"The problem with the common man, is that he never wants to stop and touch first base. He thinks he can skip it, and still score.

"In our case, one is talking of the function of the body, and of the function of the mind, and, yes, the function of the soul.

"Most people go through life without even bothering to learn how the body works. Almost none of them have any idea how the mind works, let alone how the soul works."

He studied my eyes to assure himself I had understood his opening. He would leave no stone unturned in his quest to remove the question from the end of our lives, once and for all.

"We live in a world of specialization.

"We assume, except for that specialized function for which oneself is responsible, everything else is the responsibility of someone else. It is none of our business.

"The function of the body is the business of the doctor. The function of the mind is the business of the psychologist. The function of the soul is the business of the preacher.

"Common sense tells us there is only one God for there could have been only one beginning. One would ask, why the most prominent men and women through the years, have mostly died believing in the various Gods they were born into?

"Why the Kennedys have all died as Catholics? Why the Rockefellers have all died as Protestants? Why the sultans of Arabia have all died as Muslims? Why the rulers of Tibet have all died as Buddhists? Why the princes of India have all died as Hindus?

"It was none of their business. It was the business of the specialist. It was the business of the preacher.

"I have decided to make it my business; to know my body, to know my mind, and, most important of all, to know my soul. That my destiny will not be determined by a preacher who knows less about it than I do. It will be my decision. My decision, alone."

He continued toward me who struggled desperately in his web.

"You told me, because I believe in Jesus, I must know I have a soul; to believe in Jesus, is the beginning and the end of it.

"You are wrong, terribly wrong."

He reached into his stack of books and pulled one forward that I hadn't noticed before: *Confessions of the Criminal Mind*. One that had nothing to do with the subject we were caught up in.

Setting it aside, "As you know, my friend Danny is a born-again Christian. His parents tell him that when he gets to be a teenager, he must, on his own volition, accept Christ.

"He must accept, as a historical fact, Christ came to earth to rid the world of Original Sin and died for the sins of mankind. Then, only then, will he go to heaven.

"I asked Danny, what happens if someone blows up the school and kills us all? What happens to us then?

"He told me, we would all go to heaven. Jesus said: 'Blessed are little children for theirs is the Kingdom of Heaven.'"

"I checked him out and he is right. What's more, Jesus said it in many different ways; if one did not get it in one way, one would surely get it in another:. '...all little children go to heaven.'

"Too, the oldest adage of faith is: 'many are called, but few are chosen.'

"According to Christian theology, the criminal who blows up the school guarantees all of the children go to heaven. Not one in ten, not one in a hundred, but all of the children.

"This brave man not only risks his life for the children, but also his soul. For another part of the Bible tells us: 'Thou shalt not kill.'

"He sacrifices his soul for the children he loves. Children, if they were to attain adulthood, would have a long shot at eternal happiness;

172

the overwhelming number of which would otherwise be destined for the everlasting fires of hell."

I shuddered to myself. "Why was he doing this to me? Why does he make me suffer so? Why doesn't he get it over fast, instead of heartlessly playing with me in his web?"

Knowing he had me where he wanted me, he let up a bit. "We think we know when the man blows up the school all the children have gone to heaven. On the other hand, we are outraged by the horrific action because we don't know the children are in heaven. We only think we know.

"The preacher, in consoling us in the funeral Mass, reads from his holy book: 'Blessed are little children for theirs is the Kingdom of Heaven.'

"Yet, the preacher is not so foolish as to praise the hero who blew up the school, who risked not only his life in this life, but his soul in the next life, to guarantee the children go to heaven.

"So we try him in court and send him to death row. Then we send the preacher in to save him. He has a long time to sort things out, this horrific killer, to make his penance, so to speak.

"When we finally put him in the electric chair and pull the lever, all the mothers and fathers of the children he has murdered feel vengeance in their hearts. Yet, they have had no revenge at all.

"According to their faith, he, too, goes to heaven to live happily ever after with the children he had murdered in cold blood."

He returned to the world of reality, "Yet, in truth, they know they have had revenge because they know faith is not for real. They know they have had their revenge because they know he is dead.

"Just like they know their children are dead."

Confessions of the Criminal Mind

My mind was exhausted. Perhaps, it was time to bring in one of those experts, one of those psychologists to help this little fellow who had strayed off the beaten track and lost his mind.

"No!" I stopped myself. "If I did that I would be making his point." I decided to stay in the ring myself.

"This kind of thing happens in real life." He flipped through a few pages of his book *Confessions of the Criminal Mind.*

"According to trial transcripts of John List: '...Their mother and I were to be divorced. She was not a churchgoer and they would cease to go to church... they would be destined for eternal damnation. So I killed them, all five of them. Now I am at peace with myself. They are in heaven.'

"According to Christian theology, John List was a good man. One who was so good, he would risk his soul that his children would go to heaven. So great, his love for his children, he would do this."

He held off for a moment knowing he had stirred up my little grey cells to the point they were at war with one another.

The real world

"This is the real world we live and die in."

He trumped his play, "When all is said and done, we don't really believe. We don't really believe, because we only think we know.

"We don't really believe, because we know the preacher who takes advantage of our mortality to attain his political objectives, does not know. We know he does not know because he has never been there.

"John List confused <u>faith</u> with <u>reality</u>. He confused <u>fantasy</u> with <u>truth</u>. He really believed in his God. There is great danger when one really believes in the assumption one is born into.

"When one really believes in God, one is ill. Seriously ill."

"Aghast!" is the only way I can describe it.

He read my thought, "We will see... Yes, we will see..."

Testimony reprinted from the 1990 public transcript of the trial of John List.

174

Times That Try Men's Minds

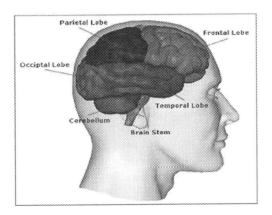

"Since you brought it up, I had to skip a few squares and touch on the soul. Yet, to really understand the function of the soul, one must first understand the function of the mind. Again, we must first understand what we are in this life before we go on to the next life."

I reminded the little make-believe theologian, "You will not find the slightest hint in Christian scripture, the mind as we have known it to be in this life, will survive into the next life."

He agreed, "Yes, the Christian is intent on saving his soul. Not his mind. Yet, again, we must set aside the assumptions we have been born into. We must consider all the religions of the world, and some of them do claim the mind will survive into the next life."

He hesitated a moment. "Still we must keep in mind—though not supported by Christian scripture or doctrine—there is a widespread misconception among Christians that the mind will survive the grave.

"Nevertheless, if we are to define the human soul—something we do not know; we must first define the human mind—something we do know. Here, again, we must benefit from things we do know and construct a reasonable bridge to things we do not know."

With a click of his remote, the diagram of the human brain lit up on the screen of our entertainment center.

"This is going to be a tough one. If I go too fast, slow me down." As he went along, he pointed to each part of the brain he was talking about with an old radio antenna.

175

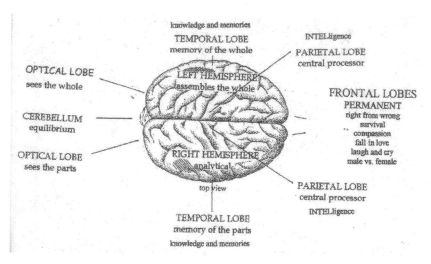

knowledge and memories
TEMPORAL LOBE
memory of the whole

INTELligence
PARIETAL LOBE
central processor

OPTICAL LOBE
sees the whole

LEFT HEMISPHERE
assembles the whole

FRONTAL LOBES
PERMANENT
right from wrong
survival
compassion
fall in love
laugh and cry
male vs. female

CEREBELLUM
equilibrium

OPTICAL LOBE
sees the parts

RIGHT HEMISPHERE
analytical

top view

PARIETAL LOBE
central processor

INTELligence

TEMPORAL LOBE
memory of the parts

knowledge and memories

"The brain is divided down its center into two main sections.

"We call these 'hemispheres.' Aside from controlling the motions of the opposite side of the body, the function of a hemisphere—the right hemisphere vs. the left hemisphere—is poles apart.

"If a person is left-handed, the 'right' hemisphere is the 'analytical' side of the brain. It deals with the 'parts.'

"It is the analytical side of the brain that enables one to single out the tone of a lone violin and enjoy it as an individual contribution to the whole. A great symphony.

"It is the analytical side of the brain that enables one to single out individual colors in an infinite range of shades and shapes and enjoy their individual contribution to the whole. A great work of art.

"In a left-handed person, the 'left' hemisphere tends to be the 'organizational' side of the brain. It orchestrates the 'parts' that are identified by the 'right' hemisphere into the 'whole.'

If the person is right-handed, the hemispheres have reverse functions. If right-handed, the 'left' hemisphere is the 'analytical' side, and the 'right' hemisphere is the 'organizational' side.

"Regardless, the organizational side of the brain enables one to harmonize the individual sounds of an orchestra into a great symphony. Or, for that matter, blend the individual colors and tones of a painting into the marvel of a great work of art.

"The analytical hemisphere deals with the parts. It deals with the facts. People, in whom this hemisphere is dominant, live in a world of reality. They tend to be progressive in their thinking.

"The great scientific geniuses, Faraday, Einstein, Tesla, Edison and others have come from this side of the brain. They deal with the parts. The facts. They are concerned with reality.

"They tend to be poor believers. They must have the facts. They tend to reject the assumption—the God—they were born into. The reason most scientific geniuses have died as atheists.

"Conversely, the organizational hemisphere tends to ignore the facts. People, in whom this hemisphere is dominant, live in a world of fantasy. They tend to be traditional in their thinking.

"The great geniuses of the art and music world, Tchaikovsky, Beethoven, Michelangelo, Raphael and others have come from this side of the brain. Though they live in the facts—color and sound; they are more concerned with the whole—the dream.

"They tend to be easy believers. The reason most of them die believing in the assumption—the God—they were born into.

"Although there are immense complexities and variations of the infinite lateralizations of the hemispheres of the human brain the left from the right—these are the most prominent.

How the mind works

"Yet, to determine if the mind is a part of the soul—what we are trying to save—we must look at this more closely."

He looked at me compassionately. "I think you'd better switch to a cup of coffee, a strong one. This is not going to get easier."

Passing up the coffee, I poured myself another Jack Daniels as he began pointing to each of the lobes as he went along.

"Each hemisphere is divided into four sections called lobes.

"These two in the forehead—the frontal lobes—control instinct and emotions. The two at the back of the head—the occipital or optical lobes—control vision.

"Between them, just up over the ears—the temporal lobes—serve as warehouses for memory and knowledge.

"Just above them, to the center point of the head, run the parietal lobes, which have the critical role of compiling, storing, analyzing, organizing and utilizing information that flows to them through the five senses—vision, touch, smell, taste, hearing.

"So that when one peels a banana, it will look like a banana, it will feel like a banana, it will smell like a banana, it will taste like a banana, and, yes, even sound like a banana.

The central processing unit

"The parietal lobes serve as the central processing unit of the human brain—twin processors. Here lies one's intelligence.

"Intelligence is measured in the speed and accuracy in which the parietal lobes can gather, analyze, organize and utilize information stored in the temporal lobes—the warehouses of the human brain. We call this 'IQ' - *Intelligence Quotient*.

"Contrary to what most believe, one is not born a genius.

"When we are born, we are a blend of genes and nutrition.

"Every day, geniuses are born to idiots and idiots are born to geniuses. Intelligence cannot be traced to genes.

"Yet, what is known, the framework of intelligence is provided by nutrition—namely cholesterol and its allied nutrients.

"Even the tiny hub of intelligence in the parietal lobes at birth, which enable us to know how to escape the womb, is a product of prenatal nutrients provided by the mother.

"Too much or too little of brain-building nutrients, one ends up a nitwit. The right balance of nutrients, one ends up a genius.

"Too, instrumental to IQ is the environment a child grows up in during the first five years of its life.

"At the age of five, the lion's share of one's intelligence is intact.

Chimpanzees

"In the first few months of life, both a human and a chimpanzee experience an explosive rate of connectivity. At ten months, the relative IQ of a chimp and a human being are equal. However, the chimp brain stops growing in two years, whereas the human brain grows for five years. Thus, on average, a human is smarter.

"Yet, even in this reduced time, if the chimp gets a better balance of nutrients and environment, the chimp will be smarter.

"Chimps generally rank in the bottom twenty percentile of the range of human intelligence. Few have reached upper percentiles."

He paused as if he had suddenly recalled something.

"Likewise, over ninety-percent of human beings rank in the bottom twenty percentile of the range of human intelligence."

He knew he shouldn't have said it, but he said it anyway. "The reason the preacher has so many sheep."

Worse yet, his lingering stare meant to include me among them.

"If we conclude the 'soul' has something to do with the mind..." pointing to his temple, "it follows, chimps, too, have souls."

My stare told him to stop this madness. Enough is enough.

For years, it was known blacks had no souls. For years before that, it was known women had no souls. In heaven, procreation of the human race will be at an end, women would have no purpose. Somewhere along the line things got out of control. We gave both blacks and women souls. Now he was giving them to chimps.

"Okay," he cut off my glare. "Let's take another approach."

I tried another stare. It didn't work.

"Chimps share upwards of ninety-eight percent of our genes.

"As a matter-of-fact, they are much closer genetically to us than they are to other higher primates—the gorilla, the orangutan, the baboon, the lemur and so forth. Chimpanzees are much more human beings than they are animals.

"Like us, they have intelligence and can invent and use tools. They have a conscience and have both emotions and instincts.

"The fundamental difference between us is that chimps lack vocal cords which would allow them to communicate like we do.

"As a result, they are unable to pass onto future generations all that they learn in a lifetime. If not for this, they would have been able to build civilizations, perhaps not on a par with us, but progress.

"As each chimp comes along, he or she must learn from scratch in the same way Adam and Eve—before the time of fire, wheels and boxed oatmeal—had to learn from scratch."

"But ..." I lost my words.

"What you are trying to say is they have no God, no religion. Therefore, they cannot have a soul which is a part of God.

"If we conclude humans have souls and chimpanzees do not have souls, then the soul is here," he pointed to his vocal cords, "and not here," he ran his finger from his heart to his temple.

He gave me a long time to allow that one to sink in.

"Did you ever wonder why chimpanzees have no God?"

I decided not to go near that one.

He took another sip of his coke. "They can't write a check.

"If chimps could write a check, profits—excuse me, prophets—would have risen up through the ages claiming they had talked to the Chimpanzee God and promised them eternal life in palatial mansions in heaven, if they followed their rules. There would be chimpanzee churches and greedy preachers to take their money.

"Nevertheless, if we surmise the soul is here," pointing to his heart, "controlled by what is here," placing the palm of his hand across his forehead, "all animals, not only chimpanzees, have souls. For all animals have instincts and emotions."

He paused, "That is, of course, if we, ourselves, have souls.

Aptitude

"So much for intelligence. Yet, we have to also consider aptitude.

"It is the relative balance and interaction of the parietal lobes on the top of our heads—intelligence—that encompasses aptitude.

"Vincent Van Gogh and Michael Faraday were of relatively equal intelligence. The speed and accuracy at which their parietal lobes could gather, store, analyze, organize and utilize data was relatively equal." He ran his fingers from the top of his head down to his ears.

"In Faraday's case, the analytical side of the parietal lobes—intelligence—was dominant, making him a scientific genius.

"Conversely, in Van Gogh's case, the organizational side of the parietal lobes was dominant, making him a genius of the arts.

"Though aptitude operates independent of intelligence, it is instrumental to the application of intelligence.

"Although they were both macro-geniuses, had Van Gogh spent his life in physics, we wouldn't have *Sunflowers* and *Starry Night*. Conversely, if Faraday had spent his life in art, we wouldn't have radio, television, cell phones, the Internet, and so forth.

Computers

"Finally, we must consider computers.

"Of the four lobes of the human brain, only the frontal lobes which contain instinct and emotion are unique to living creatures.

"Computers have no instincts or emotions—no frontal lobes." He pointed to his forehead.

"Yet, the parietal, occipital and temporal lobes—those parts of the brain housing intelligence, sight and storage—can be duplicated in computers, and, in the case of computers, they have infinitely greater capacity than they do in human beings.

"A computer can store information contained in all of the human minds that ever were and process it at immensely greater speeds and accuracy than all the geniuses who have ever lived combined.

"A simple PC can raise a fifty-digit number to the one-hundred-twelfth-millionth power in a split second with zero chance of error, which would take a mathematical genius months to accomplish with considerable chance of error. It can solve a formula in a few minutes, it would have taken Einstein years to solve."

The great painting

Passing his hand over the diagram of the brain, "Regardless, these are the think tanks of the human person. Yet, how do they do our thinking for us?" he seemed to ask himself more than me.

"Take sight. How does it tell us what color is what color, what form is what form, what composition is what composition?"

He pulled forward another book. A picture of his patron saint dominated its cover. "We are speaking here of one more aspect of Einstein's work, the 'photon.' A subatomic particle we call 'light.'

"One looks at a painting, a great work of art. Unlike what one might believe, the chain of events does not begin with the eye, or, for that matter, with the brain. It begins with the painting.

"In this immensely complex chain of events, the painting emits multi-trillions of individual impulses of light—photons—which are transmitted in three channels of empty space—trichromacy—to the retina, which, in turn, transfers them through the optic nerve to the occipital lobes in the back of the head which record these trillions of particles of light in the primary colors of red, blue and yellow in an infinite number of shapes, sizes and tones.

"It is these particles of light that strike the eye, not the other way around. If there is nothing there, one would see nothing.

"Yet, how do these particles of light reach the occipital lobes located at the back of the head?" He asked, this time with a look of apprehension, as if by chance I might come up with the answer, which, of course, would have been devastating to him.

His question did nothing more than to confuse me.

"The chemical balance of the brain," he exclaimed. "The brain is simply a housing. It is the chemicals within it that do the job.

"Now, what is a chemical reaction?" he asked.

"I guess it's when you put two different types of chemicals together and they interact with each other?"

"Not bad," he tossed me a satisfying wink of enlightenment.

"It is when one puts two or more particles of energy together. Chemistry is the study of the interaction of different placements of energy." He paused to allow this one to sink in.

"In the case of the painting, trillions of tiny specs of light are transmitted in an infinite range of chemical reactions to the occipital lobes. At that point, the parietal lobes interact with the occipital lobes, so that one can see the painting as a whole.

"In the same instant, the parietal lobes gather the resulting composition of energy and deposit it here in the temporal lobes," pointing with his fingers to either side of his head just above his ears, "so that one can remember what one saw.

"Hence, the job is done, and, the only question is, how long will it remain there? How long will one remember what one saw?

Memory

"If the capacities of our temporal lobes were infinite, then we would remember everything our five senses witness. But, as you know, we remember very little. The reason we remember very little, is that our temporal lobes are greatly limited in capacity.

"A man of sixty is likely to remember the names of two or three children he went to grade school with, and he is less likely, without the aid of a photo, to remember what they looked like.

"Even, in the short range, memory is quite limited. Hence, we make a list when we go to the store. One retains in memory only an infinitesimal fraction of what one has been exposed to.

"It is the size of the temporal lobes which determine how much one remembers, not their efficiency. In themselves, they have no efficiency. At birth they are empty warehouses of the human brain. We quickly fill them up in the first few days of life.

"This is why elephants, though of very little intelligence, have such good memories. They have the largest temporal lobes of any mammal, the largest storage capacity of any brain.

"Because of our very limited capacity, humans are constantly subconsciously purging their temporal lobes to make space for more interesting and more important information.

"All of us have the image of the *Mona Lisa* in our minds, yet few of us can describe the dress she is wearing.

"If it were not for our ongoing ability to subconsciously purge our temporal lobes, our memories would be a mishmash of everything we had ever been exposed to. We would be unable to single out any individual experience at any given time.

Four hundred thousand years old

"There are two types of information stored here in the temporal lobes," he cuffed his hands up over his ears.

"There are things we have been exposed to—memories.

"Then there is the more important of the two—knowledge. One can live without memories. One will not get far without knowledge.

"If one does not 'know' the stove is hot, one will burn oneself time and again. If one does not 'know' one cannot fly, one would not hesitate to leap from a cliff to get from here to there.

"Man's knowledge is the accumulation of the memory of his fellowman, other men, both of today and yesterday, which has found its way into his temporal lobes. It is what, through all of his life, has enabled him to live beyond the apes in the forest.

"When we give our age as ten, or twenty, or eighty, concerning this part of us—knowledge—we go back to the beginning of time. We are all about the same age. We are four hundred thousand years old.

"By comparison, a chimp, lacking vocal cords and unable to convey to future generations what he has learned in his lifetime, counts his age from birth.

"I wonder...? I wonder...?" He stopped.

"Wonder what?" I waited with anticipation.

"I wonder if there are bathrooms in the chimpanzee heaven?"

I, as not to give him the edge, "In heaven, chimps have bathrooms. We live in the jungle."

He smiled as he clicked the remote. "Let us summarize this:

Lobe	Location	Function	At birth
Parietal	top of head	intelligence & aptitude	core
Temporal	over the ears	memory & knowledge	nothing
Frontal	forehead	survival & compassion	intact

"What is important to what we will be talking about here is that we are born with the basic instincts of survival and compassion. One thing more." He annunciated the fact, "they will never change."

He shot me a look of worried concern. "Anyway, this next one is going to be a real tough one. You'd better get another drink."

Description herein of the brain is a gross simplification. It is intended only to convey a practical understanding of how the human mind works. Something every child should learn in grade school.

Jekyll and Hyde

Dr Jekyll and Mr Hyde

I had to admit that what he had told me was quite interesting. I never really knew how the brain worked. After all, it wasn't something one had to know.

It was none of my business. It was the business of the psychiatrist, the business of the psychologist, the business of the specialist in that sort of thing. I had not yet sat down when he started up again.

"When a patient goes to a psychiatrist with a problem, what do you think is the first thing the doctor has to determine?"

The master answered his own question. "He has to determine if the problem is a condition of the frontal lobes," pointing to his forehead, "something the patient was born with..." He let that sink in for a bit.

"Or is it a condition of the temporal lobes," cupping his paws above his ears, "something the patient acquired in life.

"He has to determine if it is a chemical imbalance of the brain, or is it just something the patient picked up along the way.

"He does this to determine treatment.

"The psychiatrist knows a disturbance of the frontal lobes—a chemical imbalance of the brain—will not respond to therapy. It can only be treated with chemicals—medicine.

"Conversely, a disturbance of the temporal lobes—something the patient acquired—can only be reconditioned with therapy. It will not respond to chemicals—medicine.

185

"Schizophrenia is the most prevalent mental instability one can be born with. A hundred years ago, the psychiatrist would treat this condition with therapy because, at that time, he was unaware of the chemical balance of the brain." He looked at me.

"Tell me, where were all the schizophrenics then?"

I gave him what he was looking for. "In mental institutions."

"Yes. At the time, the doctor thought he was dealing with a mental illness, whereas, he was actually dealing with a physical illness—a chemical imbalance manifesting itself in abnormal mental behavior.

"Where is the schizophrenic today?" He woke me up.

I fed his fire, "Out here, living together with the rest of us."

"The doctor now knows he is dealing with a chemical imbalance of the brain. He also knows, the only way to correct a chemical imbalance is with chemicals. Medicine.

"Schizophrenia is something one is born with, it cannot be acquired. It can only be treated with medicine.

"The psychiatrist gives a sedative patient an exhilarating drug to bring the chemical composition of the brain into reasonable balance. He gives one with an exhilarating personality, a sedative drug to bring the chemical composition of the brain into reasonable balance.

"Even the homicidal maniac can be controlled by a simple drug and live out his life together with the rest of us and never be a threat to either himself or anyone else. As long as he takes his medicine, it will control his condition. The psychiatrist now has the remedy that will change Mr. Hyde back into Dr. Jekyll.

"As you might remember, in the mid-twentieth century, when doctors first suspected the disturbance was here," the little self-made psychologist touched his forehead, "they drilled holes—lobotomies—to try to correct the condition mechanically. It was not until the sixties, they realized it involved a chemical imbalance of the brain. They then solved the problem with chemicals. Medicine."

Pointing to his forehead, "These tanks—the frontal lobes—are reservoirs of what we are mentally when we are born—our basic instincts. They will be with us to the end of our days. They will never change. Schizophrenia is not curable. It is only controllable.

"If the good Doctor Jekyll fails to take his medicine, he will revert back to the evil Mr. Hyde. He will begin to think when he has done something wrong, he has done something right.

God-made vs. Man-made killers

"Homicidal maniacs have been known to kill children.

"John List murdered his children in cold blood. Yet, he was not a homicidal maniac. That is, he was not a schizophrenic.

"His problem did not involve the frontal lobes, something he had been born with. It involved the temporal lobes, something he had learned along the way.

"His condition would not have responded to medicine. Yet, it would have responded to therapy. Sadly, it was not caught in time.

"His mind had been conditioned by the preacher to believe his children would go to heaven if he killed them.

"The preacher wrongly convinced him the book he was reading had been written by God. He wrongly convinced him that God had said: 'Blessed are the little children for theirs in the Kingdom of Heaven.'

"Had his condition been treated in time, the doctor would have proved to him, God had not really said 'Blessed are the little children for theirs in the Kingdom of Heaven.' He would have explained that he was reading a book written by politicians... ancient politicians.

"The doctor would have proved to him his children would not go to heaven. They would be dead. He would have been cured.

"Nevertheless," pointing to his forehead, "Here in the frontal lobes is our God-given ability to know right from wrong.

"Yet, there are other things in the frontal lobes that define us as the unique person each of us is. They, too, are things that will not change for the rest of our lives?" He waited.

I couldn't think of any other. I remained silent.

Instead of giving me the answer, he decided to help me. He asked, "What is the ability to know right from wrong?"

Unable to come up with anything, he gave me the answer, "It is an instinct. So, what are some other instincts?"

Once more, he had to answer his own question, "Survival and compassion are our basic instincts. All the others emanate from these two, including our ability to know right from wrong.

"When we do something, we either do it for ourselves or we do it for others. There are no other alternatives.

"The instinct of survival drives one of these, while the instinct of compassion drives the other. When we are born, the instinct of survival drives us to the teat. The instinct of compassion moves us to one side to allow our little sister to have some too.

"We usually think of helping others as good—as Christ taught us. Conversely, we usually think of doing things for ourselves as bad— selfishness. To hell with the others.

"There are countless manifestations of the basic instincts of survival and compassion.

"There is the instinct that tells us who we are. Is one a boy? Is one a girl? Is one a heterosexual? Is one a homosexual?"

"You can't prove homosexuality is God-given," I challenged.

"No, 'I' can't prove it. Yet, that does not overrule the fact that the psychiatric community has already proved it.

"Until the middle of the twentieth century, as I have said, the psychiatrist treated schizophrenia with therapy. He thought the problem was here," pointing up over his ears. "He did not know the problem was here," placing his palm across his forehead.

"It was the psychiatrist's success in treating schizophrenia in the sixties that led to his discovery a decade later that homosexuality also has its roots in instinct," pointing to his forehead, "and not a condition one acquires in life," pointing just above his ears.

"We don't know that," I corrected him.

Not surprised he would have to explain to a man who had spent a decade in college what he should have learned in grade school. "I think we had better define what we are talking about here.

"When the world of psychology ruled on homosexuality, it did not take a vote of its constituents. There is not a psychologist or psychiatrist in the world who would tell you homosexuality is not a function of the frontal lobes— a matter of instinct we are born with.

"Homosexuality is defined by what kind of person one has the instinct to fall in love with. This is a manifestation of the instinct of compassion. Not necessarily who one has sex with.

"As was true in the case of John List, acquiring the motivation to kill his children, the desire to engage in same-sex acts can be acquired by a heterosexual. A heterosexual who is confined to prison, for example, might acquire a preference for homosexual behavior and like John List the problem is here." He pointed up over his ears.

"Yet, no matter how he tries, he will never be able to fall in love with his partner. His instinct," he pointed to his forehead, "allows him only to fall in love with one of the opposite sex.

188

"If children were taught at an early age the basic functions of the brain as we have been discussing them in these few minutes, we would better understand one another. We wouldn't have many of the problems we have in the world today."

"You mean, Bible thumpers showing up with 'hate' signs at gay funerals would realize they have a shortage here..." I pointed with the tips of my hands up over both ears, "knowledge?"

"Their real problem is here..." He planted the palm of his hand firmly on top of his head: "Intelligence!"

Disturbances in the frontal lobes can drive disturbances in the temporal lobes and vice versa. Hence, treatment usually requires both medication and therapy.

The film '*Awakening*' starring Robert De Niro and Robin Williams recounts the work of the doctor who first used chemicals (LSD) to control schizophrenia

The psychiatric world declared homosexuality no longer a mental illness in 1963. Psychiatric organizations exclude from membership greedy psychologists who capitalize on the whims of preachers and practice sexual orientation change therapy.

The Greatest of Sins

"We have made of sex the greatest of sins, whereas it is nothing more than human nature and not a sin at all."

Albino Luciani

Sitting down, his dark mysterious eyes roamed around the room and finally came to rest on mine, "We have reached that point at which we have to put on the table precisely what we are talking about when we speak of heaven.

"How does one define precisely this merchandise for which we spend our faith all of our lives?

"To determine what we are talking about when we say, 'heaven,' in the case of the Christian, we must first define morality—right from wrong—as it exists in Christian scripture and doctrine, as opposed to how it is defined in society."

I cut him off, "There is no difference…" He cut me off.

The Confessor

A fifteen year old boy told of his confession with the priest Luciani in which he ranted on and on for twenty minutes about his sexual exploits and awaited his penance. *"Good, you have told me of your God-given nature. Now tell me of your man-made sins. Tell me of malice in your heart for any of God's children whether they be black, bastard, gypsy, queer, atheist, communist, Russian, Chinese, Jew …"*

Morality

"Christianity holds the human body to be sinful and shameful.

"This has its foundation in the stories of Adam and Eve and Original Sin, Sodom and Gomorrah, the promiscuous patriarch of the Canaanites—Hamm, Noah's Ark and countless other stories which permeate the books of Moses in the Old Testament.

"The tale of eating of the apple is generally construed by scholars to have been the first sin of the flesh for which Adam and Eve forfeit immortality. In *Sodom and Gomorrah*, God orders the destruction of cities for sins of the flesh. In the case of the promiscuous descendants of *Hamm*, God orders the murder of the Canaanite nation for sins of the flesh: 'every man, woman, and child, leave not one alive.'

"In the case of *Noah's Ark*, God destroys the entire world for sins of the flesh: 'God looked upon the earth, for all flesh had corrupted its way.'

"There are eighty-seven condemnations of sex in the Bible.

"Those in the Old Testament call solely for the death penalty; Adam and Eve having forfeited eternal life for the first sin of the flesh. Except for Christ's condemnation of Jews: '...those enemies of mine who did not want me to be king over them, bring them here and kill them in front of me;' those in the New Testament call for eternal punishment: 'on the Day of Judgment they will be cast, both body and spirit, into the eternal lake of fire.'

"By comparison, there are only six condemnations of murder in the Bible. Those in the Old Testament call for the death penalty: 'an eye for an eye.' The only one in the New Testament calls for the ultimate penalty: 'they will be cast, body and spirit, into the eternal lake of fire.'

He had made his point. *'Sex is the greatest of sins.'*

The big cover-up

"Too, there are countless condemnations of mere nakedness in the Bible. For example: 'If a man see her nakedness, and she see his nakedness; it is a wicked thing... the eyes of both of them were opened; they knew they were naked; they sewed fig leaves together, and made themselves aprons.'

"Yet, in the eastern world, the story is much different."

He pulled the book of the Hindu culture, the Vedas, forward and read: '"He saw her in her nature. And he saw that she was good and beautiful. And she saw him in his nature. And she saw that he was good and beautiful. Together they knew they were good and beautiful. They praised Brahma He had bestowed such a gift on them that they could come together.'

"Whereas, one-third of the leaves of the Bible deal with the shamefulness and sinfulness of sex, one-third of the leaves of the Vedas deal with the beauty and godliness of sex.

"In the east, temples have thousands of carvings depicting every imaginable sexual act built into their facades, honoring this great gift the God Brahma has bestowed upon His people.

"Conversely, in the west, churches have covered up genitalia in the works of Michelangelo, Raphael and other masters.

Eastern temple façade   Vatican now and then

"The gospels, themselves, magnify the misconception sex is sinful. So much so, they make Jesus out to be asexual, one without sin.

"They go so far as to make His conception 'Immaculate,' free of the filthiness of the great sin of fornication.

"One cannot possibly profess to believe in the Bible and ignore the overwhelming message of its 'politicians.' particularly Paul's epistles in the New Testament: *The Greatest of Sins is Sex.*

"Driven by the overwhelming preponderance of evidence in the Bible, in the sixteenth century, the Council of Trent elevated celibacy above all other ways of life: 'If one saith the marriage state is to be placed above the state of virginity, or of celibacy, and that it is not more blessed to remain in virginity or celibacy, than to be in matrimony, let him be excommunicated.'

"It follows, canon law defines morality in the Roman Catholic world today as to what goes in the bedroom, rather than what is really right or truly wrong.

"Today, all sex outside of what a sitting-pope considers marriage, including impure thoughts and masturbation is mortal sin. The reason

192

the definition of marriage within the Catholic Church is: 'permission to a kind of people by a sitting-pope to have sex without committing mortal sin.'

"Yet, westerners, like their eastern counterparts, are coming to know sex as being good and beautiful. A gift from God. We no longer think of sex as being sinful and shameful. Influenced by those in the east and by conscience," pointing to his temple, "we now think of it as being good and beautiful. A great gift from God."

He thought a moment, "Except... except, of course..."

"Except... what...?" I opened another door for him.

"Popes, bishops, priests, monks and nuns think there is something wrong with sex. The reason they think themselves holier-than-thou in abstaining from it."

I kept my mouth shut, gambling he'd drop the subject.

Genophobia and Homophobia

Instead he went in for the kill, "It is an illness, you know."

"An illness? What are you talking about?"

"Fear of sex. People who think there is something wrong with sex are suffering from a mental illness. Genophobia," he explained.

"You're suggesting the clergy are nuts?" I laughed.

"As was true of John List, Genophobia is a condition of the temporal lobes," pointing up over his ears. "Something one picks up in this life. Its victims believe what ancient and medieval men wrote—themselves suffering from Genophobia—is God's instruction.

"Like the illness which drove John List to murder his children, Genophobia costs thousands of lives every day.

"When a priest convinces teens, God ruled masturbation is mortal sin, many of them kill themselves for nothing more than responding to a natural biological function of their bodies.

"Homophobia is, too, a dangerous illness.

"Homophobia? You mean people who hate homosexuals?"

"Yes. Tens of thousands of gay teens, whose minds are deranged by priests and evangelical preachers who suffer from homophobia, take their own lives every year.

"You're suggesting preachers are mass-murderers?"

193

"You said it. I didn't." He gave me an out.

"Yet, popes and other clergy afflicted with these dreaded diseases can be cured.

"As in the case of John List, they can be treated with therapy because the problem is here," he pointed up over his ears.

"Like John List, the psychiatrist would convince these preachers that they are only reading a book. One not written by God, but written by men who, themselves, suffered from these same illnesses.

"The psychiatrist would convince them: *'We have made of sex the greatest of sins, whereas it is nothing more than human nature and not a sin at all.'* He would convince them, sex is good and beautiful, a gift from God. He would convince them, not to kick the gift-horse in the mouth. He would convince them, not to kick God in the mouth."

He couldn't restrain himself, "Yet, the psychiatrist's success depends entirely on whether or not his patient has something up here." Winking he pointed to the top of his head. "Intelligence!"

"Nevertheless, according to canon law today, hatred of sex is a virtue. To put it another way, hatred of love is a virtue." He paused.

"To put it as is really is, 'The greatest of sins is love.'"
Nevertheless, realizing he had driven me to the limit with this one, he decided to break the ice a bit.

"I first became suspicious of Father John's loathing for sex when I was three years old.

"Three years old?" I was shocked.

"Yes, Mom caught me playing with my testicles in the tub.

"I asked her, 'Are these my brains?'"

Curiosity got the best of me. I wondered how Audrey had handled that one, "What did she say?"

She told me, "Not yet." He laughed.

Headline quote: The most prolific message of Albino Luciani's ministry.

The Confessor: *L'Unita* 15 Sep 1955. As a cardinal, Luciani moved to raise the earliest age of confession to fourteen, citing the great preponderance of sins seven year olds confess are sins of the flesh rendering them prey of pedophile priests.

The Descriptions of the Heavens

He had reserved a rainy afternoon for this one. Hopefully, the rain would drown out most of what he had to say.

"Before we get lost along the way, a brief outline of what we are talking about when we say 'salvation' or 'heaven.'

"When we speak of immortality, we mean survival beyond death of one or a combination of these:" He scribble on his blackboard.

Mind = instinct, intelligence, memory

Body = breathe, eat, drink, defecate, urinate, fornicate

Spirit = akin to the mind - oneself without one's body

Soul = akin to the heart – undefined in scripture

"By faith, immortality is quite different."

Spiritualist = survival of the spirit on earth

Christian = survival of a mindless body and soul in heaven

Muslim = survival of the body and mind in Eden

Hindu = divine transfer of the soul to a new body on earth

Buddhist = scientific transfer of the mind to a new body on earth

Our home theater did the rest:

195

Spiritualism

Source: Neanderthals
Salvation: spirit escapes the body at death
Requirements: belief in ghosts

Before the last ice age, the hereafter was limited to coexistence with the present. The spirits of the dead coexisted with the living.

Practiced by primitive societies that survived into modern times uninfluenced by modern deities: Eskimos of the north, aborigines of the South Pacific, witchdoctors of South Africa, the American Indian.

Of modern religions, only Catholics communicate with the dead. So much so, most of their prayers are to plaster idols of the dead.

Hinduism

Source: The Vedas
Salvation: successive reincarnations of the 'soul'
Requirements: love thy neighbor as thyself

In Hinduism, reincarnation is a theological concept; not a scientific process. Shiva, the Redeemer, guides the 'soul' into the next life.

The successful Hindu progresses through a succession of lifetimes up through a five-level caste system, from the peasant at the bottom, to the scholar at the top. He finds his ultimate reward in eternal peace.

The unsuccessful Hindu ceases to exist.

The Hindu has a relatively low level of confidence in his salvation. He depends on the supernatural—the existence of a Ghost and there is no description of what he is trying to save—soul—in his scripture.

Buddhism

Source: Tripitaka - Mahayana Sutras
Salvation: Reincarnation of the 'mind' as a scientific process
Requirements: love thy neighbor as thyself and meditation

The Buddhist is the only practitioner of faith not dependent on the supernatural. The Buddhist has no God—no Ghost with a capital G. He banks his hopes on the theory, the composition of one's mental energy finds a new host as a function of the natural order of creation.

Because the Buddhist does not depend on the supernatural, he enjoys a relatively high level of confidence in his immortality.

Judaism

Source: The Tanakh—includes the Torah, the five books of Moses
Salvation: The body and mind cease to exist at death
Requirements: live this life to the fullest

In the Hebrew Bible, the prophecy of Isaiah does not speak of the coming of a Savior, but of a New Jerusalem. It does not speak of an individual Deity, but of the people of Israel as a whole.

Hence, there is no facility in Jewish scripture for an afterlife: 'from dust thou hast come… to dust thou wilt return.' The Jew ponders his own fate.

197

Christianity

Christianity accepts man's mortality. The mind and body—as they have been in this life—will cease to exist at death.

Suspension of the soul upon death until a Day of Judgment when it will be rejoined with a mindless body. The unsaved are cast into eternal fire; the saved are suspended in eternal adoration of Deity

It is that he pins his hopes on the existence of something he does not understand (soul), and it makes no sense there are bathrooms in heaven, the Christian has a low level of confidence in his salvation. Hence, he prays for miracles to save himself from impending death.

Catholicism

Source: Neanderthals, Old Testament, Nicene Council
Salvation: Resurrection of the body via forgiveness of sin by priests
Requirements: idol worship, pomp and pageantry, mysticism, occult, apparitions of dead people, communication with the dead, baptism.
Canon Law based primarily on prejudices of the Old Testament.

Protestantism

Source: Old and/or New Testament
Salvation: Survival of the 'soul' and a mindless asexual 'body'
Requirements: baptism, scriptural readings, miracles solely by God

Most protestant churches have broken from idolatry, vain repetitions, belief in ghosts Catholicism is immersed in. Various sects are based on selective parts of the Bible that support the political ambitions of their founders. Consistent with the Bible, prayer is restricted to God. Some sects have moved away from prejudices of the Old Testament.

Islamism

Source: The Koran and excerpts of the Toran
Salvation: Survival of the 'body' and the 'mind' in Eden
Requirements: Prayer to God. Love thy neighbor. Kill idolaters.

Islamism is the only faith in which the body and the mind including sexuality, as they have been in this life, will survive into the next life.

The successful Muslim finds his salvation in the Garden of Eden. The Koran speaks of the soul as being synonymous with survival of the mind and body and not as a separate dimension of man.

In early years, Muslims have high confidence in their salvation.

'Kill the idolaters' is the most prominent hostile verse in the Koran. Muhammad targets Orthodox and Roman Catholics who are heavily immersed in idol worship. There are no idol images in the Mosque.

Religions are shown in the order in which they evolved

There are variations within Protestantism, some sects embracing the gospels' 'Love thy Neighbor as Thyself' with adoration focused on Christ, and others embracing the Old Testament's persecution of neighbors (not like self) with adoration focused on the God of Moses as in Catholicism. Mormonism—consistent with the gospels—restricts salvation to the soul. Christ spoke only of souls in His Day of Judgment.

Catholics immersed in idolatry and mysticism reduce Jesus to a mere sacrifice to satisfy the bloodlust of the God of the Old Testament who subordinates women and others. The Sacrifice of the Mass is offered up to Moses' God. Not to Christ.

The soul is often likened to the emotional nature of a human being—akin to the heart. Yet, there is no description of the soul in the world's scriptures.

The Bible is explicit that the mind will cease to exist at death. One can imagine the horror of the mind—consciousness—being suspended in time for thousands of years without a body as the mind is overwhelmingly occupied in controlling bodily functions. Hence, western religions peddle survival of the body in the afterlife.

199

The Impenetrable Fortress of Faith

The little fellow spoke with authority. "As an absolute fact, there are only two dimensions of man—the mind and the body.

"As we have said, the first Neanderthal to pick up a shovel to bury his enemy added the 3rd dimension of man. The spirit.

"With 'survival of the mind' and 'survival of the spirit' to pick from, why add the '4th' dimension of man. The soul?" He waited.

He answered his own question, "We all know what the mind is. We perceive the spirit to be what we are without our bodies.

"But we don't know what the soul is. The dictionary is vague: 'the soul is akin to the heart.' The universal theological definition: 'the soul is just something we don't understand...' In truth, we have nothing.

"Faith preys on ignorance. The adversary of religion can destroy the possibilities of survival of the <u>mind</u> and survival of the <u>spirit</u> because he <u>knows</u> what they are. But he can never destroy the possibility of survival of the <u>soul</u> because he <u>does not know</u> what it is.

"Hence, the soul is the impenetrable fortress of faith.

"As we have already established, the idea grew up early in the 2nd millennium BC in Hinduism because the eastern prophets had never heard of the western belief of resurrection of the body.

"Though the word <u>soul</u> is no more than a synonym for the word <u>spirit</u> in the Bible, by the time the Nicene Fathers came along in the 4th century, east had met west. Hence, they built it into Christianity as a fourth dimension of man—'...something that we just don't understand.'

"Nevertheless, let us take them one by one. Can the body? ...Can the mind? ...Can the spirit? ...Can the soul? ...survive death."

The Case for the Body

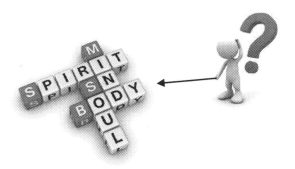

'When the thousand years is finished, the sea gave up its dead, and the depth gave up its dead... I saw the dead, small and great, standing before God, and the books were opened...

They shall hunger no more, neither thirst no more, neither shall the sun light on them, God shall wipe away all tears, there shall be no more death, neither sorrow, nor crying, neither shall there be pain, nor light of day, nor darkness of night, for these things have passed away... They are before the throne of God and serve Him day and night for all time...

In the New Jerusalem... there was no sea.'

Book of Revelations

"Nevertheless, I will tell you of my vision." He waited.

"Your vision?" Aghast. This little hypocrite, who had so often criticized the visionary saints, was, himself, a visionary.

"Yes, my vision. I was privileged to visit each of the heavens of the world's religions." He stopped to clarify precisely what he was talking about. "...tales told by ancient politicians.

"As the Christian heaven came into view...

'...the great city was made of pure gold, as pure as glass. The streets paved of pure gold, like transparent glass. The houses built of jasper, of sapphire, of chalcedony, of emerald, of diamond, of ruby, of beryl, of amber, of amethyst... all together, making for magnificent rays... The twelve gates to the New Jerusalem were huge solitary pearls of dazzling splendor... there was no sea, no forest, no mountains, no valleys, no waterfalls to shroud the golden metropolis...'

He told it exactly as it was. "In this life, achievement of vast wealth is the Christian dream. The reason he thrives in a capitalistic society.

"This is precisely what his God gives him in the next life.

"A palatial urbanization without a pigeon to stain its opulent buildings, nor a puppy to muddy its golden streets. A city of pure gold without aquariums, zoos, parks or botanical gardens: 'there will be no sea life, no animal life, no plant life...'

The living dead

"Let us assume the Pharaoh Narmer and the Nicene Fathers were not telling tall stories to attain their political objectives when they claimed the body will resurrect on a day of judgment.

"In what form would one come back? As the ugly, aging, frail, balding, white-haired, wrinkled up bag of bones one died as? Or would one want to come back as Matt Damon or Jenifer Lopez?

"Few of us would choose to come back as the person he or she died as. Most of us would prefer to come back as the epitome of what we perceive a human being to be.

"Sadly, this will not be. There is no provision in the Bible for one to rise in any form other than one died in.

"This may be the promise of the preacher, 'He who sat upon the throne said, Behold I make all things new.' But not true of his scripture.

"Literally, this means we will come back as fertilized eggs or infants. Yet, this is inconsistent with other descriptions of the Day of Judgment in *Revelations*: 'Four and twenty elders sat before God...'

"Regardless, what is really important is what will Jesus look like? After all, we will be in adoration of Jesus for all time."

He couldn't answer his own question. "No one really knows what Jesus looked like. They didn't have cameras in those days.

"The closest renditions of what He may have looked like are the earliest icons which have survived.

"In the eighth century, Byzantine emperors ordered destruction of all existing icons and commissioned a kinder, gentler likeness to be created which forever changed our perception of Jesus, from the mid-eastern man He actually was, to the western Hollywood icon we think of Him today.

"Yet, a few of the early icons did escape destruction. They portray Him as the mid-eastern man He actually was.

"It was Charles Manson's remarkable resemblance to the earliest icons which have survived, that enabled him to convince his followers of his possible divinity."

The little man lit up the screen of our entertainment center.

Earliest known icon   Charles Manson

He took advantage of my shocked reaction, "Why are we such hypocrites, we cannot accept Jesus as he actually was.

"Why do we play with our minds and visualize Jesus as what He never was? Why are we ashamed of what He really looked like? How do you think Jesus feels about our deception?

"How would you feel, if after you are gone, I did not like what you actually looked like, and asked an artist to paint an imaginary picture of a Hollywood icon to remember you by?

"Can it be the early fathers decided the truth would not be good for business? Can it be the current fathers know the truth would not be good for business?

"I have said this before. I will say it again. If we are ever to realize the truth, we must begin with the truth." He paused for a time to let it sink in, that he would not have to repeat it again.

"Regardless, we will all come back in the form we died in.

"There we will be, the newborn infants, the children, the lame, the deaf, the blind, others suffering from AIDS, leprosy, cancer and various afflictions, the ugly, the frail, white-haired, wrinkled-up skin and bones we died as. Even Jesus will display the blood-soaked wounds in His arms and feet and a gaping hole in His side.

"Hands and feet," I corrected him.

Wrong again, "Not true. First century crucifixion involved the

203

driving of spikes into planks placed over the arms into the cross beneath the bone line. The early icons placed the nails in the palms as it was more artistic and all artists since have followed this practice.

"It would not take a PhD in structural engineering of the anatomy to tell one that razor-sharp first century nails in the palms would never support the weight of a human body.

"Regardless, that one comes back as one is in this life is crucial, as there would be no other way to tell us apart. Consistent with all Christian scripture and theology, our bodies will be accompanied only by their souls and not by their minds.

"Mentally, if there is any mentality at all, we will all be the same. Who we are, what we are today, our memories and the way we think, will not survive in the Christian heaven.

"We will no longer possess decision-making abilities.

"We will not be able to choose between good and bad. In heaven, all will be good. Our decisions will all be the same.

"We will have no memory of loved ones or things of this life. 'Thou shalt not take thee a wife, or siblings, or sons, or daughters into this place'

"In eternity, all of one's love will be for Christ alone.

'He shalt clothe me in the garments of salvation, hath covered me with the robe of righteousness, as a bridegroom decketh himself with ornaments, as a bride adorneth herself with jewels. He who is saved will be as the bride of Christ.'

The greatest of sins

"Yet, Egyptians, Muslims and others, that realize resurrection of the body, will have a big advantage over Christians." He waited.

"Advantage?" I gave him the opening he was looking for.

"Sex." he replied, "Yes, sex.

"There is no room for sex in the Christian heaven as there is no room for sin in the Christian heaven. As we have discussed, according to Christian doctrine, sex is the greatest of sins.

"Christians will rise in a state of total castration. Eunuchs so to speak. The only thing man fears more than his mortality in this life, will be his reward in the next life."

I thought it was embarrassment I felt at the time, Today, as I think back, I know it was fear. Utter fear.

"Nevertheless, there will be no need for sex.

"There will be no pregnancies in the Christian heaven.

"That which we perceive as this life's greatest rapture, the enchantment of growing up, the pursuit of happiness, finding the love of one's life, of having children, of watching them grow up in search of their pursuit of happiness, will not be. On the Day of Judgment, the bell would have rung. Human procreation will no longer be.

"There will be no highs, no lows, no ups, no downs, no pleasure, no pain, no illness, no cuts, no bruises, no sadness, no joy, no good times, no bad times. How will we know when we are happy, if we don't know what it is to be sad?

'Only when one has walked in the shadows of the deepest valley, can one realize how magnificent it is to be at the pinnacle of the highest mountain.'

"It will be the same thing, day after day..." He stopped.

"Did I say, day after day? I stand corrected.

"There will be no day, no night, no sun, no moon, no twinkle of the stars, no yesterday, no tomorrow, no this year, no next year. Heaven will be a sameness suspended in sameness, for all time...

"There will be no football, no baseball, no tennis, no golf, no winning, no losing, no television, no movies... no fun at all.

"Every day will be Sunday. Perpetual adoration of the Magi, for all time..." He couldn't hold back a smirk as he clicked the remote.

He corrected himself, "Perpetual? Well, not entirely nonstop. Every so often, we will get a break."

"A break?" I repeated with a hint of surprise.

"Yes, every so often we would have to go to the bathroom. We will be human, you see.

205

"Too, every so often, Christ, Himself, would have to excuse Himself from His audience and pick up a copy of Playboy and head off to His great white throne in the royal bathroom."

I finally had him, "Justin, you're reading it wrong. We won't have to go to the bathroom in heaven." I quoted from memory the Book of Revelations: "'...there will be no thirst or hunger there.'"

If nothing more, I had at least raised his curiosity. "What's this? Human beings who don't have to go to the bathroom?

"No mouthwatering porterhouse steak with the baked potato and sour cream? No zesty cheese omelet with sausage and the hash browns? No stack of crepe suzettes with the wild berry sauce? No chips and dips? No Ben and Jerry's ice cream with the mountain of chocolate sauce and whipped cream with a cherry on top? No thirst quenching soda pop for me, or a beer for you?

"Yes, I stand corrected, '...there will be no thirst or hunger there.'

"The next thing you will be telling me, we won't have to go to the barbershop to get our hair cut. Mom won't have to go to the salon to make herself beautiful for the adoration. We won't have to go to the gym to keep in shape. We won't have to clip our nails. Or scrub our feet. Or clean behind our ears. Or brush our teeth.

"Yet, what puzzles me most about the Christian heaven, there will be no sea."

"Why is that such a mystery to you?" I waited.

"In the beginning, water was all that there was," he shot back.

I drew a blank, "Water was that there was?"

"Remember the day we discussed the story of creation in *Genesis*. God did not create the waters. They were always there.

'Let there be a firmament in the midst of the waters which are there, and let it divide the waters from the waters. And, God divided the waters which were under Heaven from the waters that were above Heaven... Then God said, Let the waters under the Heaven be gathered together, and let the dry land appear; and it was so. And, God called the dry land earth; and the gathering together of the waters He called the sea. And He saw that it was good.'

"This tells us the founding fathers got it terribly wrong. '...life everlasting' is just not in the cards for us."

"You can't prove that." I stopped him.

He didn't bat an eye. "Yes I can. Water is synonymous with life. When the astronaut lands on the distant planet and finds water, he knows life exists." He said it with an air of certainty. "There will be no life in heaven as we know it here on earth.

"We may 'exist' for all time. But we will not 'live' for all time.

"Our many friends in the sea will not be. You and I won't be able to go fishing in the old mill pond. Or go hiking to search for the cascading waterfall at the trail's end. No longer will I be able to beat you down the slopes. For there will be no snow, you see.

"There will be no seasons of winter, of spring, of summer, of fall. No rumbling of clouds, no roar of thunder, no lightning on a midsummer's night. No pitter-patter of rain on the window pane.

"Of all the world's religions, only Christianity accepts man as he has been on this earth is mortal.

"It is the explicit testimony of both the Old Testament, the New Testament, the doctrine of the Roman Catholic Church, the doctrine of the Orthodox world, and the doctrine of all Protestant churches, the mind, as it has been in this life, will not survive into the afterlife.

Burn, baby, burn

"Perhaps, our greatest anguish will be that we will not be able to hug one another as all our love will be for Christ alone.

"Of course, we will suffer the torture of knowing those of our loved ones who didn't make it. Our only hope would be that we will be unable to hear their screaming down below.

"Just who will be screaming down below?

'...on the Day of Judgment their souls will be rejoined to their bodies and they will be cast, both body and soul, into the eternal lake of fire.'

"Embryos and unborn fetuses for sure. They would have died short of the baptismal prerequisite for salvation: 'I say unto you, unless one believeth in me and be born again of baptism, one cannot enter the Kingdom of God.' Backed up by the Bible's explicit edict ensoulment takes place at birth: '...when thou camest out of the womb, I sanctified thee.' The reason no Christian church baptizes before birth.

"Those of distant lands not aware of baptism will be there.

"All those who engaged in sex outside of what the preacher considers marriage will surely be there.

"Homosexuals and even heterosexuals who don't marry and all those evil teenagers God catches masturbating will be there.

"The young who die suddenly will be there; they are likely to be caught in a state of un-repentance with their pants down.

"Perhaps, the largest group will be the remarried.

"Those who having made a mistake at twenty, found the love of their life at thirty, and chose to live out their lives in long term loving relationships not sanctioned by the man in Rome, will surely be there; burning their penises and vaginas off, for all time…

"As Father John told me, 'there are no penises or vaginas in heaven, only those burning down below have them.'

Heaven

"Sure gives a lot of truth to the age old adage; 'many are called… few are chosen.' Just who will be those lucky few?

"Popes, bishops, priests and nuns will surely be there. That is, provided they kept it in their pants." He grinned.

"Even those clergy, who slip up and allow the monster within them to get the best of them, and pedophile priests who murder their tiny victims to silence them, will be there. After all, the clergy keep their repentance up to date.

"Many of the elderly will make it; old folks are conscious of impending death and keep their repentance up to date. Too, they are less likely to be caught with their pants down.

"The young, who die long slow deaths, will be there as they, too, would have had the opportunity to repent."

"How about the children?" I would sweeten his broth.

"Thank you for reminding me. 'Blessed are the little children for theirs is the Kingdom of Heaven.' Yes, they, too, will be as the bride of Christ…" scratching his brow as if confused, "provided, of course, they keep it in their pants.' He leered.

"Nevertheless, it will be a strange world, this New Jerusalem.

"Do you think, do you really think, this is what Jesus wants of us? To fall down before Him and adore Him, for all time…?

"Or, rather, do you think He would want us to be out playing with our friends, going to the football games, going to school, taking the girl of our dreams to the junior prom, falling in love, and having children, so they, too, can realize their dream?"

He allowed me time to think. Perhaps, to soak up what he had just said, or, perhaps, to ready me for what he was about to say.

"Regardless, what all this tells us is that the human body is not a viable vehicle for eternal life. For if the resurrected body was truly human, it would have its ups and downs, it would grow up, and grow old, and eventually die, and die again, and die again.

"Too, the human body is a composition of trillions of Einstein's little friends from body cells to bacteria, all the way down to the atom, each one, an entity unto itself. Each one, with a brain, a nervous system, a cardiovascular system, a pulmonary system, a digestive system… most important of all, a reproductive system.

"Resurrection of the body requires each of these microcosmic creatures would also live on. For them, it would be quite a reward, as in this life many of them live for only a few seconds.

"All in all, Hollywood comes remarkably close to the Christian dream in its movie *Night of the Living Dead*. Mindless zombies madly-in-love with a Charles Manson look-a-like, for all time…

The lucky few

"We are lucky, aren't we?" His seriousness demanded an answer.

Confused by his question, "What do you mean, lucky?"

"The earliest known Homo erectus 'Lucy' lived three million years ago. God didn't send His Son to save mankind from sin until two thousand years ago. We have been lucky to have come along in the 1/6,000th percentile of humanity with a shot at immortality.

"Huh?" I scratched my temple. "I wonder why God waited so long to send His only begotten son to save mankind from sin?"

He read my mind, "He never thought of it.

"He got the idea from the Greeks. As I have said, Zeus sent His only begotten Son—Zagreus—to save mankind from sin more than a thousand years before our God copied the Grecian idea of a Savior."

I had him, "Then, why did God wait a thousand years?"

He had set me up, "In Greek Mythology, as we have discussed, just three hundred years before Jesus, the reincarnation of Zagreus (Dionysus) is born again. This time of a human virgin:

> 'Zeus flies over the realm in the guise of an eagle... falls in love with the virgin princess, Semele. He comes as a thief in the night upon her... Dionysus is born again... this time as man... becomes God from man... rules eternal life...'

"In the same way, Matthew and Luke added the virgin birth."

"In the same way?" I questioned.

"As I have said before, religion evolves just like any other social practice, each prophet building on those who came before him.

"By the time Matthew and Luke wrote of the Holy Ghost in the form of a dove impregnating the Virgin Mary, Dionysus had been adopted by the Romans as the Son of God, born of the human virgin Semele, impregnated by the God Zeus in the form of an eagle!"

Verses: 'Thou shalt not take thee a wife, nor siblings, nor sons, nor daughters into this place...' and '...when thou camest out of the womb, I sanctified thee:' *Jeremiah.* Verses attributed to Christ: gospels of *Matthew* and *John.* 'Creation' verse: *Genesis.*

Other biblical verses are from the *Book of Revelations.* The phrase '*...pinnacle of the highest mountain*' is of Richard Nixon's farewell address August 8, 1974

Source of earliest concept of Son of God in Greek mythology Zagreus-Dionysus: *Callimachus* 1610BC- 1230BC *Nonnus* (British National Museum). Dionysus is born of a mortal virgin in *Phrygian* mythology 349BC (Library of Alexandria).

Dionysus reigned as the Roman God born of a human virgin sired by the God Zeus in the form of an eagle the 1st through the 4th centuries when he was replaced by Jesus, born of a human virgin sired by Moses' God in the form of a dove.

The Case for the Chopsticks

"You forgot about the atheists of the eastern world. According to both the Bible and the Koran, they, too, go to hell."

He was quick to respond. "Yes, you are correct. In name, according to both the Bible and the Koran, they go to hell. But in action, according to all world scriptures, they go to heaven.

"Children brought up in atheist families have an infinitely better chance of heaven because they grow up free of prejudices peddled by religions to achieve political ambitions. They are much more likely to fulfill the will of the Universal God as we discussed the day I sold my bike: 'Love thy neighbor as thyself.'

"The reason the most fundamental adage of religion: 'many are called, few are chosen,' doesn't hold water in China."

"In China?" I sniggered.

"China is the largest atheist country in the world." He waited.

"Not true," I stopped him. "The Chinese practice Taoism, Confucianism, Buddhism and a host of other religions."

He agreed. "Yes, they do practice Taoism, Confucianism and Buddhism. But these are not religions. Though they are guiding lights to this life, not one of them recognizes the existence of God.

"Regardless, in my vision, I have had the good fortune to have visited those places which lie beyond the wall for the unbeliever. I have found—true also of the believer—he will live beyond the wall as he has chosen to live on this side of the wall.

How to use the chopsticks

"First, I was granted the privilege of seeing the Atheist Hell.

211

As I peered in through the gates, I saw a small room with a few tables. On these were so many bowls of cooked rice in as wide a range of gourmet delicacies as one could ever imagine. Properly spiced, aromatic, inviting.

The diners were seated there, filled with hunger, two at each bowl, one facing the other. Then what?

To carry the food to their mouths, they had chopsticks affixed to their hands, but so long that no matter how great their efforts, not a single grain of delicacy could reach their mouths. Here, the diners were angry, though starving, they could not eat.

Then, I was able to peer into the Atheist Heaven.

Here, I saw an immense room with many long tables, the same long chopsticks affixed to the diners' hands, the same delicacies, properly spiced, aromatic, inviting.

Here, the diners were happy, smiling, and satisfied. Why?

Each, having picked up food with the chopsticks, raised it to the mouth of the companion sitting opposite, and all was right."

He allowed me time to picture his vision of the Atheist Heaven.

He made his case: *"We must learn here as we make our way toward the great wall, how to use the chopsticks, else we will not know how to use them when we are on the other side of the wall.'*

The Hindus

"Likewise, the Hindu grows up relatively free of prejudice.

As we have discussed, unlike our God, the God Brahma is not a politician. Like the Atheist, the Hindu is more likely to fulfill the will of the Universal God: 'Love thy neighbor as thyself.'

"Nevertheless, in my vision…

"I wandered in a paradise of fresh air, of living plants, of towering trees, of crystal lakes, of running rivers, of sparkling brooks, of snow-peaked mountains, of green valleys, of cascading waterfalls; of dogs and of cats and of our friends in the forest; of marigolds, of violets, of tinker bells, of buttercups, of birds and bees and butterflies which go from here to there; of reds, of greens, of

212

oranges, of blues, of yellows, of violets; of apples, of apricots, of strawberries, of peaches, of plums, of watermelons, of limes.

"A realm of the sun, of the moon, of stars, of mountains, of valleys, of forests, of the sea. Where creatures live in waters as deep as high does the eagle soar. Not a perfect world. Yet, one where one can look forward to growing up, taking the girl of one's dreams to the junior prom, of falling in love, of hugging children, of watching one's child grow up, and take the girl of his dreams to the junior prom, of falling in love, of having children...

"The Hindu wanders in a land of ups and downs; he can walk in the shadows of the deepest valley and climb the tallest mountain.

"The Hindu chance is based on reincarnation. A minimum of five of them as he progresses up the caste system toward his ultimate reward of a perpetual state of eternal peace.

"Upon death, the soul rises to heaven, falls as rain which nourishes plants, nourishes man, nourishes semen/egg, cumulating in rebirth.

"Unlike the Buddhist, the Hindu has a God to guide his rebirth.

The Muslim Heaven

"I emerged out of a dense forest into a vast grotto. Towering walls of granite hemmed in cascading waterfalls plunging downward into a crystal blue pond.

"To one side, was spreading greenery with tints of red, white, yellow, blue, orange. Whatever colors the Master happened to have dipped into when He executed this breathtaking work of art.

"Much of the color was in motion. Butterflies and fireflies hovered above waters reflecting a living rainbow of fish glistening in an endless array of silver, gold, orange, red and what have you.

"Silent winds crept about the evergreens forming a crescent enclosing the pond as if to reflect the moon which was not there.

"As the mist made its retreat, slivers of the sun's rays pierced through the trees trying to take out a frog or two which sat on island rocks of gray surrounded by isles of green lily pads.

"All told, like a family reunion posing for a picture.

"The quiet of this infinite diversity of species broken only by the hum of bees, the chirping of birds, the croaking of frogs, the chirping of crickets, the squeaking of field mice, and, alas, a rabbit rustling through nearby bushes. And, one more.

"Voices, human voices. I heard the chattering of clusters of delighted youths eating and drinking in eternal banquet."

"The youths were outnumbered seventy-two-to-one by the naked bodies of voluptuous maidens...

He pulled the Koran in front of him: "'The good Muslims shall return to the Garden of Eden, whose portals shall stand up to them. Therein reclining, they shall call for many a fruit and drink... With them shall be virgins of their own age, with modest retiring glances. This is what ye were promised at the day of reckoning.... And youths shall go round them beautiful as imbedded pearls. Fruits in abundance will we give them, and flesh as they shall desire... '

"It is this promise of sex with the virgin of one's dreams that drives so many young men of the Muslim faith to become suicide bombers. They really believe what they have been unable to get in this life, will be theirs for certain in the next life.

"Too, unlike the Christian, the Muslim will be reunited with loved ones he has known in this life: 'To those who have believed... we unite them with their offspring...Enter ye and your wives into Paradise. Dishes and bowls shall go round unto them. There they shall enjoy whatever they desire and whatever their eyes delight in; therein ye shall abide forever.'

"One thing more. In Muhammad's paradise there will be a lineup at the outhouse." He smirked. "They would be human, you see.

"Of all the world's religions, only Islamism provides man as he has been on this earth, mind and body, will survive into the afterlife.

"Yet, like the Christian, the Muslim is dependent entirely on his God for his salvation... tales told by ancient politicians..."

The Jews

Suddenly, I realized he had missed one. I could hardly wait. I could finally score. "You forgot about the Jews?"

His eyes lit up. "Yes, thanks for reminding me. Yes, the Jews. Where do they go?" He scratched his head as if thinking deeply.

214

"I have always been puzzled about the poor Jews. To me, it makes no sense to go to church, week after week, and accept what God has given one in this life and not greed for more."

I knew I shouldn't have said it, "Like we good Christians..."

He shot me a look of utter despair.

"Nevertheless, I have found out what happens to the Jews."

"You found out?" I cried out. "Just how did you find out?"

"I asked them?"

"You asked them?"

"Yes, I asked Mrs. Goldstein on the steps of the synagogue, "Dear Mrs. Goldstein. Where do you go when you check out?"

"What did she say?" my ears perked up in great anticipation.

"Well, the old woman thought a long time... a very long time...

"Finally, she told me..." he paused long enough for my ears to perk up, one last time. "'We usually go to Philadelphia,'" he laughed. "'But if it's a nice day, we go to the park!'"

The 'Atheist' heaven (Chopsticks) is reprinted from Albino Luciani's book *Illustrissimi*. Confucianism, Taoism, Buddhism and other atheistic ways of life are practiced in China. Judaism is a guide to this life. It is the only 'religion' that there is no promise in its faith of an afterlife. Yet, the Jew still has hope.

The Case for the Spirit

"There is the guess of the Neanderthal which survives in the world of occults, mystics, séances and goblins: the spirit escapes the body at death and coexists with those who come after it.

"A ghost, who every so often gets the chance to speak out in the dark at the silent table of the counterfeit medium.

"The spirit is perceived as being the mind without the body. What one is really speaking of is a tiny fragment of the mind as in this life the mind is overwhelmingly occupied controlling bodily functions.

"That the spirit escapes the body at death and lives on in the present setting would be a torture much too terrible to endure. As we have said, imagine the horror of going about eternity without one's body.

"Yet, the mystic has no God. The mystic is up the river without a paddle. The reason he has few followers.

"Of course, all religions peddle belief in the supernatural and ghosts. After all, God, Himself, is a Ghost with a capital G.

The King Kong of the Supernatural World

"The Nicene Fathers built the Roman Catholic Church on Christ's archenemy—money. Pay the pastor for resurrection of the body:

> 'We are the ambassadors of Christ who has passed solely to us the power to forgive sins and pave the way to life everlasting... If the dead are not raised, Christ has not been raised...'

"Recognizing that few men are thieves, murderers and so forth, and everyone is guilty of sex, they cleverly made sex the greatest of sins; the central moral canon of the Roman Catholic Church today.

"It was the power of priests to forgive sexual sins and the exclusive power of popes to grant certain kinds of people the right to engage in sex without committing sin (marriage) that propelled Catholicism into the largest congregation in the world.

"Jesus did not give his disciples the authority to forgive sin.

"Too, Jesus never mentions sex in the gospels. He did not say: 'It is easier for a camel to pass through the eye of a needle than it is for a masturbator to enter the kingdom of heaven.'

"Despite Jesus' overwhelming testimony in the gospels *'greed is the greatest of sins,'* one will never hear in the confessional box: 'Father forgive me, I made too much money this week.'

"Catholicism has been built on greed, and it continues to thrive on greed today. To put it as it truly is, it preys on poverty.

"The closer one is to the ground, the more vulnerable one is to vendors of the supernatural. The closer one is to starvation, the more vulnerable one is to vendors of the supernatural. The closer one is to death, the more vulnerable one is to vendors of the supernatural." Raising his voice to leave no doubt as to his summation, "The Roman Catholic Church is the King Kong of the Supernatural World.

"Poverty stricken people are uneducated and will believe most anything one tells them that gives them hope for a better life in the next life. Prosperous people are educated and will not believe anything that does not make sense. Very little of what the Vatican has to say makes sense. That is, in first world countries.

"Yet, in third world countries, everything the Vatican has to say makes sense. In the most heavily AIDS infected countries of Africa, believers won't use a condom despite the risk of spreading AIDS and inviting pregnancies which will yield AIDS children born only to suffer unbearable lives and die unspeakable deaths.

"The Catholic Church knows if one were to rid the world of poverty, it would lose most of its congregation. One reason why the Vatican is the great enemy of Marxism—everyone an equal share.

"Canon law is based on the prejudices of Moses that Paul cleverly wove into his epistles: subordination of women, damnation of homosexuals, bastards and others who don't fit in with Moses' God.

"Among upwards of a half-million words in canon law, one will find only one verse from the gospels: 'He took bread and broke it. This is my body. He took wine. This is my blood. Do this in remembrance of me.'

217

"As we have already discussed, this verse was taken completely out of context by the Founding Fathers who ingeniously reduced Jesus to no more than a sacrificial lamb to satisfy the bloodlust of their God.

"He raised his voice in upper case. Only an imbecile would miss it:

'...TAKE YE NOT THE LIFEBLOOD OF THE BULLOCK. I GIVE THEE THE HERBS OF THE SOIL. LOOK UP THY EYES AND LOOK IN THE FIELDS FOR THEY ARE RIPE TO HARVEST. I GIVE YOU THE FRUIT OF THE VINEYARD. LOOK UP THY EYES TO THE BRANCHES FOR THEY ARE FIT TO DRINK. HE BROKE BREAD, 'THIS IS MY BODY. HE TOOK WINE, THIS IS MY BLOOD. DO THIS IN REMEMBRANCE OF ME.'

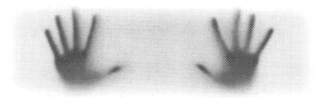

Stop killing animals.

"Too, among those same half-million words, one will not find a single mention of 'Love thy neighbor as thyself.'

"When a pope encourages women to play a more active role in the management of the Church, he does not make them priests so that they are able to play a more active role in the management of the Church. His God—Moses' God—decreed: 'only the sons of the sons of the sons of Aaron' can be priests.

"When a pope says of homosexuals—'Who am I to judge'—he remains sworn to preserve cannon law which condemns them as: 'degenerates destined for the damnation of hell.' Moses' law decrees: 'He that lieth with a man as he lieth with a woman shall surely be put to death.'

"To disturb canon law would be to disturb the foundation upon which the Roman Catholic Church is built: Adoration of the God of the Old Testament and adherence to His laws.

"Regardless, the Nicene Fathers molded their sheep into idolaters. Mindless zombies mumbling empty repetitions to rumbling beads before plaster idols. As if a plaster doll can hear what one has to say?

"Fools mesmerized by the 'Great Houdini' on the stage changing bread and wine into the body and blood of a God before their eyes.

"They molded their gullible sheep into the Hypocrites Christ so often condemned, posing in magnificent cathedrals to be seen and heard of men, while children all over the world starve to death.

"Zombies, magic, pomp and pageantry; anything for a buck."

He stopped for a time to allow what he had said to sink in.

Islamism

"This is a major difference between a Muslim and a Christian.

"Muhammad believed literally in Jesus. In fact, he mentions 'Jesus' much more than he does himself in his Koran.

"Re: forgiveness, he agrees with Jesus: 'Only Allah can forgive sin'

"He makes Jesus' commandments: 'Love thy neighbor as thyself' and 'Sell all thou hast and give to the poor.' his sole requirement for salvation:

> 'Give all thou hast to your neighbor. I am your neighbor. If the wealth ye have gained, and the merchandise ye fear may be unsold and dwellings wherein ye delight, be dearer to you than God, dearer to you than your neighbor, then God too will be dearer to Himself and you will not reside with Him in His house.'

"Muhammad concluded the Nicene Fathers had made a mockery of Christ's substitution of bread and wine in exchange for the life of the lamb in their cannibalistic ritual of their Blood Mass.

"Canon law had cleverly replaced Christ's will to rid the world of starving children with the pomp and pageantry of entranced sheep.

"Muhammad knew the Nicene Fathers had based their church on Greek mythology: 'Zeus flies over the realm in guise of an eagle... gazes with love upon the virgin princess Semele. He comes as a thief in the night upon her... Dionysus is born again as man as God... rules eternal life.'

"He raised his voice: "ONE WOULD HAVE TO BE A NITWIT TO MISS IT." He paused as if assuring himself this nitwit had not missed it.

"Too, Muhammad struck directly at the Eucharist. In a nutshell, man must save himself from sin, not by ceremony, but by deed.

> 'It is not your meat nor your blood that satisfies Allah. It is solely your personal sacrifice for others that satisfies Allah.'

"As I've said, 'Jesus' is mentioned more than 'Muhammad' in the Koran. Sadly, 'Moses' is mentioned more than anyone else. As is true of the Bible, Moses does the dirty work in the Koran:

'Slay the IDOLATERS wherever you find them... Fight against them until idolatry is no more... Make war on the HYPOCRITES. Their ultimate abode is hell...' is repeated many, many times in the Koran.

"Specifically who is Muhammad's Moses speaking of?

"IDOLATERS? Catholics who believe the path to heaven is on one's knees talking to plaster idols. In Muhammad's world, the only path to heaven is on one's feet helping others.

"In Muhammad's time, all Christians were members of the Roman Catholic Church deeply immersed in IDOLATRY. When the political expert claims there is nothing in the Koran responsible for what is going in the Mideast today, he'd better guess again.

"HYPOCRITES? Again, he is referring to Catholics who make a mockery of Jesus' instruction to 'stop killing animals for the dinner table' by engaging in a mishmash of the Eucharist and steak dinners.

"Regardless, we have covered them all. Jews, Christians, Muslims, Hindus, Mystics, Atheists... We know where each of them is going.

"Realizing he had said something wrong he stopped. He corrected himself, 'We know where each of them thinks they are going.

He stopped for a long time now. I would guess to assure himself that I had fully grasped what he had said.

Still he left the door open, "We shall see... Yes, we shall see...

Priest's authority to forgive sin and resurrection of the body: *Corinthians*. Both principles contradict the gospels. Re: chapter The Crown Jewel of Christianity E.g., only God can forgive sin: all four gospels and in the *Koran Al-Hajj*-22:37 Kill the Idolaters (Catholics): *Koran* 2:191 2:193 9:73 and dozens more...

According to the gospels, consistent with the prophecy in I*saiah*, Jesus lived as an ethical vegan – one who thought it wrong to kill animals for nourishment when God provides the fruit of the vine and the wheat of the fields. Jesus did eat fish.

Through the centuries some monasteries and Christian churches practiced vegetarianism as required by Jesus.

The Case for the Mind

"Our only chance of immortality is that there exists in the natural order of creation a vehicle that enables us to save what we want to save. All we need do is to identify that vehicle and get on board."

Albino Luciani, Gregorian University, doctoral dissertation, Feb 27, 1947

"We have come to that point at which we must provide the 'proof of the pudding' so to speak. Is it possible to know before we die in this life that we will indeed survive into the next life? Is it possible to remove the question mark from the end of one's life, once and for all?

"If we fail to do this, we are no better than all the political vendors of gods who have come before us or will come after us.

"The Neanderthal who buried the ghost of his enemy, to the Cro-Magnon whose gods lived in the deepest and darkest of caves, to the sly witchdoctor of Africa whose gods lived in the jungle, to the shrewd Egyptian whose gods lived on the other side of the Nile, to the cunning Aborigine whose gods of the South Pacific lived in the sea, to the bloodthirsty Maya whose gods lived in the underworld, to the clever Celtic who dreamt up the Banshee who lived in the forest, to the devious Eskimo whose god Agloolik lived under the ice, to the Greeks whose God Zeus roamed the realm in the guise of an eagle searching for the love of His life—the virgin Semele, to the offspring of that union, Dionysus, who lives on with us to this very day in the guise of Jesus Christ who lives somewhere up there.

"Unscrupulous men who capitalized on man's mortality through the ages to attain political ambitions. Unscrupulous men who leave us scrambling for miracles when the doctor tells us:

221

'You are about to meet your Jesus!'

"When the master detective applies the grey cells. When he separates the facts… from the probabilities... from the possibilities… from the politics of men; he will find he has only one real shot at immortality."

I reminded him "You just proved that we aren't going anywhere."

"Yes, according to ghosts. All gods are ghosts. When we speak of ghosts we are speaking of the world of make-believe."

He reminded me. "We have not yet discussed the facts. We have not yet discussed science. We have not yet discussed reality."

"Reality?" The thought popped into my mind. "There is no more certain definition of 'fact' than when you are dead, you are dead!"

Setting my thought aside, he began.
"When he comes to the end of the day, what is he trying to save?

"Is he trying to save his body? Something he knows.

"Is he trying to save his mind? Something he knows.

"Or, is he trying to save his soul? Something he does not know."

He stopped to allow time for me to etch the alternatives in my mind, before taking them away from me, one by one

"When he lays on his deathbed, he will realize what he is.

"If he is old and gray and wrinkled and frail, he will have a body that he really wouldn't want to keep. If he is young and vibrant, he will know his body will eventually grow old and gray and wrinkled and frail, a body, which in the long run, doesn't count at all.

"Unless he is a fool, he will realize the forefathers of his faith had lied to accomplish political ambitions. Unless he is an imbecile, he will realize Moses was right: 'Dust thou art and to dust thou wilt return.'"

I stopped him with the Christian's pledge of allegiance to his faith: "'I believe in resurrection of the body and life everlasting...'"

He cut me off, "Don't kid yourself. There are no bathrooms in heaven. Not even for chimpanzees."

I gave him more of the same: "'...Christ descended into hell...rose from the dead... ascended into heaven...'"

He cut me off again, "...not even for Gods.

"Regardless, when he comes to the end of his days, he will not be trying to save his body which he 'knows' will return to dust.

222

"Nor will he be trying to save his soul, something he has never known and doesn't understand. He might reserve this whim of the preacher in the back of his mind as an imaginary safety net in the event what he really wants to save, doesn't work.

The way he thinks

"When he comes to the end of the road, he will be trying to save what he knows himself to be without his body.

"He will be trying to save his mind - the way he thinks.

"More specifically, he will be trying to save that which makes him different from the rest of us. He will be trying to save that which defines him as an individual. He will not be trying to save that part of his mind he shares with the rest of us. He will be trying to save that part of his mind that is unique to his own existence. He would not be trying to save anyone else. He will be trying to save himself.

"If we define the 'individual' as he is at the time of death, though intelligence, aptitude and instincts would be a part of him, they do not define him as the individual he is apart from the rest of us."

Lowering his voice, he said it in an unwavering tone: "When he comes to the end of his days, he will realize he is something far greater than a mortal body that has met its date in time. Something far greater than the whisker of intelligence and instinct he had been born into.

"He will be a collection of 'memories,' some wonderful ones, some dreadful ones, some distant ones, some recent ones. And, most of all, he will be what he 'knows.'

"Of all the people in the world, of all the people who ever were, of all the people who will ever be, only he possesses this unique combination of 'memories and knowledge.'

"This is him." The little man struck his fingertips up over both his ears in a repetitive motion. "This is what defines him as an individual apart from the rest of us, more than anything else.

"This, more than anything else, molds the way he thinks."

He asked himself. "Yet, is this what we seek in immortality?

"Is this what we are trying to save? Is this what we are trying to make last forever? This unique formation of electrons stored in the temporal lobes just up over the ears?"

"It sort of looks like that," He took it away from me again.

"Not so. What is here in the temporal lobes will change from time to time. When we are born, there is nothing here." curling his fingers up above his ears again.

"If one were to say, what is stored in the temporal lobes defines a person, a person would be a different person every day of his life.

"If a man were to die at sixty, he would be saving an entirely different man than if he had died at thirty. At sixty, he may have been a progressive, whereas at thirty, he may have been a conservative.

"Regardless, this is what we are at the time of death.

"It is our memories and knowledge that determine what we are without our bodies, much more so than anything else.

"If the composition of our memories and knowledge—which mold the way we think—cannot survive death, we are mortal."

He nailed the lid shut: "We will cease to exist at death.

"Nevertheless, we have arrived at the moment of truth, the moment of reason. Can the mind—the way we think—survive death?"

I reminded him, "Not possible. According to Christian doctrine, the human mind as it has been in this life will not survive in heaven."

He grew annoyed. "Again, you are talking about ghosts.

"Even with a capital G, God is still the make-believe world of ghosts. When one is on one's death bed, one is dealing with the real world one lives and dies in. Not the whims of ancient politicians.

"We have already firmly established that if there is a God—a Ghost with a capital G—we know when we are dead we are dead.

"To think otherwise, is to contradict the natural order of God's creation. As much as if to say 'God is Stupid' with a capital S.

"The fantasy that of the trillions and trillions of infinite variations and aspects of God's creation only man is immortal, may be enough to fool the mindless sheep of the preacher; yet, it does not get past the lowest rung on the ladder of human intelligence."

He put his hand on my shoulder. "Listen carefully. I am going to define our only chance at immortality. I am going to say it, not as one of those mindless gullible sheep, but as an intelligent human being.

"Our only chance of immortality is that there exists in the natural order of creation a vehicle that enables each of us to save what we want to save—'the way we think.' All we need do is to identify that vehicle and get on board. This we will do now."

The Case for Reincarnation

He began, "One possibility is reincarnation of the mind.

"The Buddhist, the principal practitioner of reincarnation, stakes his salvation on the existence of a scientific process that guides the composition of one's mind into a new body upon death.

"On the surface, it seems, he has much to support his ideology."

My mind drew a blank.

"There is the remarkable chain of coincidences in the search for a successor Dalai Lama, one is always found.

"The present Dalai Lama was found at age six in a remote part of Tibet speaking in the ancient language of the Buddha. One of many signs the reincarnation of the medieval Dalai Lama has been found.

"Then there is the practiced Buddhist, himself, as he reaches into his past through meditation.

"To the onlooker, one would think he is searching into the future. In reality, he is searching into the past for the strength developed in past lives to guide his mind into future lives. We know he must be having some level of success, lest he would cease to meditate.

"Then, one has Mozart." He waited for me to repeat it as a question.

"Mozart?" I gave him what he was looking for.

"Yes. Mozart. The remarkable phenomenon of genius.

"How is it possible, Mozart, at the age of six, knew more about music than one could possibly accumulate in six lifetimes?

"As we have said, intelligence cannot be traced to genes. Every day, geniuses are born to idiots and idiots are born to geniuses...

"Likewise, aptitude has nothing to do with genes. Edison was not born into a family of inventors. Einstein was not born into a family of physicists. Tchaikovsky was not born into a family of composers...

"Michelangelo was born into a family of bankers. Da Vinci was born to a notary and a peasant who had no background in art or invention. Rembrandt was born to a miller and a baker's daughter...

"All of these exhibited at an early age astounding knowledge of the vocation which would eventually immortalize them.

"How could these children have amassed a greater knowledge of their respective fields of endeavor at the age of six than they could possibly gain in six lifetimes? Unless they had lived those lifetimes?

"Then, we have transgenders.

"A condition that manifests itself in early infancy.

"From the start, the transgender little boy will reach for the doll, and, from the start, the transgender little girl will reach for the truck.

"Then again, how is it possible the normal little girl knows that she should reach for the doll, and the normal little boy knows he should reach for the truck, unless one has been a girl or a boy before?

"Moreover, we have ourselves.

"Many of us can remember the details of life in another part of the world which we have never been to, or even read or heard about. Things that happened long before we were born.

"Often, one meets someone for the first time, and thinks he has known them all of one's life. What's more, one has either good or bad vibes, and in time often finds one's vibes were right.

"Too, we have the mental transfer of energy decidedly felt by both the giver and the taker as we discussed the day when we talked about the birds and the bees.

"What's more, we know thoughts can be transferred to others without the use of the five senses. It happens every day.

"In the conference room, at the breakfast table, or even in the classroom, if one knows something one does not want to pass on to others, one will try to think of anything else. One knows if one dwells mentally on the subject at hand, others will pick it up.

"We know that some of us are good transmitters of thoughts while others are good receivers of thoughts—the world renowned physic reading the minds of his subjects with uncanny accuracy.

"As we discussed, the day we spoke of the miniature world that goes on beneath us, each thought is made up of physical things— electrons—the same particles which make up electro-magnetic sound waves which are transmitted and received in wireless radio.

"Similarly, the brain is a wireless transmitter and receiver of thoughts—electrons; visibly demonstrated by the neuroscientist's brainwave-sensing-headband permitting a paralyzed person to drive a computer keyboard solely with human thoughts.

"Yet, in all these cases, we are speaking of simple thoughts, and the existence of another mind or receptor to provide the chemical or electronic base necessary to receive those thoughts.

The scientific possibility of reincarnation

"On the other hand, in reincarnation one is not speaking of individual thoughts, but the entire composition of a mind finding another host.

"Consider the scientific environment necessary to accomplish this remarkable phenomenon.

"We know this cannot possibly happen after the body is brain dead, as there would be no existing chemical base to sustain thoughts. That is, to sustain a composition of electrons. If reincarnation takes place, it must take place before the brain—the transmitter—is dead.

"What's more, the host would have to be living.

"It could not scientifically occur at conception, as there would be no existing chemical base to receive thoughts. If reincarnation takes place, it would most likely involve a child in its first five years of life when the brain is developing and most receptive.

"This tells us that reincarnation is scientifically possible only if the benefactor and the host coexist when the transfer takes place.

"The practitioner of reincarnation acknowledges this requirement. Countless studies in India have tried to establish a coalition between Buddhist monks and Alzheimer's disease. Yet, to no avail.

"Nevertheless, there is a more conclusive reason that reincarnation—the transfer of one's memories and knowledge at a given point in time to another body at death—does not occur." He waited.

I decided to let him answer his own question. "Common sense. There would be no point to it. One would be saving a different person every day of one's life. The infant who dies at birth and the old man who dies of Alzheimer's would save nothing at all.

"So we know reincarnation is not a viable vehicle to achieve our goal. We don't want to save 'the way we were' nor do we want to save 'the way we will be.' We want to save 'the way we are.'

"To say it as it really is, we want to save…

'The way we think'

227

"This leaves us with only one shot at eternal life."

Wisely, I decided to let him answer his own question.

It struck like a dagger through my heart. "The human soul."

Closing his books and carefully setting them aside, he peered over at me. "Aside from resurrection of his body, which common sense tells him is sheer fantasy; the good Christian is bent on saving his soul, something he does not understand.

"Doesn't make a lot of sense, does it?" He waited.

I gave him the first one. "You are right about resurrection of the body. It makes no sense there are bathrooms in heaven."

Anyway I had him on the other. "One still has the soul. You will never be able to prove or disprove the existence of the human soul."

He wormed his hook, "Why not?"

I took the bait. "For starters, you don't know where it is. In truth, you don't really know what it is."

Reaching over and grasping my arm, he held my eyes.

I nearly fell off my chair. "But I do know what it is. I have found my soul. What's more, I have the proof."

Not good enough. He spelled out precisely what he meant by proof:

"It is possible to know in this life that what we are trying to save —the way we think——will live on for all time..."

The room fell respectively quiet. I waited anxiously for the little man to make his astounding revelation...

There are an infinite number of ideologies of reincarnation in eastern sects.

The modern Buddhist' definition—scientific transmission of the 'mind' to a new host—is discussed herein. Conversely, the Hindu relies on divine transmission of an undefined 'soul' to a new host and eventual peace in Nirvana.

Again, the Hindu has a God whereas the Buddhist has no God. There is a misconception the Dalai Lama is the reincarnated spirit of Buddha. Not true. The Dalai Lama is the reincarnated spirit of the first Dalai Lama (1391-1474AD).

The Case for the Soul

"Don't knock yourself out over smart monkeys and Adam and Eve. Each of us is responsible for our own evolution. We can choose to remain as mortal men, or we can evolve as Gods."

Albino Luciani, Gregorian University, doctoral dissertation, Feb 27, 1947

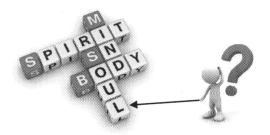

He had cleared the table. He sat there with a single book and a deck of cards. It was the first time I had ever seen him with only one book. I read its face, *The Hinayana.*

"Some kind of a game," I thought.

He read my mind, "Yes, you are right, we are about to play a game. An ancient game. Yet, not a game of chance. It is a game of certainty. I call it, *The Sure Bet.*

"As we have determined, the survival of the body and the survival of the mind as they have been in this life is just not in the cards for us. This leaves us with only one chance, the soul."

I shot up my hand as if I was stopping a line of traffic. "You told me when one faces the moment of truth—when one faces the question mark at the end of one's life—one is not going to stake one's eternity on something one does not understand—on the whim one has a soul."

"That's right, as the soul has been said to be given us by God.

"I am speaking here, not of the mythical soul claimed by political preachers to be created by God in heaven. I am speaking here, of the real soul man makes for himself here on earth."

I shot him a look of despair, as if he had gone mad.

229

"I will say this one more time." He said it slowly and decisively.

"Our only chance of immortality is that there exists in the natural order of creation a vehicle that enables each of us to save 'the way we think.' All we need do is to identify that vehicle and get on board.

"I have struck upon that vehicle. I have struck upon the winning card."

I thought it was time to bring an end to his nonsense.

"Ridiculous. You are wasting your time. It cannot be done. No matter how one reads the cards and plays the game, there will always be a question mark at the end of one's life." I didn't have to wait long.

"Not in my case. As I have said, I am not going to risk my eternity on the unfathomable chance I have a God-given soul. I am not going to pin my hopes on tales told by ancient politicians.

"The Christian, despite his foolish impulse to think otherwise, doesn't enjoy the slightest confidence in his destiny.

"When the doctors tell him, he is about to meet his Jesus, he falls on his knees and prays for a miracle to save him from meeting his Jesus. He does not really want to meet his Jesus. He does not want to meet his Jesus, because he 'knows' his Jesus is not really there.

"He does not trust the preacher who sold him his condominium in the sky because he knows the preacher has never been there.

"When he comes to the end of the game, he knows his chance of winning is a much longer shot than the ridiculous tale of the 'burning bush' he has gambled his eternity on. After all, he holds only one card. The 'mythical assumption' he was born into."

Picking up the deck of cards, he fanned them across the table in a cutting thud. "This is the real world we live and die in.

"There are fifty-two cards in this deck. There are infinitely more cards in the vast deck of eternity. Yet, in the vast deck of eternity there is only one winning card." His eyes roamed around the room as if to assure himself the walls were not listening. He paused for a moment or so to set the stage for his astounding revelation.

I waited with baited breath. He was not to disappoint me.

Lowering his voice just above a whisper, "What is important for me, I have found it. I have struck upon *'the vehicle that exists in the natural order of creation that enables us to save 'the way we think.'"*

An octave lower, "What is important for you, I am about to share it with you.

The Man-made Soul

"As we have determined, man is without a soul. That is, he is not born with a supernatural soul. God did not give him a soul.

"If I have no God-given soul, then I must find another form of guidance. All surviving religions would be meaningless to me as their salvations depend entirely on the existence of a God-given soul.

"Buddhism is the only viable choice.

"No, not in its more recent, more popular, northern variety, the Mahayana, with its endless parables of reincarnation, embarrassing puppets dedicated to the pornography of worship, its emphasis on meditation, its futile promise of salvation in another body.

"No, the possibility lies in the more distant Hinayana, the less popular ancient instruction that dictates man is without a God-given soul. The Hinayana holds that his deeds, themselves, will create his soul, which will live on in his fellowman, for all time…

"An ideology which emphasizes contribution to mankind, rather than paying men to dress up in fancy gowns and tall hats to prance about altars of marble and gold in adoration of a mythical creation of ancient politicians.

"Death, the Christian fears above everything else, the Hinayana welcomes. The Hinayana is the only practitioner of any faith who is certain of his destiny for he is certain that what he has done here in this life, will live on, for all time…

"The Christian can only imagine his afterlife. Sadly, not even his own imagination, but the imagination of ancient men.

"For him, life ends in a question mark? When his number is up, he prays for a miracle to save himself from going to meet his God.

"Yet, this type of Buddhist, the Hinayana knows.

"He knows it is the composition of this life that will become the substance of his afterlife. He is certain of his afterlife, as he is building it every single day of this life. One believes, while the other knows. The Christian can only believe, the Hinayana knows."

He had raised my curiosity, "You mean, if someone makes a great contribution to society, we will remember them?"

"It is much more than simply remembering someone."

He took on a tone of absolute certainty which totally obscured all the uncertainty we had found ourselves engulfed in up to that point.

231

"The Hinayana wastes no time falling on his knees before mythical creations of gods other men place before him.

"He does this because he knows they are false gods. He knows they are false gods because..." pausing to highlight his astonishing declaration, "He knows He, Himself, is God."

I recall it, as if it were yesterday, his remarkable affirmation. At first, I took it he was talking off the top of his head. I had no idea, at the time, he was about to prove it.

> *'We can choose to remain as mortal men...*
> *...or we can evolve as Gods.'*

"We have determined a man is defined by how he thinks, much more so than by his body which will decay to dust."

Slowly, raising his hand and pointing to his temple, he reminded me, "Remember, it is the composition of our minds—the way we think—we want to live on, for all time.

"I have stumbled upon the secret of how our minds—the way we think—can live on, for all time...

"I have stumbled upon the secret of eternal life. To live on, for all time... not just as a simple pawn in adoration... but as a God.

"What's more, unlike the preacher who talks through his hat and has not a single fact to back up what he has to say..."

Reaching over and grasping my shoulder, he held my eyes.

"I have the proof.

"Take Lincoln, for example.

"Before his time, Christians in America believed in slavery. They thought it was good.

"What's more, they thought there was something holy about it; their God explicitly protected the right of one man to enslave another in His Tenth Commandment: 'Thou shalt not covet (desire to take from) thy neighbor's property, including his house, his wife, his slaves, his ox, his ass.'

"Today, no one thinks slavery is good. We all know it is wrong. Lincoln has obtained immortality for today He is part of the way we think. What's more, He is a part of the way—not one of us thinks as in simple reincarnation—but the way all of us will think, for all time...

"His consciousness, the way he thought—the composition of his mind—what He was trying to save—lives on, for all time...

232

"Today, Lincoln is much more than the simple soul the faith he had been born into had promised him. He is much more than the simple man who spoke hallowed words at Gettysburg: 'Four score and seven years ago… the world will little note, nor long remember what is said here…'

"Today, Lincoln has survived as a God—that part of each of us that tells us right from wrong." He pointed to his temple.

"As for the fair sex, among others, we have Susan B. Anthony.

"When Susan first came along, she and other little girls, like other animals, were mere property of men.

"Again, everyone thought it was right. They thought there was something holy about it. After all, it was written in their holy book that women, like other animals, were mere property of men: 'Thou shalt not covet thy neighbor's property, including his house, his wife…'

"Today, no one thinks of women as mere property of men.

"Susan has obtained immortality. What She wanted to save—the way She thought—is the way not one of us thinks as in simple reincarnation, but the way all of us will think, for all time…

"She has survived as a God—that part of us that tells us right from wrong." He pointed to his temple.

"In more recent times, we have Elizabeth Taylor.

"When the dreaded disease first surfaced, many of us thought those afflicted with and dying of AIDS were evil. The preacher convinced his sheep that it is God's punishment for having lived sinful lives.

"Yet, today, Elizabeth has changed the way all of us think. We no longer think of people of disease with hatred and scorn. We think of them with love and compassion.

"She, too, etched hallowed words into time: 'I call upon all of you, to draw from the depths of your being, to prove we are one human race, to prove our need to love outweighs our need to hate…'

"Words that have found their way into our hearts and minds. They have become a part of each of us, the way each of us thinks—not one of us thinks as in simple reincarnation—but the way all of us will think, not for just a day, not for just a year, but for all time…

"As I have promised, I have the proof." He dealt the winning card.

233

"Elizabeth is still alive today. A living person who has no question mark at the end of her life. A living person who knows beyond a shadow of a doubt 'the way she thinks' will live on for all time…

"When she comes to the end of the day, when the doctors tell her that her time is up, she will not fall on her knees begging for miracles to save her from going to meet the mythical assumption she had been born into. She will not fall on her knees because she <u>knows</u>—beyond a shadow of a doubt—long after her body returns to dust, what she is trying to save—the way she thinks—will live on… for all time…"

He locked up his case. "…not merely as the simple pawn in eternal adoration of the Magi that the 'assumption' She had been born into had promised Her… but as a God." He raised the tips of his fingers to his temple, "That part of each of us that tells us right from wrong!"

All Gods… great and small

"You say, 'we will remember them.' In truth, we remember few of them. For the most part, we never hear of them.

"Every day the *rampaging locomotive of immortality* comes one's way. All one need do, is not pass it up, but get on board."

It came from deep within him, striking deep into my heart, reaching deep into my very soul: "*'All one need do, is to take a chance, and have on one's arm, the homeliest girl at the dance!'*

"This is the kind of stuff souls are made of.

"Men and women who make the world a better place to bring the world's future children into, create their own souls, which will live on for all time… a part of this thing we think of as *'that part of each of us which is a part of God—that part of each of us that tells us right from wrong.'*" He pointed to his temple one last time.

"Unlike the Christian, who crawls on his knees before statues and altars of marble and gold in adoration of a mythical creation of men's imaginations, the Hinayana <u>knows</u> He will go on, for all time…

"Unlike the Christian, who fears death most of all, who runs into a big question mark at the end of the day, who prays for a miracle to save himself from going to meet his Jesus; the Hinayana does not fear death. Rather He welcomes it. He <u>knows</u> for Him it is not the end; it is the beginning… the beginning of His eternal destiny…"

Finale

He paused for a long time now. His mind undoubtedly concentrated on what would be the composition of his finale. Of how this little man would sum up in a single phrase, all that he had said.

As for myself, I was still trying to put together what he had already said, while at the same time trying to catch my breath. Suddenly he interrupted my mind.

He spoke steadily, very slowly, as if to make every word count, pausing after each phrase, as if to give the Creator time to etch each of them into the sacred scroll of eternity.

The room fell respectfully quiet.

The rigid gaze of a pair of cockatiels in a cage off to one side focused on the little general like soldiers standing at attention.

Our old ragged dog, Rusty, crawled up out of his basket, sat up straight, perked up his ears in watchful attendance.

A fly, zooming around the room for the past hour, perched on the crest of an overstuffed wingchair in a frozen stare.

The logs in the fireplace ceased crackling, as to allow each of its flames to bear witness.

Even the air stood still as it waited anxiously for what Justin was about to say...

"When we began this journey—when we first walked in the woods together with Albino, Pinocchio, the Cat and the Fox, and the Poodle Medoro—we decided, if we are ever to define the human soul and its role in eternal life, we must first determine the truth of the assumption we have been born into.

"Now, we have come to the end of that journey.

"We now know the assumption we have been born into are tales told by ancient men to accomplish political ambitions.

"What's more, we know these same tales are used by modern men to accomplish their political ambitions today.

"We now know the soul is not the mythical assumption we were born into. The soul is not our birthright. The soul is not a free ride. The origin of the human soul is not of heaven. The origin of the human soul is of this earth.

"The soul is not made by God. The soul is made by Man.

"What's more, it is the sacred responsibility of each one of us to build it every moment, every hour, every day, of our lives.

"It is up to each one of us, to create our own soul. It is our sacred responsibility to create a world in which every child, who comes after us, has an equal chance at a good and healthy life.

"On Napoleon's tomb is etched the code of the Hinayana, *'Man's only immortality is what he leaves behind in the minds of men.'*

"What we are in this world—how we think and what we do—will determine whether or not we will live on, for all time...

"On the other hand, those fools, grumbling on their knees with rumbling beads before plaster dolls and marble altars for selfish favors in this life and demanding a better life in the next life, will survive into eternity, no more than the empty air they speak to."

He paused, one last time. Perhaps to allow the one above time to catch up with him. He carefully stacked the cards back into the deck. He closed his book.

"As for me, I would want to live a life of great contribution, for I know the only way I will live on forever, is in my fellowman; in his ambitions, in his hopes, in his struggles, in his pursuit of happiness, in the realization of his dreams.

"When all is said and done, and I come to the end of the day, when the last sigh has been spent, when all the dials return to zero, when this machine has finally read its last book and drawn its last conclusion, when it has done its last deed, when it has played its last card, that I would know in my mind, and in my heart, that I would go on forever in my fellowman—like Abraham Lincoln, like Susan B. Anthony, perhaps, like Elizabeth Taylor, Herself.

"That I would have made my mark and know that it will never be erased by time. I will remain here for all the days beyond the end of the earth. Not just as a simple pawn in endless space as fantasized in faith, but as a God on earth as known in reality.

"That I would have fulfilled my mentor's commission:

'Don't knock yourself out over smart monkeys and Adam and Eve. Each of us is responsible for our own evolution. We can choose to remain as mortal men, or we can evolve as Gods.'

236

His audience held its breath as he dealt the absolute proof.

"For mankind has never died. Not even once. You see..."

He stopped, transfixed in boundless apprehension, as does a great actor who stands on the grand stage at the end of an epic performance, awaiting applause.

It came. It came in a smile. My smile. My reassuring smile.

I decided not to say a thing. Nothing I could have said could begin to add to what this little man had put before me.

Getting up, I headed for the stairs.

"I wonder, I wonder," I repeated as I struggled up the stairs. "Soul? Soul? I wonder if... I wonder if... I, too, have a soul?"

I reminded myself, "I wonder? I wonder? I wonder? Perhaps, I, too, don't have a soul?"

As I staggered into the kitchen in a state of shock, together with a frozen stare as Hollywood builds into its living dead, Audrey greeted me with her playful, whimsical, all-knowing smile. "Well, did he find his soul? Or, did you lose yours?"

Quote attributed to Abraham Lincoln—the Gettysburg Address. Quote attributed to Elizabeth Taylor— the Academy Awards March 29, 1993 when she accepted the Jean Hersholt Humanitarian Award for her work in AIDS.

In the following encore—'Prejudice'—the author creates little known incidents in the lives of Susan Anthony, Elizabeth Taylor and other famous people that caused them to rise up as champions of human justice.

10th Commandment is per all bibles predating 1881. In modern bibles the word 'slaves' changed to 'servants' 'Slaves' no longer good for business.

Because Albino Luciani's thesis was known to have involved a 'Man-made Soul,' in the wake of the Pope's death, the Vatican confiscated his original thesis and cleverly replaced it with a fraud which dealt with the genetic orientation of the soul. Taking his thesis entirely out of context.

237

Afterword

After his death, an alleged 'original' of Albino Luciani's doctoral thesis was displayed in the Vatican Museum.

A tourist—a typewriter manufacturer—recognized it as having been typed on a typewriter he had developed in 1958, more than a decade after Luciani had executed the work.

The 'thesis' disappeared from view.

Shortly afterwards, a second 'original thesis' was distributed to libraries in Europe. This one typed on a 1940s vintage typewriter. Yet, even this rendition was typed in both upper and lower case letters.

Albino Luciani typed his doctoral thesis on a Remington portable typewriter given him in 1929. It typed only in UPPERCASE letters.

All documents attributed to Luciani that have survived, from the time he entered the Seminary at Belluno in 1929, until he became Chancellor of Belluno in 1947, are typed in UPPERCASE letters.

Nevertheless, the 'Vatican Fraud' belittled Luciani, suggesting he wasted his doctoral years examining the possibility of genetic orientation of the human soul. It doesn't take a PhD to tell one, if the soul was of genetic origin it would decay at death.

Though the fraud is consistent with Albino Luciani's thesis—the soul is not made by God, it is made by Man—common sense tells one that the 33-day Pope did not speak of genes, but of deed.

Justin's chats in *The Reincarnation of Albino Luciani* are consistent with those Albino Luciani presented in defense of his doctoral thesis *The Origin of the Human Soul According to Antonio Rosmini* at the Gregorian University in Rome, February 1947 and other things this pope said and did in the twenty years he was a bishop and a pope.

Unbeknown to the author—knowing his father had at one time been an acquaintance of Albino Luciani—the boy studied Luciani's life at his local library. In truth, the philosophical content of Justin's conversations in this nonfiction novella weren't his own, but those of Albino Luciani. Hence its title *The Reincarnation of Albino Luciani*.

Reminiscent of sessions as they occurred, Justin's dialogue has been embellished by the author and updated to modern times.

Six months after this last episode, Justin and his mother Audrey lost their lives in an airplane tragedy.

He was eleven years old.

"...that I would have made my mark and know that it will never be erased by time..."

To those who made it possible.

To Audrey, to Justin, to Albino Luciani, to Abraham Lincoln, to Susan B. Anthony, to Elizabeth Taylor, and to all those who we have never heard of who ceased to be mortal beings, and evolved as Gods...

Yes, one more.

The youth, you are about to meet, who now so very long ago, came in from the street, and left his tears in my shop.

Justin's real name was Lucien, the reason the author uses the penname 'Lucien Gregoire' Pseudonym is used to avoid confusion with the pen name.

In modern times, upon the death of a pope, Vatican teams are dispersed to diocese and other places the deceased pope had spent his life. All original documents, no matter how minuscule, are removed to the Vatican. Popes are prone to sainthood and original works of saints are relics.

This would be particularly true of Albino Luciani, who had spent his ministry speaking out against the Church's policies against women, homosexuals, atheism, contraception and what have you. His thesis was particularly dangerous to the Roman Catholic Church in that it questioned the existence of a God-given soul.

Luciani's original doctoral thesis, together with his other controversial works, are under lock and key in the Apostolic Library Archives under St. Peter's Basilica.

Antonio Rosmini was a monumental nineteenth century homosexual progressive whose propositions for change in the Church were condemned by the Vatican. Albino Luciani adopted Rosmini as his philosophical mentor at an early age.

Not Quite yet a Man

At war's end

Many years ago, I returned from the front and changed from my
military gear into my civilian uniform, an old shirt and blue jeans.

I got on a phone, then I got on a plane, then I got on a train, then I
got on a bus, then I got in a car, then I walked the rest of the way to
the crest of the pond.

As I moved along its edge, the mystery of nature was all around
me. The water reflected all it could see. Darkened blues and greens
splintered with glistening reds and yellows laced in silver and gold.

All was silent, not even the whisper of a breeze. The lifting of the
dew hazed out over the pond intending to never go away. Dark clouds
loomed off in the distance as to foretell what was about to come.

The hum of a bee going about its work on a nearby bush broke the stillness of the dawn. The song of a whippoorwill made its entrance from a nearby tree. Right in front of me, came the trumpeting of frogs. Off in the distance, the rumbling of thunder followed by a crash of lightning. Each one speaking in its own tune, as if the great maestro above was sleeping.

I came to the place where Audrey and I had once walked and talked of things that were yet to come. I knew her then, and I thought back to that time when I had said my last goodbye.

As she lay there, the pallor of her lips eclipsed the radiance of her smile. She was in death every bit as much as she had been in life.

I had not known a human face and form, if not translated into art by a great master, could be so beautiful. Mere mortal flesh, bones and hair, I reminded myself, trying to dispel the wonder one feels in witnessing perfection.

As I reached over and touched her hand to confirm to myself this was forever goodbye; one of those things one calls tears climbed up out of my heart, started from the crevice of my eye, and crept toward the lid.

I glanced around the room, first, to the right, then, to the left, again, to the right, and, finally, to the left, once more. All the time, fearing someone might notice and expose me; destroy me, so to speak. For I was a man, and men don't cry.

I stealthily rolled the tear back into the corner of my eye.

Justin

As I stood before him, I couldn't see him, for the mutilation had been much too terrible to allow the body viewed. As I began to realize he was now still, I recalled what he once was.

His was a simple, silent greatness; one whose words would not long be remembered, whose deeds would long be forgotten; yet, whose dream would live on in his fellowman, for all time...

As I reached over and lay my hand on the coffin, just above his heart, to confirm to myself, this was forever goodbye; one of those things one calls tears climbed up out of my heart, started from the crevice of my eye, and crept toward the lid.

I glanced first, to the right, then, to the left, again, to the right, and, finally, to the left, once more. I carefully held it there, hovering on the edge of the cliff.

I stealthily rolled the tear back into the corner of my eye.

The old man of the pond

On the other side of the pond was a small cottage, most would call a shack. An old friend lived there, alone, pacing his time until he, too, would go to join my loved ones.

I proceeded out away from the edge of the water onto the dirt road which circled the pond. As I came up to the pathway leading to the cottage, an overflowing trashcan greeted me.

There, atop the debris, was an old violin bedecked with a fresh sprinkling of rain spots. With it, a bow.

I took them with me toward the door. The old man stood there, "I'm so rich," he laughed, "I threw away my Stradivarius."

Taking up the violin, he held it in such a way, light shone into the opening atop the instrument.

As I peered into the violin, sure enough, there, to my surprise, was a label: *Antonius Stradivari*. He told me thousands of these had been made around the turn of the twentieth century.

Nevertheless, he let me take the violin with me, and I made him promise not to tell anyone, I had been picking trash.

A year later

The following year, I received a note from one of his neighbors, my old friend had died. I went to the corner of the room where the violin lay. Picking it up, I took an overstuffed chair that sat by the fireplace, and thought of the old man.

I thought of the good times… the bad times… the changing times.

Once again, the tear started to move toward the edge of the lid. I cautiously looked around the room, first, to the right, then, to the left, again, to the right, and, finally, to the left, once more. As if a ghost might be watching, I forced it back.

The next day, intending to have the violin restored and place it on my wall in memory of my friend and my dearest Audrey and my pal Justin, I took it to a musical instrument shop.

Without giving me the courtesy of checking the label, the man behind the counter told me: "It will cost you five hundred dollars to restore this thing. If you make this investment, you'll be able to sell it for fifty bucks to anyone who knows anything about violins."

Picking up the bow, he stretched it out from the level of his eye, as if he were zeroing in on a doe. "You might have something here."

He waved it a few times through the air, first, to the right, then, to the left, again, to the right, and, finally, to the left, once more.

Taking up a miniature screwdriver, he removed the ivory casing enclosing one end of the bow.

I presumed he was searching for the name of the maker.

Yet, etched into the wood was nothing more than the letters 'IHS' followed by a row of Roman Numerals. I recalled from catechism class, 'IHS' was a monogram for Jesus Christ.

The old man thought a moment, and offered, "Five hundred?" Not knowing what he meant, I hesitated.

He corrected himself, "A thousand?"

Puzzled, I asked, "What do you mean, a thousand?"

He countered, "Okay, I'll give you two thousand in cash."

I thought of the old man of the pond, of my dear Audrey, and of Justin. Gathering up the violin and the bow, I headed toward the door.

He called out, "Three thousand. Five..."

Charging out after me, he yelled: "Ten thousand dollars!"

I hurried away down the street, all the time, glancing, first, to the right, then, to the left, again, to the right, and, finally, to the left, once more.

Reaching my house, nervously fumbling for my keys, I unlocked the gate, hastened along the walkway and up the steps to the door.

I went directly to my toolbox and moving quickly into the great room, I hung the violin together with its bow up over the fireplace.

All the time, glancing, first, to the right, then, to the left, again, to the right, and, finally, to the left, once more. Struggling desperately to hold the tear that hovered precariously on the edge of the cliff.

Years later

Through the years, I prospered. There occurred a downturn in markets in which I had invested heavily. I fell on bad times.

I moved back to Baltimore, hoping to start over again.

I opened a small shop near the Peabody Conservatory of Music. The prestigious factory that has produced such products as Stravinsky and a wealth of others.

In a desperate attempt to pay off what was insurmountable debt, I was selling off most of what I had. One day, I sold my computer to one of the students.

The next day one of the instructors of the great institution came into my shop, "I understand you have a computer desk for sale?"

We proceeded out of the shop and down the street to the old rooming house in which I had taken a room. Midway down the street, I stopped. Stooping down, I picked up a dime.

He asked, "Lucky dime, huh?"

I lied, "Yes." I put it in my pocket together with the other eight 'lucky' dimes I had collected earlier that month.

Once upon a time,
I came upon a dime.
With the other eight,
There were nine.

We climbed the creaking steps.

On reaching the landing, we proceeded down the long dark dismal hallway which had the same paint on its walls it had when the building had been built, I would guess a hundred years before. I blushed as we

245

passed by the open door to the less than sanitary bath I shared with a dozen welfare cases who lived on the floor.

As we entered the room, thinking this could be a homeless shelter or a halfway house of some kind, "Do you have to pay to live here?"

"Not very much," I replied as I led him to the desk and began the sales pitch.

My words fell on deaf ears. There, next to the desk, was the violin with its bow poking itself out of a packing crate.

Like the man in the shop in Chicago, he ignored the violin.

He picked up the bow in his hand in such a manner as if he were handling God's scepter itself.

His motion came with such an air of divinity, 'IHS' popped into my mind. I kept the thought to myself. 'Jesus had worked in a woodshop as a child. Could it be Jesus, Himself, had made the bow?'

He put it to his eye and stretched it out toward the light as if he were going for a great stag. Like the man in Chicago, he waved it through the air, first, to the right, then, to the left, again, to the right, and, finally, to the left, once more. He paused and exclaimed, "Wow!"

I offered a screwdriver. He refused.

I asked, "Don't you want to know who made it?"

He told me, "I already know. I knew when I first saw it."

He grew silent. Thinking deeply. Thinking very deeply…

I looked at the spot I had reserved on the wall.

I thought of the old man, and of my Audrey, and of Justin. I knew that someday, when I would go to join them, the violin and its bow would remain behind on the wall, perhaps forever.

Clearing his throat, he stuttered, "Would you consider…"

I cut him off, "Perhaps, perhaps, there is a needy student; one that could use the bow?"

The instructor looked about the room.

Splinters of the old wooden floor poked their way, here and there, through the worn linoleum which spread itself across the room. The only visible thing, that might work, was a solitary light bulb that hung from a ragged chain in the center of the room and a five-and-dime hotplate in one corner. An old army cot occupied the other.

Between them, perched on the windowsill, a roach seemed to be cleaning its whiskers. Just outside was a carton of milk and a bottle of orange juice trying to keep cold.

He looked at me as one looks at one who is about to jump off of a tall building.

I continued, "Let's say you replace the strings and polish it up a bit, and you carefully search out a student who is in great need. Let's say, one, who without the bow, could not go on?"

A tear appeared in the corner of his eye.

He looked around the room as if to reassure himself that no one was watching. He looked, first, to the right, then, to the left, again, to the right, and, finally, to the left, once more. He glanced back at me as to assure himself, I, too, hadn't noticed.

So as to save him from exposure, to preserve his manhood, so to speak, I led him quickly out of the room with bow in hand and carefully closed the door behind him.

The crate with the violin remained on the floor. Feeling I had separated two friends forever, I looked, first, to the right, then, to the left, again, to the right, and, finally, to the left, once more. I carefully rolled the tear from the edge of the lid, back into the corner of my eye.

A few months later

In the weeks and months that followed, busy with my new shop, I had forgotten about the incident.

Then, one day an Asian youth came into my shop.

He carried with him a small case together with all the beauty and aspiration one usually associates with youth. His jet black hair splashed down evenly from its center part stopping just short of his ears. The wonderment and enlightenment of his dark eyes did much to obscure the mysterious gloom behind them.

Stopping at the counter, he looked across at me. Forcing a slight smile, he asked, "Lucien?" I nodded.

A thud struck at my heart. "My name is Paul. I have your bow."

He told me of his journey from Tiananmen Square to America. Together, with his friend Len, they had come to reap that promised by that lady who lifts her lamp beside the golden door.

"We had everything going for us. Then Len was diagnosed with AIDS. The medical bills have chewed up everything we had and, perhaps, everything I will ever have. Hal gave me the bow in memory of Len the day we buried him. I've not been well since or I would have come in sooner."

As he went on, the tear moved from the corner of my eye to the edge of the lid. Once again, I looked, first, to the right, then, to the left, again, to the right, and, finally, to the left, once more; then, back at the boy, to be certain he had not noticed.

Reaching down into his case, he pulled forward the bow.

With unwavering emotion, his voice vibrating with every word, "With this, which you have given me, I will make such music," raising his voice and glancing upwards toward the ceiling in utter conviction, "it will be heard in the heavens above."

Lowering his voice and looking deep into my eyes, "Thank you, thank you," very much deeper, "from the bottom of my heart."

With two great tears rushing from the corners of his eyes, he turned and reaching the door, Not Quite yet a Man, they broke out onto his cheeks and fell to the floor. "I will never forget you." He was gone.

I whispered to myself, "Yes, it is still there, still on the edge of the cliff." I looked, first, to the right, then, to the left, again, to the right, and, finally, to the left, once more. I carefully rolled the tear back into the corner of my eye.

Christmas Eve a few years later

With my new business, I had regained my ground and purchased a nineteenth century house in Baltimore's affluent Federal Hill district. The house fronted on a cobblestone street and its rear decks loomed out over the city's harbor which glistened with the season's lights.

One day, a letter postmarked *New York City*, forwarded from my old address, arrived. Sitting at my desk to one side of the fireplace, flanked on its opposite side by an overdone Christmas tree, I took up a letter opener and sliced the envelope open.

Out fell a partially dried up rose and a newspaper clipping: "Young Artist Stuns Carnegie Hall."

Carefully laying the letter on the desk, I read:

Dear Lucien:

Forgive me for addressing you by your first name. While I have known many much longer, I know no one better.

Last night I stood at the pinnacle of life.

I have saved here for you a part of the roses and ovation. For they, in truth, belong to you. At least, mostly, to you.

Yes, it was my hand that scratched out the simple concerto that was meant for the lone instrument I held. But, it was your gift that translated my meager work into the great symphony heard in the grand hall last night.

The bow, itself, is only a simple composite of wood, ivory, string, and what have you. Yet, what sets it apart from all the others is not its age, nor for that matter its maker, but what you have unselfishly added to it. That you have chosen to weigh compassion above material wealth, and, perhaps, even your very survival, has made you forever a part of it.

Believe me, for as long as I live, perhaps, long after you are gone, and, perhaps, even long after I am gone, whenever the hand touches the bow, it will move across the strings of a thousand violins, it will whisper the hum of the bees, it will bring up the howling of the wind, it will call forward the power of the brass, it will echo the thunder of the drums; it will orchestrate all these things to the final crash of the cymbals.

Bees will hum, whippoorwills will sing, trumpets will blare, thunder will roar, and lightning will strike deep into the hearts of all those who are privileged to listen.

We together, you, I and this simple composite of wood, ivory and string, will gather up the tears from all their hearts, move them from the corners of the eyes, to the edge of the lids, watch them drop onto the cheeks, and crash to the floor. In their place, we will leave something more. The same thing you left in my heart that day when I left my tears in your shop.

We will do this, Lucien, not for ourselves, but for him, and for her, and for all humanity.

Paul

As I looked up, I thought of the conservatory instructor, of the old man of the pond, of my beloved Audrey and of my pal Justin.

One of those things one calls tears climbed up out of my heart, started from the crevice of my eye, and moved toward the lid.

I looked, first, to the right, then, to the left, again, to the right, and, finally, to the left, once more. Yes, it was there.

I would carry it there all the remaining days of my life.

The Great Theater

Many years later, I was led into an immense theater, as many people as could hold all the stadiums of the world.

As I glanced around, I saw some seats still available.

In the lodge, were Mom and Pop, and just below them was my old high school chum, Jack. Just above in the balcony were Grandma and Grandpa and some others from my past, scattered, here and there, throughout the great audience.

I was ushered all the way down to the front row.

There was my mentor Albino Luciani, together with my emissary the conservatory instructor, Paul's friend Len, the old man of the pond, my cherished Audrey, and my dear, dearest Justin.

In the center seat, the one who bore the nametag IHS beckoned me: "When the wolves came, you bravely stood your ground and risked your life for your neighbor's cub. Now come here to my side."

I took my place beside Him.

As I looked up, I recognized the great stage that lay before us.

It was the grand stage of the great symphony hall in Vienna; the same forum which had witnessed the miracles of Beethoven, Mozart, Handel and other grandmasters of notes and song. Enveloped in a mysterious haze, I could not make out where it joined the theater.

Momentarily, the curtains shielding the vast platform began to part. The lights of the immense theater grew dim. The drone of all those present hushed silent. Presently, all was dark.

In the light of a spot, stood Paul. In his hands, a violin and the bow.

Once more, I heard the hum of the bees, the song of the whippoorwill, the blare of the trumpets, the roll of the drums. I looked over at the one who sat beside me.

He suddenly looked, first, to His right, then, to His left, again, to His right, and, finally, to His left, once more.

With the final roll of the drums and the crashing crescendo of the cymbals, I saw them climb up out of His heart, watch them run from the corners of His eyes, to the edge of His lids, splash down onto His cheeks, and fall to the floor.

I looked up at Paul, as he took his bow to the cascade of roses and the roar of the crowd. I looked back at the one who bore the nametag IHS, with His tears still crashing down onto the floor.

I thought: "Not Quite yet a Man!"

Up until *The Great Theater*, this story recounts an incident in the life of the author.

No, the violin bow referred to in this work was not made by Jesus in His workshop.
    The author never learned the value of the bow.
    What he does know is 'IHS MDCCXLIV' was carved under its casing. This record was made when his artwork was inventoried by an insurance company. Insofar as 'IHS' symbolizes Jesus Christ, he believed the bow to be of significant religious importance, judging from the substantial offer made for it.
    After he first published this story, it fell into the hands of a violinist of a symphony orchestra who told him in the world of violins: 'IHS' stands for *Giuseppe Antonio Guarneri*; the bow referred to in this work is a *Guarnerius* bow dated 1744.
    As Guarneri died in that year, it was possibly the last bow the master made and the accompanying violin, with which it was to share its life, was never made. Integral parts of the same instrument, it is unheard of for a bow to be separated from its violin if created by one of the great master craftsmen.
    Being an orphan, it is reasonable to believe the bow got matched up with one of the Stradivarius copies made around the turn of the twentieth century. *Guarnerius* and *Stradivarius* violins are among the most highly valued musical instruments in the world. The violin remains on the author's wall today, alone, without its bow.

The History of Christianity

130000BC *Neanderthals Crete*: Origin of ideology of 'Survival of the Spirit.'

3100BC *Pharaoh Narmer Egypt:* Origin of ideology of 'Resurrection of the Body.'

629BC *Zagreus Tablets Cretan/Cyprus*: Origin of ideology of a 'Savior.' The God Zeus sends His Son Zagreus to save the world from sin:

> *'Zeus, King of Gods speaks, Hail my offspring who come upon thou to save thou from sin... rejected by His chosen people... suffered unto death... descended into Hell... shall rise again without lust (virgin birth) ... shall rule eternal life...'*

349BC *Phrygian Tablets Turkey:* Dionysus—the reincarnation of Zagreus who is killed by his chosen people—Titans—is reborn of a human virgin sired by a God:

> *'Zeus hovers over the realm in guise of an eagle... comes upon the Virgin Semele her in the night... Dionysus is reborn of a human virgin... becomes God from man... rules eternal life...'*

253BC *Septuagint, Philadelphus, Alexandria:* Greek ethical vegans, in the Greek translation of the Hebrew Bible, add the prophecy of the God of Isaiah (7: 14-16) who promises to send His Son (an ethical vegan) to save mankind from sin:

> *'Behold, a virgin shall conceive and bear a son... Butter and honey shall he eat so that he may know to refuse the evil, and choose the good... numbered with transgressors... bare the sin of many... poured out his soul unto death... descended into Hell... rose again... shall come to rule eternal life...'*

6BC-32AD *The Greatest Story Ever Told:*

> *'The Holy Ghost hovers over the realm in guise of a dove... comes upon the Virgin Mary in the night... Jesus is born of a human virgin ... becomes God from man... saves mankind from sin... rejected by His chosen people... suffered unto death... descended into Hell... rose again... rules eternal life.'*

---

300 year gap between Jesus and the writing of the gospels as we know them today

---

325-490AD Gospels as we know them today are written – Greek Uncial Codices.

Facts vs. the Politics of Men

The Politics of Men: those who wrote the gospels were contemporaries of Christ.

When one separates the facts… from the probabilities… from the possibilities… from the politics of men… this is nothing more than someone saying something to support one's political agenda.

Fact: we don't know when the gospels were written other than—according to their content—they could not have possibly been written earlier than 70-95 AD.
We don't know what Mark, Mathew, Luke and John or even Paul may have written as not the tiniest reliable scrap predating the 4ᵗʰ century exists.

Fact: the Christian Bible is sourced from the uncial codices—Old/New Testaments as Christians know them today—written more than three hundred years after the time Christ is said to have lived. There exist no earlier biblical record of Jesus Christ.

*4ᵗʰ century Greek Codex Sinaiticus & Codex Vaticanus
5ᵗʰ century Greek Codex Alexandrinus & Ephraemi Rescriptus.*

Fact: with a three hundred year vacuum between the writing of the gospels and Paul's epistles—as we know them today—and Christ's alleged time, without any technological means to record events as they may or may not have occurred, one could have written most anything to support one's political agenda.

Fact: even these 4ᵗʰ and 5ᵗʰ century texts have been materially changed to meet the changing politics of modern preachers (see 'Changing Times' pgs. 79-81).

Fact: there have survived more than a thousand engravings of events in the Mideast and Rome dating to the first and second centuries, including events in the lives of historical figures in Jesus' life—Herod and Pilate. Yet, no trace of Jesus Christ.

Fact: if it were possible to attend, in one's lifetime, all the history classes of all the universities of the world since the beginning of time, one would never hear the words 'Jesus Christ.' The reason the *Apostles Creed* begins: "I believe…"

Readers are encouraged to search reliable sources on the Internet and in libraries

The History of World Religions

"Religion evolves just like any other social practice. Each prophet building on the imagination of those who came before him."

Albino Luciani

Earliest known occurrence <u>underlined</u>

400000-130000BC - Neanderthals did not bury dead. Humans had no spirit or soul

130000BC Crete. Beginning of <u>Spiritualism,</u> Neanderthals begin to bury their dead. The bigger the man the deeper the grave. Earliest fear of spirits of the dead.

40000-12000BC Origin of <u>Love thy neighbor as thyself</u>. Cro-Magnon cooperatives protect against bears and famine. Isolated families risked starving to death.

27000BC Chauvet France, Cro-Magnons, altar of bear skulls. Earliest archeological evidence of possible belief in a <u>Supreme Being</u> in the west. The Bear God.

11000BC Pottery etchings, Japan. Earliest archeological evidence of possible belief in a <u>Supreme Being</u> in the east.

9130-7370BC Turkey, *Gobekli Tepe Temple*, Earliest known <u>Worship of Gods</u>.

7000BC-3000BC Egypt. <u>Gods of Nature</u> evolve: Aten, the sun god, creator/ruler of human realm, lion: creator/ruler of animal realm; crocodile: creator/ruler of water realm, falcon: creator/ruler of bird realm, beetle: creator/ruler of insect realm.

3940BC *Adam and Eve* are created; the fundamental thesis of the Bible.

3100BC Egypt, *Pharaoh Narmer* is first man to convince a major population of his <u>Divinity</u> and of the <u>Resurrection of the Body</u> after death.

3087BC Abydos Egypt, *Menes-Narmer*. Earliest tomb with elements of life: clothing, weapons, tools, bowls, grain and portable toilets.

2000BC prox. India. *Hinduism,* earliest concept of an undefined <u>Indestructible Soul</u>.

1750-1350BC Egypt, *Hieroglyphs*. Twelve million figures depicting life in Egypt for the 400 years Hebrews are said to be in Egypt. NOT A HEBREW AMONG THEM.

1500-1200BC India, *Rigveda*. <u>Reincarnation of the Soul.</u> At death, soul rises to heaven, falls as rain, nourishes plants, nourishes man, nourish semen/egg = rebirth.

1440-1320 prox. Moses is claimed by the Bible to have lived

1375BC Egypt, *Hieroglyphics.* Earliest archeological proof of a <u>Day of Judgment,</u> Osiris—the Redeemer—judges the dead in the *Book of the Dead.*

1352BC Egypt, *Pharaoh Akhenaten* declares there is only one God, Aten—the Sun God. Earliest known belief in a <u>Monotheist God</u> in the west.

1201BC Beijing, National Museum. *Hinduism.* Earliest <u>Holy Trinity,</u> Three persons in one God: *Brahma* the Creator, *Shiva* the Redeemer, *Vishnu* the Enlightener.

1186BC Egypt. Earliest concept of <u>Hell</u> - *Hieroglyph Day of Judgment.* Evil doers are cast into fire; the good raised to serve Pharaoh, for all time.

650BC *Elephantine Papyri*, Brooklyn Museum. According to history and archeology the earliest Jews in Egypt. Small detachment of soldiers on the island of Elephantine.

629BC *Cretan/Cyprus tablets, epic Alkmeonis*: Earliest belief in a <u>Savior</u>. God Zeus sends His Son Zagreus to save the world from sin. Rejected and killed by his chosen people. Zagreus is reborn of the virgin goddess Persephone as Dionysus:

> *'Zeus, King of Gods speaks, Hail my offspring who come upon thou to save thou from sin... suffered unto death... descended into Tartarus...Thou wilt rise again without lust (virgin birth) ... save man from sin ... rule eternal life.'*

525BC India, *Buddha,* the beginning of the ideology of <u>Reincarnation of the mind</u>: perpetual survival of the mind in successive hosts.

517BC *Temple Anat-Yahu Elephantine* The earliest community of Jews in Egypt— NEVER HAVING HEARD OF MOSES' GOD—worshipped pagan-god *Anat-Yahu.*

400-100BC: *Hebrew Bible* decrees <u>God is everywhere</u> and emerges as the political foundation of western society. *God of Moses* decrees the mortality of man; explicitly refutes resurrection of the body: *'dust thou art, to dust thou wilt return.'* The reason the Jews have no afterlife.

349BC, Turkey. *Phrygian Tablets,* Dionysus had been born of a virgin goddess. In Phrygian mythology he is reborn of a <u>human virgin impregnated by a God:</u>

> *'Zeus hovers over the realm in guise of an <u>eagle</u>... gazes with love upon the <u>virgin Semele</u>... comes upon her in the night... <u>Dionysus born of a mortal virgin</u>... becomes God from man... rules eternal life...'*

356-323BC *Alexander the Great* said to be 'Son of God' born of a mortal virgin. That he lived 33 years set established the myth all Sons of God live 33 years.

253BC Alexandria, *Septuagint*, Ethical vegan Greeks, in the Greek translation of the Hebrew Bible add the prophecy of the God of Isaiah (7: 14-16) who promises to send his Son (an ethical vegan) to save mankind from sin:

> *'Behold, a virgin shall conceive and bear a son... <u>Butter and honey shall he</u> <u>eat so that he may know to refuse the evil, and choose the good</u>... numbered with transgressors... bare the sin of many... poured out his soul unto death... descended to hell... rose again... comes to rule eternal life...'*

1st century BC, Greek God *Dionysus* is adopted by the Romans as God of the Vine (ethical vegan), born of a mortal virgin, sent to save mankind... rules eternal life

6BC-32AD Christ's life. If His ministry spanned three years, Jesus lived 38 years

53-65AD *Paul* founds Christianity as a money-making business—passing the hat for silver and gold in exchange for forgiveness of sins and resurrection of the body:

> *'We are the ambassadors of Christ who has passed solely to us the power to forgive sins and pave the way to life everlasting...'*

70AD or later* *Mark* said to write the first gospel. He repeatedly refers to Christ as Son of Man. Christ denies He is God three times. No virgin birth or resurrection.

85AD or later* *Matthew* plagiarizes *Mark* taking care to change the phrase 'Son of Man' to 'Son of God' and adds the Virgin Birth and Resurrection:

> *'The Holy ghost hovers over the realm in guise of a <u>dove</u>... gazes with love upon the <u>virgin Mary</u>... comes upon her in the night... <u>Christ born of a mortal</u> <u>virgin</u>... becomes God from man... rules eternal life...'*

85AD or later* *Luke* plagiarizes Matthew; gives a different story of Christ's birth.

95AD or later* *Gospel of John*. Christ's refusal to eat the meat of the Passover. He orders his disciples to <u>stop killing animals for nourishment</u> and sacrifice:

> *'...Take ye not the lifeblood of the bullock... I give thee the herbs of the soil... Look up to the vines for they are fit to drink... He took bread and broke it, 'This is my body. He took wine, This is my blood. Do this in remembrance of me.'*

> * Each of the gospels contain historical events which did not occur until the earliest dates they could have been written. The gospels—the uncial codices—as we know them today were written in the 4th and 5th centuries. See below 325AD-490AD.

222-233AD *Hyppolytus* (Rome) *Origen* (Alexandria), *Gospel of Thomas*. Oldest record of Christ known to exist. Not a gospel per se. 114 verses which contradict the canonical gospels. No mention of virgin birth, resurrection or attributes of God.

229AD Syria, *Dura-Europus*. Earliest Christian church in the Mideast.

259AD *St. Dionysus*. First titular bishop of Rome. Council of Antioch.

280AD *Marcenas Foundation* (Basel). *Gospel of Judas.* Contradicts the betrayal of Judas in the canonical gospels as we know them today. Not a gospel per se.

300AD *East* meets *West*. Those in the *West* first become aware of the Hindu Holy Trinity of the *East*—three persons in one God: *Creator - Redeemer - Enlightener.*

313AD *St. Miltiades*. First bishop to actually reign in Rome. *Edict of Milan*

325AD Nicene Council bases the Christian Trinity on the Hindu Trinity: *Creator - Redeemer - Enlightener*. Constantine founds the Roman Catholic Church on priests' forgiveness of sins. Knowing few men are thieves, murders, etc., it declares sex as the greatest of sins. The Church becomes immersed in pomp, pageantry, idolatry, the occult and mysticism. Its market comprised of meat eaters, it cleverly turns Christ's plea for the lives of animals into a mockery in the symbolic Eucharist.

352AD Rome, Basilica of St. Peter, first Christian church in Rome, is completed.

325-360AD *Codex Sinaiticus*. New Testament and about half of Old Testament—Greek *Septuagint*. Insofar as *Sinaiticus*—the oldest surviving gospels—contains the *Eusebian Canons*—a product of the Nicene Council—is compelling evidence the gospels—as we know them today—were not written by Mark, Matthew, Luke and John in the 1st century, but were a product of the Nicene Council in the 4th century.

350-380AD *Codex Vaticanus*. Greek. Partial Old Testament and New Testament.

352AD Rome, Basilica of St. Peter, first Christian church in Rome, is completed.

373-450AD *Codex Alexandrinus* Greek. Most of the *Septuagint* (Greek translation of the Old Testament) and the New Testament.

435-490 *Codex Ephraemi Rescriptus.* Greek. Contains all but one book of the New Testament and six books of the Old Testament.

603AD Rome, Pope Gregory answers Jesus' plea for animals. Knowing he would risk schism, if he forbade eating meat entirely, he mandates Friday abstinence from meat hoping his successors would add days of the week until Christ's will was done.

610AD Muhammad decrees Catholicism made a mockery of Christ's 'bread and wine' in its idol worship of the God of Moses. Idolatry (Catholicism) becomes his bitter enemy. 'KILL THE IDOLATERS' is the most prevalent hostile verse in the *Koran*.

850AD *Torah*. Oldest surviving 'Hebrew' five books of Moses. British Library

985AD *Aleppo Codex*. More than a thousand year gap between this oldest surviving copy of the Hebrew Bible and the alleged time it was written. British Library

Scriptural Sources

Hebrew ideology: Old Testament verses are taken from the 10th century AD *Aleppo Codex* - the Hebrew University and the 9th century AD Torah - National Library in London

Christian ideology: Old Testament verses are taken from the 4th century AD *Sinaiticus* (the Greek *Septuagint*) held by the National Library in London. Christians do not believe in the Hebrew Old Testament; for example, the Hebrew Book of Isaiah doesn't include the prophecy of Christ. It speaks of the coming of the New Jerusalem. Jews have no Savior.

New Testament verses are taken from the 4th century Greek *Codex Sinaiticus* held by the National Library in London or the 4th century Greek *Codex Vaticanus* held by the Vatican.

Hindu verses: 12th-10th century BC *Vedic Sanskrit* and 2nd-6th century BC *Brahma Sutras*

Buddhist verses: canons of the 6th-1st century BC *Tripitaka, Mahayana* & *Hinayana Sutras*

Islamic verses are taken from the 7th century AD *Topkapi Quran Manuscript*

Greek-Roman Mythology

Despite it predates it by many centuries, unlike western scripture which no original writings survived, the original writings of mythology have survived in either tablets or reliefs. Likewise, the original writings of the Egyptian gods have survived in the hieroglyphics.

Greek Cretan/Cyprus Tablets, epic Alkmeonis, Phrygian Tablets - Zagreus/Dionysus: British National Museum, the British Library and the Royal Library of Alexandria

Zagreus/Dionysus Sculpture/Reliefs: National Archaeological Museum of Athens

Roman God Dionysus Sculptures/Reliefs/Tablets: National Roman Museum and elsewhere in Rome and Italy

Roman God Dionysus is also known as Bacchus 'God of the Vine.' Greek God Dionysus was adopted by the Romans about the turn of the first millennium.

If one searches *Dionysus* on the Internet or in libraries one will find an endless variations of how He came about. Yet, at the time those who wrote of Jesus picked up their pens:

'Dionysus was the Roman God of the Vine... sired by God Zeus in guise of an eagle...

born of the human virgin Semele... became God from man... shall rule eternal life...'

260

Intermission

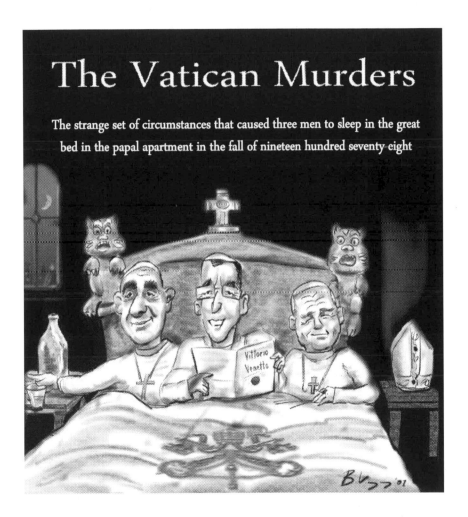

Did his struggle for women, homosexuals and the poor
cost him his life?

Two books in one book: Biography & True Crime

Prologue to Prejudice

"The kind of stuff souls are made of..."

The Icicle That Would Not Fall

"Pneumonia!" Doctor Rosenbaum cried out. "You've come down with pneumonia. I'm going to have to put you in Saint Vincent's. At your age the most we can do is hope for the best. Above all, you must keep warm. A slight draft will kill you."

He was eighty-three. The love of his life, Robin, had been gone ten years. They had lived out their lives together in a quaint little lane tucked away in a tiny borough just south of Sheridan Square in New York's Greenwich Village for more than fifty years.

No one knew he was there. Now, he had little to live for other than to leave a trace of evidence he had ever been there.

Creativity had been his birthright.

At the early age of six, he had astounded those around him with what he could do with a simple brush and palette. His father had put him through the best art schools in the world.

He had worked all of his life in search of a whisker of recognition. In doing so, he had exhausted the family fortune left him.

Yet, with all of his genius and all of his money, he never came close to what one would consider a masterpiece. He had tried and tried through the years yet fame had escaped him.

His works would never hang in the Louvre, nor in the Met, nor in any of the great galleries of the world.

The best he had ever done was to get a few bits of his efforts onto the canned goods which lined his grocer's shelves.

Now death was knocking on his door. He pleaded with his maker. "Please, give me a few more months, a few more years, to see the light, to leave my mark in time."

It was a frigid Christmas Eve. He nodded to a group of carolers in the street as he trudged through the snow up to the hospital entrance with his inseparable brush and palette in hand. Penniless, he would share a room with a welfare case on the second floor next to the laundry.

Though he could have shuffled up to his room, the nurse planted him in a wheelchair and pushed him down the corridor. On the way, she stopped in a small visiting area.

Sitting opposite him, she told him of his roommate.

"You will be sharing a room with a little boy, Tommy. He just had his eighth birthday. Only his will has been keeping him alive. If we can get him through the winter, he will most likely live out his natural days. But if he gives up, he will never see another day, much less another birthday. It is important you don't say or do anything that might discourage him. Now, I will take you to your room."

The boy stirred as the old man was wheeled into the room.

"This is Mr. Bentley," she told the boy. "We want you to take good care of him." She turned to the old man. "This is Tommy. We will leave you in his care." Tommy nodded as she laid a newspaper on the bed and disappeared out of the door.

The boy gazed out past the snow heaped windowsill.

All he could see was the aging brick wall of a building a stone's throw away. A row of icicles poured from a gutter which ran along the edge of its roof. A sliver of sun poked its way through the clouds taking out a couple of them. "Eighteen, seventeen..." the boy counted.

The old man whispered, "Eighteen, seventeen, Hmmm...?"

The boy counted again, "...sixteen, fifteen, fourteen..."

Curiosity got the best of him. "'...sixteen, fifteen, fourteen...?' Why are you counting backwards?"

The boy's eyes remained frozen on the icicles, "The icicles. Yesterday, there were over a hundred of them. Now it is easier. Much easier. There are only thirteen left."

"Easier?" the old man pondered.

"Yes, easier." The little boy's words struck at the old man's heart. "When the last one falls, I, too, will go. Yes, I have made up my mind. When the last one falls, I, too, will go."

The old man shuddered. It was late afternoon. It seemed the icicles were safe for the day. He picked up the newspaper and turned a page. "Snow, sub-zero temperatures tonight... sunny, warmer tomorrow." He shuddered, once more.

Tommy counted again, "Thirteen, twelve, eleven, ten..."

The boy's words stabbed at his chest.

He looked out at the icicles. They seemed to be safe for the night. Yet, tomorrow they would surely fall.

He thought of his selfish plea, "...give me a few more months, a few more years, to see the light, to leave my mark in time."

He looked out at the icicles, then back to the boy, then back to his brush and palette, then back to the icicles, once more.

That evening, he waited for Tommy to fall asleep.

With brush and palette in hand, the old man crept silently across the floor. He snuck stealthily down the hospital corridor and went out into the frigid night.

The next morning, Tommy awoke.

He looked at the bed where Mr. Bentley had died. They had taken him out in the early morning hours.

He was alone again. He peered out the window.

The sun was taking its toll. "Nine, eight, seven..." he counted. His breathing more rapid now, "...six, five, four..."

He thought of paradise, "...three, two..." he held his breath.

The last icicle clung to the edge of the roof threatening to fall. Of what had been a magnificent crystal glass menagerie, it was the grandest of them all. A shimmering rainbow, it struck halfway down the side of the building into the alley below. It sparkled in the early morning sun as does a colossal diamond in a king's crown.

Tommy never thought a simple icicle could be so beautiful. "It is as if God created this masterpiece just for me. He chose to give me a breathtaking glimpse of heaven before I go."

He counted again, "Nine, eight, seven, six, five, four, three, two…"
He held his breath again.

In the coming days, he would count, "Nine, eight, seven, six, five, four, three, two…" and hold his breath, many times, more.

It was mid-April and Tommy was going home.

He wandered over to the window. It was still there. Glistening in the sun. He peered down into the alley below. A ladder leaned up against the wall directly under the icicle.

By mid-summer, police barricades had been set up to control the crowds. Many more people than could hold all the museums of the world. People, from the far ends of the earth, who came to see

The Icicle That Would Not Fall!

The Icicle That Would Not Fall was inspired by O Henry's *The Last Leaf* in which the old man paints the last leaf. Here, he paints an icicle. Yet, the similarity ends there.

The old painter is scarcely mentioned in *The Last Leaf*. Yet, he is the leading character in *The Icicle That Would Not Fall*. The young boy Tommy does not appear at all in O Henry's story which involves two old maids in Greenwich Village. The dialogue in *The Icicle That Would Not Fall* is entirely original.

The Icicle That Would Not Fall has been published in newspapers and journals.

Prejudice

The author recreates incidents in the lives of famous people that caused them to rise up as champions of human justice

An invisible monster from the ancient past stalks about our time.

He climbs the tallest mountains. He lurks in the shadows of the deepest valleys. He crosses the widest seas.

He toddles upon the cobblestones of the tiniest hamlet. He parades up and down the grand boulevards of the greatest metropolis.

He calls on the humblest of huts, the homeless under the bridge, the farmhouse in the country, the split-level in the suburbs, the hi-rise in the city, the cottage on the lake, the mansion in the sprawling estate.

He knocks on every door.

He sits in the pews of the smallest of chapels. He speaks from the pulpit of the most magnificent of cathedrals.

He makes his noise each day, in factories, in schools, in taverns, in the hallowed halls of parliament, in the highest courts of the land.

He has no preference as to who he touches with his icy hands. He smites his victims, rich and poor, young and old, black and white, straight and gay, Christian, Jew, Muslim, Hindu and Tao.

He has no heart, he has no soul.

An endless path of death and destruction, he leaves his mark in time.

I Want to Learn to Count

"God is the Father, more so, the Mother."

John Paul I, September 10, 1978

"One, two, three, four, five…" her little brother stopped.

He looked around the room as if someone had hidden the next number behind the chair, under the rug, perhaps, in the closet?

He started up again, "One, two three, four, five, six, seven…"

The boy seemed lost. He tried again, "One, two, three, four, five, six, seven, eight, nine…?" He stopped again.

His eyes searched along the floor, glanced up to the ceiling. He found it under the dust in the corner, "…ten!" he beamed.

Susan told her mother, "I, too, want to count. I, too, want to learn to count."

Her mother laughed, "Girls don't have to know how to count."

The blackboard had three panels. Each day one of them changed. The one in the middle. The one reserved for the lesson of the day.

The *Pledge of Alliance* was written on the one on the left, as if by this time one could not have possibly learned it by heart.

I pledge allegiance to the flag of the United States of America, and to the republic for which it stands, one nation under God, indivisible, with liberty and justice for all.

The *Ten Commandments* were listed on the right panel. As if by this time one could not have possibly learned them by heart.

I am the one and only God, bow down and adore me.
Thou shalt have no graven images before thee.
Thou shalt not take my name in vain
Thou shalt keep the Sabbath
Honor thy mother and thy father
Thou shall not kill
Thou shall not commit adultery
Thou shalt not steal
Thou shalt not bare false witness
Thou shalt not desire to take from thy neighbor
  his property, his house, his wife, his slaves, his ox, his ass.

Ichabod Falwell was an old wrinkled up prune with chalk dust wedged into its fingernails. He scrubbed down the center panel as a mixed-bag of ragged and dressed up boys and girls shoved their way boisterously into the one-room schoolhouse behind him.

He picked up a piece of chalk and wrote,

The Minutemen

What those brave young lads at Concord
took those first bullets for in 1775...

He struck his stick. The chatter stuttered to an end.

He pointed to the left panel.

The children stood up and clasped their hearts and droned to an old flag which seemed to have fought the war itself.

The master struck his pointer toward the panel on the right.

They droned again, this time to the board itself. Not one of them had made it his or her responsibility to learn them by heart.

The wrinkled up old prune spread his arm toward the center panel. "Today we are going to talk about the Minutemen. We are going to talk about those brave young lads at Concord. What they took those first bullets for in the spring of 1775?"

Susan raised her hand. Getting a green light she stood up.

The old man was disturbed, "Why didn't you go before class?"

She interrupted the snickers, "It's not that. It's something else." She mustered up the courage, "I want to learn to count."

The class broke into a frenzy. The old man laughed, "You don't have to learn to count. You are a girl."

He ordered, "Sit down." Susan hesitated a bit and sat down.

The old prune with chalk dust wedged into its fingernails turned to the class, "Now, let us get back to the business of the day. 'What those brave young lads took those first bullets for in the spring of 1775?'"

This time Susan didn't wait for the okay. She stood up again. "That's what I'm talking about. 'What those brave young lads took those first bullets for in the spring of 1775?'"

"Nonsense." The old man, frustrated by the little girl's persistence, bellowed, this time at full volume, "Sit down!"

The little girl held her ground, "You don't understand. I have the right to learn to count."

This time the class didn't laugh. It had never asked itself why boys were taught how to count, and girls were not taught how to count. If nothing else, its silence demanded an explanation.

The old prune with chalk dust wedged into its fingernails frowned, "You're wrong. You don't have the right to learn how to count. There is no reason for you to learn how to count. You are not among the counters. You are among the counted.

"See, here," he pointed and read the Tenth Commandment: *'Thou shalt not desire to take from thy neighbor his property, including his house, his wife, his slaves, his ox, his ass.'*

"Only a man counts his property, his money, his slaves, his cows, his wife, his children and everything else he owns.

"According to Almighty God, under whom our great nation has been built, according to its constitution, like other animals, girls are property of men. Being property they cannot own property. Having no property to count, they have no reason to learn how to count."

Susan didn't blink an eye, "I'm not an animal. I'm a human being." The boys doubled up laughing. The girls looked up at Susan as if they had just come back from the dead.

The old prune with chalk dust wedged into its fingernails nailed his case shut. "Not according to God, not according to the facts." He pointed once more to the Tenth Commandment. The boys giggled. The girls seemed to yield to their fate.

The old prune with chalk dust wedged into its fingernails glanced around the room. Excepting his adversary, it was clear he had convinced the lighter sex of their role in life. He had done a masterful job of presenting the facts. He had won his case. He had removed the question mark from each of their stares.

What's more, he had made a fool of this impudent little girl.

"Now let's get on with the business of the day. 'What those brave young lads took those first bullets for in the spring of 1775?'"

Susan was not quite finished. "That's not what it says."

"It is exactly what it says." The old man repeated again, "'*Thou shalt not desire to take from thy neighbor his property, including his house, his wife, his slaves, his ox, his ass.*'"

Taking up his chalk he underlined '*his property*' → '*his wife*'

"Not there, over here." She pointed to the other side of the board, *The Pledge of Allegiance*. With a defiant smile she demolished the case of this old prune with chalk dust wedged into its fingernails.

Susan read: "'*...liberty and justice for all.*'"

Her classmates looked to their master for an explanation. He answered their stare. "My mistake," the old prune chuckled. Taking up the chalk, he added the word '*men.*'

Standing back, he read, "'*...liberty and justice for all men.*'

"That's better" he announced. "This is what those brave young lads took those first bullets for in the spring of 1775."

The little girl kept the thought to herself. "This is not what those brave young lads took those first bullets for in the spring of 1775. They took those first bullets so that I, too, can learn to count.

"Furthermore, I am going to learn to count. What's more, I am going to make it possible for all those little girls who come after me to be able to learn to count.

"I am going to change Ichabod Falwell's blackboard back to what those brave young lads took those first bullets for in the spring of 1775: '...*liberty and justice for all!*'"

On April 9, 1775, British troops fired on Minutemen at Concord. Two fell dead and four others were wounded by *'the shot heard round the world.'*

Until the mid-20th century, there were virtually no women engineers in the United States, engineering requiring a strong aptitude in mathematics.

Susan B. Anthony was a precocious child having learned to read and write at age three. In 1826, at the age of six, a teacher refused to teach her arithmetic because of her gender. That night, Susan announced to her family she was going to learn how to count, so that all little girls who would come after her would have the same right to learn how to count.

Her father, a cotton manufacturer and abolitionist, groomed her into the human rights activist she became—one dedicated to women's rights, particularly as they concerned themselves with custody rights of their own children.

She would change the definition of *'woman'* in the Constitution from *'property'* to *'human being'* which in turn changed the definition of marriage. Marriage would no longer be a barter between two men—a father trading his daughter to a suitor for a cow—but the mutual decision of any two people who are in love.

The Red-faced Chaplain

"Never be afraid to stand up for what is right, whether your adversary be your parent, your peer, your teacher, your politician, your preacher, or even your God."

Albino Luciani, Basilica di San Marco, Venice, March 5, 1973

Montgomery had chased Rommel back and forth across North Africa for months. Among others, the battles of El Alamein, El Aghela, Gazala, Alam El Halfa, and, El Alamein, once more.

Finally, it had been George Patton's turn. The battle of El Guettar.

It had been two weeks since he had given Rommel that one last kick in the ass and sent his tanks running off over the hills. Since he had thundered out over the battlefield: "Rommel, you magnificent son-of-a-bitch, I read your book!"

Now he stood at Tunis on Africa's coast—a stone's throw from Sicily. His triumphal entrance into Italy would mark the beginning of the end of Hitler. He was not aware it would also mark the beginning of the end of discrimination in the western world, together with its champion, the Roman Catholic Church.

As he contemplated his advance on Palermo, the phone rang. He

275

picked it up, "George Patton, here."

"Major Foley, Chaplain Corps."

"Go ahead, Major."

"General Patton, Sir. We have a problem. Sir…"

"Shoot."

"I suggest we leave the black battalion behind and transfer them to the Third Army in France."

The general shot back, "Why would we ever do that?"

"Blacks are not allowed in Italy," Foley asserted.

Patton grew annoyed, "Blacks are not allowed in Italy? This is war. We don't go by the enemy's rules. We go by our rules."

"With all respect General, you don't understand. If we march the black battalion into Palermo, we will offend His Holiness."

"His Holiness? What has he got to do with it?"

"It is Canon Law to preserve the purity of the white race. Blacks are not allowed in Italy."

The general sneezed.

"It is the Pope's rules we must follow. Not necessarily those of the enemy. As a matter-of-fact, we follow them ourselves. The reason why we have a black battalion to begin with. The reason why we bury them separately away from the rest of us so they don't contaminate the purity of our white race in the afterlife." The chaplain waited.

The general lost his cool, "I don't give a damn what the Pope thinks. My black battalion is going to march into Palermo."

The young chaplain dealt his trump card. "General, it is much more than just the Pope. It is the will of the Almighty Creator. You will be thumbing your nose at the Lord, Himself."

Patton stopped. "Major Foley. Let me think about this. I will get back to you." He hung up. He struggled with the thought.

During the long haul from Casablanca, the casualty rate had been thirty percent among his black soldiers whereas it had been only half that among the rest of his forces. He knew why. He had used blacks for high-risk reconnaissance missions behind enemy lines as they could blend in as natives.

He thought of the times he had carried himself into battle, into the pit. Of the times he had pulled the boy out of the mud and searched for where the mud left off and the blood began.

He thought of his impending triumph into Palermo. It would be a celebration, one of liberation for its people, but more so, a celebration of the lives he had left behind. Yet, he also thought of his impending doom, for this time his enemy was his God.

He thought back to West Point. To that day the instructor told the class: "A soldier must never cower in the face of an enemy no matter how great that enemy may be."

He picked up the phone and dialed. It buzzed in his ear.

"Major Foley, here."

"George Patton," the general paused. "Major Foley, thank you for bringing this matter to my attention. I have thought this over. I have decided to change my plans for Palermo."

"Good. God will be pleased." The major heard a click.

The following week, jubilant crowds lined the streets of Palermo as the Seventh Army band marched to the tune of *The Stars and Stripes Forever*. Eyes strained anxiously down the street for a glimpse of the famous general. Yet, Patton was not there.

Heading up the black battalion was a young white army chaplain with a cross held high. His face more red, than white.

Headline quote: Albino Luciani honors Abraham Lincoln and Susan B. Anthony for having had the courage to defy their God's Tenth Commandment which protected the right of one man to enslave another and held women to be property of men.

The Battle of El Guettar: Patton thought he had defeated Rommel. Months later, Patton learned Rommel had flown to Germany on the eve of the battle leaving General Arnim in charge.

Prior to the war, pressured by the Vatican's decree to maintain the purity of the white race, blacks were not allowed in Italy, Poland and other predominately Catholic countries in Europe—the reason few blacks died in concentration camps.

The young army chaplain filed a complaint with Eisenhower that Patton had ordered him against his will to head up the black battalion. Ike reprimanded Patton.

The following year Patton would officiate jointly with Albino Luciani in Milan at the grave of a gay soldier who had sacrificed his life to save twenty-eight Italian school children. The complete record of that event is in the author's book 'The Vatican Murders: The Life and Death of John Paul I

The Dumb Chinaman

"We must learn here how to use the chopsticks, or we will not know how to use them when we are on the other side of the wall."

Albino Luciani, *Illustrissimi*

The story is told of the young Christian who went into the cemetery and placed flowers on his parent's grave.

While he stood there talking to the air, an Asian youth came along and placed bowls of rice on the adjacent graves.

"Dumb Chinaman," the American chuckled to himself.

He asked the boy, "When do you think your mother and father are going to come up and eat the rice?"

The youth thought a bit and replied, "I would guess, the same time your mother and father come up to smell the roses."

This story is the only thing in this book not original to its author. Yet, it is important to this work because it pinpoints the differences between cultures.

China is overwhelmingly atheist (Taoism, Buddhism, Confucianism, etc.). Hence, it has only <u>reason</u> to guide it. America is overwhelmingly Christian, As Albert Einstein told us: "<u>faith</u> is the opposite of <u>reason</u>."

No, we don't know when they will come up. But what we do know, if they ever do come up, every single one of them will pass up the flowers, and go for the rice.

The author of this story is unknown.

First, onto my shoulder…

"Freedom without equality is not what it pretends to be. The diamond would be made of paste."

General George Patton, Milan, March 29 1944

For the last year of my military service, I was stationed at Fort Hancock in New Jersey. I took it as a reward for my time at the front.

The base was situated on what is today Sandy Hook State Park, a peninsula jetting out northward from the surrounding highlands into New York Harbor.

As a young officer, I enjoyed waterfront quarters and it was my routine each morning to peel out of the sack and take a dip or two in the ocean surf before heading off for the day.

Aside from running the Adjutant's office, I was rewarded with a number of additional duties. Among them was headmaster of the enlisted men's barracks—about two hundred young soldiers. Among them were Richard Edwards and Alan Small.

Small was nineteen, a bundle of good looks. If his deep dark brown eyes and perpetual smile didn't get you, his ever present darting personality surely would. He was the huggable type.

Edwards was a bit older. Though he didn't smoke, he was the type a cigarette company would give its net worth to have on its billboards. Above all, he had a heart that would tame a tiger.

The two had recently been named Soldier of the Year. When the time came to make the award, Edwards and Small came in 'first' and 'first'—a dead heat. There was a reason for this.

They were inseparable. Whenever and wherever you would run into one of them, you were sure to run into the other.

It had been their work with the homeless in the surrounding community which had won for them the prize.

Nevertheless, for the first time in the history of the post, two awards were handed out. I know, because I pinned the accompanying Commendation Medal on each of their chests.

Yet, we all have our faults. For them, like most others in those days, it was beer. Problem was Alan couldn't keep up with the rest of us. By the time we had our full, he was already under the table.

In October of that year, Alan was caught driving under the influence. The local headline read: *Soldier of the Year DUI.*

Though he had been barely over the limit, the colonel threw the book at him. Three months in the pen.

Each week, I would visit the stockade and interview Alan. It was a rare day, Richard was not there.

As Christmas approached, the season spirit got the best of me. I talked the colonel into letting him out a tad early. It has been my fate, I have lived with that decision all the days of my life.

It was Christmas Eve, we got the word. Alan had been beat up by thugs in a parking lot. The word was not good. He had been taken to a hospital in the nearby city of Long Branch.

I dashed to the office. As I suspected, Alan's blood type was rare. I quickly rummaged through the files and found two others with the same type. Loading them into my car, I placed a flashing red light on its roof and sped off the base.

As I came down the hospital corridor and turned the corner, Richard was there. Behind him, Alan was already under a sheet.

Rushing toward me, he fell into my arms, sobbing relentlessly. I held him there for what seemed an eternity. I could feel his tears drop... first, onto my shoulder... then, run down my back.

I had no idea a soldier could love another soldier so deeply. I had no idea a person could love another person so deeply.

After I got out of the Army, I took a job in New York City.

One afternoon, I ran into Richard. Still in uniform. This time setting up pup tents for the homeless on Manhattan's lower east side. The ribbon I had placed on his chest had been joined by the Purple Heart, a Bronze Star, and a row of others.

He told me Alan had been a victim of gay bashing. He and Alan were in love. They had planned to adopt handicapped children and live out their lives helping others less fortunate than themselves.

Today, halfway down the Vietnam Veterans Memorial Wall in Washington DC is the name, *Richard Edwards*. Shot dead by an American army officer when he tried to stop the torching of a village housing hundreds of Vietnamese women and children.

For some reason that escapes me, each time I have witnessed homosexuals struggling for the right to marry, I would feel Richard Edward's tears drop... first, onto my shoulder...

...then, run down my back.

This story recounts an incident in the author's life.

The headline quote is that of George Patton at the graveside of a gay soldier who had given his life to save twenty-eight Italian school children, Milan, March 29, 1944. The story of General Patton and Albino Luciani officiating jointly at the interment of this soldier is recounted in the author's book *The Vatican Murders: The Life and Death of John Paul I*

The Queen of Theology

"I call upon you, to draw from the depths of your being, to prove we are one human race, to prove our love outweighs our need to hate."

Elizabeth Taylor, Academy Awards, March 29, 1993

The television spoke the words of an American president as he stood on the world stage with an American evangelist talking dirty: *"They live like that. Let them die like that."*

She gasped. "People are dying and preachers and politicians are talking morality. What they think is morality."

She thought a moment, confused as to what she could do.

She had no experience in politics. But she did have a background in theology, the world of make-believe.

In fact, she knew all about the world of make-believe. She was an actress. Not just an actress. She was at the top of the game.

She knew more about the world of make-believe than did all the popes who had reigned before her and all those who would come after her. She was the queen of the world of make-believe. She was, in truth, the reigning *Queen of the World of Theology*.

She looked at her secretary, "Get Frank on the phone."

"Mr. Sinatra is vacationing in the Canary Islands. I don't think he wants to be disturbed." Ellen warned.

Elizabeth didn't skip a beat, "I don't care if he's in China. Get him on the phone. People are dying."

Ice cubes rattled out of the glass, onto the beach, crossed the ocean, went along the way, into the city of superstars, up the driveway, and into the house of the most beautiful woman in the world.

"I know where you're coming from, I would want to help, but I wouldn't go near that one with a ten foot pole."

She hung up. She would try again. "Try Sammy. Being both black and Jewish, he knows better than anyone else how cruel prejudice can be. Get him on the phone."

"Mr. Davis is in Las Vegas. Busy as hell." Ellen headed her off.

"Get him on the phone."

Ice cubes rattled out of the glass, into a land of fantasy, across the desert, into the city of superstars, up the driveway, and into the house of the most beautiful woman in the world.

"I know where you're coming from, I would want to help, but I wouldn't go near that one with a ten foot pole."

Her friends were deserting her. She would reach for a straw.

Ellen saw it coming. "Mr. Donohue is on the moon," laughing as she dialed the number.

Ice cubes rattled out of the glass, into the windy city, across the plains, over the mountains, into the city of superstars, up the driveway and into the house of the most beautiful woman in the world.

"I know where you're coming from, I would want to help, but I wouldn't go near that one with a..."

Phil stopped. He thought back to that day many years before when he had come in out of the snow.

"The kids are calling Jimmy a fairy and they push him around."

His mom told him, "Phil, you must stay away from Jimmy or they'll think you're a fairy, too."

He weighed friendship above all else. "No. He needs me now more than ever before. I'm not going to abandon my friend."

So he stood by Jimmy. As his mom had warned, they began to call him a fairy, too. It was then he acquired his most inner fear. If he helped those like Jimmy, others would think him gay.

As the most beautiful woman in the world was at the top of the world of theology, he as the world's leading talk-show host was at the top of the world of reality. He was, in truth, the reigning *King of the World of Reality.*

Throughout his reign he had reached into the prisons, under the bridge, into the sewers, and into the darkest worlds beyond. One by one, he had brought them onto his stage and gave them a chance.

He talked to them, listened to them, talked to others about them, listened to others about them. Like a world class chef he brought them together in a mixing bowl and baked a cake.

The cake had a face on it. The face had a frown. He knew why.

He had left out a certain ingredient. What's more, he had done it on purpose. He was afraid if he helped those like Jimmy, now the whole world would think him gay.

The fork in the road had come up for Phil.

He looked down the road. Off in the distance was Jimmy. This time Jimmy was dying. He was calling to Phil to help him.

The road was lined with bigots, armed with sticks and stones which could break his bones. They shouted "Queers, faggots, pansies; they live like that... let them die like that."

What's worse, they backed it up with proof: 'God hates Fags' signs quoting the Bible's condemnations of homosexuality.

Phil looked down the road to the right.

The path was clear. A golden carriage stood there.

At its open door, a beautiful angel beckoned, "Ignore Jimmy. AIDS is the work of God. It is Jimmy's punishment for having lived a life of sin. Come, we will be late for the Bigot Ball."

Off in the distance, beyond the carriage, kings and queens and princes and princesses dressed in radiant evening attire drifted up white marble steps into a grand theater of gold.

He looked back down the road beyond the angry crowds waving their sticks and stones and Godly signs.

Jimmy looked terrible. His body shriveled. His eyes drawn. His cheeks blemished. A shadow of the walking dead.

Without fear of sticks or stones that might break his bones—still fearing names might forever harm him—Phil courageously went down the road and saved his friend.

The *King of the World of Reality* told the *Queen of the World of Theology*: "I know where you're coming from. I know where you're going. Take my hand. Walk with me. I will take you there..."

On the campaign trail with gay-hater Reverend Falwell, to secure the Christian vote, Ronald Reagan remarked *'They live like that, let them die like that'* CBS August 4, 1984.

At the time of this incident, Elizabeth Taylor's friend Rock Hudson had been diagnosed with AIDS and Ronald Reagan had just vetoed another AIDS bill.

The most beautiful woman in the world took it upon herself to do a job that should have been done by an American Congress and an American President. She organized an event in the Hollywood Bowl establishing AIDS research.

This is the story of the ups and downs she encountered of those who were afraid to get involved because of the stigma attached to the dreaded disease. The Frank Sinatra and Sammy Davis Jr. incidents are the public testimony of Elizabeth Taylor.

Phil Donohue often spoke publicly of his most inner fear, people might think him gay if he helped those in the gay community. He was the first host in the history of television to give representatives of the gay community a world forum.

The Enchanting Stenographer

"Democracy which finds its strength in rule by the people can only find its sacred duty to society in preserving the basic human rights and dignity of its loneliest individual."

Albino Luciani, Christian Democratic Party Convention

I pressed the intercom. There was a whiff of jest in the receptionist's tone. "Your stenographer is here from the temp agency."

The mascara was overpowering and the lips too red.

Yet, she was a pretty girl. Good taste in clothes, a suggestive bulge in the blouse, and, the fashion in those days, a miniskirt that stopped too many inches above the knees.

I introduced myself. She smiled and shook my hand.

It had been only yesterday, I had searched the yellow pages and ordered a secretary for the boss.

Dropping her at the desk just outside his door, "This is your spot." I pointed, "Coffee is just around the corner."

Dropping her purse on the desk, she sat down and wound her left leg over the right one, as if the miniskirt couldn't do the trick by itself.

For the rest of the day, I would enjoy a pretty sight, one of the hidden benefits of the job. Aside from her imposing beauty, there was something mysterious, something enchanting about her charm.

I won't tell you of my thoughts as I lurked hungrily an aisle away.

286

After all, my mother might get her fingers on this book.

Her compact mirror caught my eye as she ran it up and down her face as one does a flashlight looking for a needle in the dark.

Suddenly, it stopped. Reaching into her bag, she withdrew a kind of surgical instrument. Taking it up, she plucked her nose.

Shortly, another contraption of sorts came up out of the bag. She went to work on her eyes.

Suddenly, sensing she was watched, she turned in my direction and shot me a glance of a dark winking eyelash curled up to her brow.

As she finished filing her nails, I saw I was wrong.

Not too much mascara. Not too much red on the lips.

She blackened the black, and reddened the red, and patted her cheeks with the rogue.

A touch of powder, here and there, she was ready for the day.

The boss stepped out of his office.

I snickered as he struggled to control the joy of the marvel of it all. I was surprised he got it right. "I am Harry Dobbs. Welcome aboard. What is your name?"

Fluttering her eyelashes in a double roll, she looked up at him with a baffling and seductive smile.

Then in a deep voice, as if a frog had lodged in her throat, "I am Roger Baker. Could I ask? Where is the men's room?"

This story recounts an incident in the author's life.

Transgenders have been among the most persecuted of human beings. Until recently, those not in the entertainment industry found work only in temp agencies.

Included are homosexuals whose sexual orientation drives a preference for apparel/mannerisms of the opposite sex—butch females and effeminate males. Few homosexuals are transgender. Also included are transsexuals whose preference for apparel/mannerisms of the opposite sex is driven by sexual identity. Also included are transvestites who acquire a fetish for apparel of the opposite sex for reasons other than sexual orientation or sexual identity. Postoperative transgenders are forbidden to serve in any role—priest/monk/nun—in the Roman Catholic Church.

Quote: Albino Luciani, 1963 Christian Democratic Party Convention, Milan

Ten Little Indians

"And then there were none."   Agatha Christie

It was the year of our lord fourteen hundred and ninety-two.

The sails of the three tiny vessels fluttered in the wind as they rocked about the waves.

Struggling onto shore, the crew was greeted by an astounding sight. Ten little Indians, dressed up in feathered hats and beaded skirts, dancing around the trunk of a tree.

Striking the flagpole into the sand, the captain proclaimed, "I claim this land in the name of Almighty God and Isabella of Spain."

The captain laughed. "These Indians are like little children. They dress up in women clothes and tall hats and prance around the trunk of a tree. We will teach them of the true God."

"And Then There Were None"

Many years later there were none, almost none.

The only thing that had changed was their dwindling numbers and a near naked man now nailed to the trunk of their tree.

makes no sense   makes sense

The Massacre at Wounded Knee

In December 1890, an American Christian Militia attacked a Lakota Sioux settlement at Wounded Knee in the Dakotas. Three hundred Indian men, women and children were protesting for religious freedom to worship the Great Spirit Wakan Tanka. When all was said and done, there were none. They were all dead.

Christian soldiers answering their Lord's command: 'Take to the sword, the infidels, every man, woman and child; leave not one alive.'

Sadly, this was not the beginning of the slaughter. It was the end of it.

In the wake of *Wounded Knee*, less than two percent of America's original inhabitants were alive. Those few entirely converted to Christianity.

This would reoccur in 1955 when Pope Pius XII and President Eisenhower entered into an alliance with the ruthless Catholic dictator Ngo Dinh Diem to annihilate Buddhists (atheists) in South Vietnam. Hundreds of thousands of men, women and children were murdered in the villages of Vietnam and Cambodia.

In 1963, Buddhist monks burned themselves to death in protest of American brutality. When John Kennedy realized he was engaged in the Vatican's war to annihilate atheism, he moved to end United States intervention in Vietnam.

One of the more plausible theories of Kennedy's murder, was based on his intention to get out of Vietnam. Kennedy started to withdraw troops on August 10, 1963. Twelve days later, he was dead. If America withdrew from Vietnam, it would forever block the Vatican's expansion of Catholicism into China.

When the author was growing up, his mother did not allow him to go to Cowboy (the good guys) and Indian (the bad guys) movies.

The motion picture industry's mal-portrayal of the American Indian has only been surpassed by its mal-portrayal of Moses; it paints him out to be a good and holy man whereas, in truth, Moses has led the western hemisphere into twenty-five hundred years of hatred, prejudice, persecution, suffering, destruction and death: 'Take to the sword, the infidels, every man, woman and child; leave not one alive.'

'Ten Little Indians' Agatha Christie's bestselling novel

'And Then There Were None' Agatha Christie's famous play

Why Am I Killing These People?

"Let not one remain alive."   God the Father, Book of Joshua

It was the year of our Lord nineteen hundred and sixty-eight.

With mud all over our faces and eyes dressed in mascara, we peered out from the jungle growth engulfing us. A pig snorted a stone's throw away, threatening to blow our cover.

Aside a thatched roof shanty, an old man resembling a Buddhist monk in a yoga position stared off to nowhere. For him, it was just one more day on a long journey into the next life.

Children ran to and fro, laughing... shrieking... squealing... For them, it was just one more day on a wonderful journey into this life.

On the front porch, a young mother rocked in a chair nursing an infant. For her, it was the epitome of life.

An old woman, stringing clothes on a line under a nearby tree, looking back on treasured memories of this life, shouted at the children, "平靜下來!." I supposed, it meant "QUIET!"

A pair of teens walked hand-in-hand down the mudded boulevard of cherished dreams, looking forward to when they, too, would have a thatched roofed hut with children running to and fro laughing... shrieking... squealing..., with an old man staring off to nowhere, and an old woman, hanging out to dry, shouting "平靜下來!"

Behind me, I felt the scurrying of mortar sneaking into place. I heard it breathing, waiting hungrily for its moment in time.

The snorting of the pig raised an octave or two.

I recalled my time at West Point: *"When you find the enemy, hit him and hit him hard. Show him no mercy. Stick him between the third and fourth ribs. Kill him... Kill him... Kill him..."*

Too, the instruction of our Lord: *"Smote them with the edge of the sword, slay all the souls therein; leave not one remain alive, every man, woman and child..."*

I answered the Lord's valiant call: "Fire!"

The sound was a rhythmic symphony of rapid reverberation. The sight was blazing light mixed with blood in the mud. The smell was burning flesh in the dawn. The feel was the icy cold of the night.

The old man and the old woman keeled over into the next life. The girl in the rocking chair froze in place. The children finally heeded their grandmother's call for silence. The teens, strolling down this boulevard of cherished dreams, went up in a single puff of smoke.

The end came as quickly as it had come. "Hold your fire."

I cringed and asked myself, "Why am I killing these people?"

In the Massacre of My Lai, American soldiers systematically murdered five hundred men, women and children. My Lai was not an isolated incident. During the course of the war, American Christian soldiers snuffed out the lives of hundreds of thousands of innocent atheist men, women and children in Vietnam and Cambodia.

Genocide is defined as 'systematic annihilation of a kind of people.' When the Geneva Accord declared North Vietnam a Free Atheist Nation, the United States allied itself with the ruthless Catholic dictator Ngo Dinh Diem to invade North Vietnam and annihilate Atheism in Asia.

Atheists are the most scorned human beings in a Christian society.

Of 44 United States presidents, 118 justices, 1,922 senators and 17,216 congressmen, only one known atheist has ever been elected to office: Barney Frank who was also the first homosexual elected to congress. Yet, both elections were reelections. In his first election, he ran as a heterosexual Jew.

Today, the Supreme Court is entirely Judea-Christian. Catholics: Roberts, Scalia, Thomas, Alito, Kennedy and Sotomayor. Jews: Breyer, Ginsberg and Kagan.

Justices seeking guidance of the Holy Spirit

Open for Business

The marquee over the shop read, "Signs." Opening the door to the tinkling of bells, an old man sat there.

In his lifetime, he had made thousands of crazy signs. This one took the cake. For the life of him, he could not understand what kind of a business could sell its wares under such a sign.

Excitedly, Florence asked, "Is it ready yet?"

"It certainly is," he answered. "But could I ask... could I ask... what kind of business you are in?"

"It's on the sign," she told him. "It is on the sign."

She tucked a wad of bills into his hand. Taking up the sign, Florence hurried out of the shop and down the street to her place of business. The newly established entrepreneur hastily stepped up on a box. She hung the sign just above the door.

"Give me your tired, your huddled masses yearning to breathe free. The wretched refuse of your teeming shore. Send the homeless, the tempest-tossed to me. I lift my lamp beside the golden door."

As her sign seemed to say, Florence had no preference as to who would buy her wares. She didn't care if they were Christian, or Jew, or Muslim, or Hindu, or Shinto, or Buddhist, or Tao.

She didn't care if they were Russian, or German, or Polish, or Irish, or Italian, or French, or English, or Swiss, or Mao.

One by one, she took them out of the loneliness of the night, while the rest of the world slept out of sight.

One by one, she held their dizzy heads, rubbed their tired backs, calmed their shattered nerves, cooled their burning flesh, and soothed their tormented souls.

One by one, she took them out the gloom of their everyday lives, into a wonderland of enlightened dreams.

Like a fairy godmother, she waved her wand and changed their world, from dreary and doubt, to contentment and joy.

Joy? Yes, above all, she made them happy. Boy, did she ever make them happy.

Florence never knew deer or chamois or bear in the forest, never flew with the sparrow swooping down on specks of white and yellow buds of *Belles Dames* and *Painted Ladies,* never flew upside down under a blue sky over fields of green with the swallow and turn the sky from blue to green.

She never knew of little boys and little girls splashing in the pool. Never had to scold an insolent son, "Get over here, or I will break every bone of your body."

But she did her work, and she did it well.

She never wrote a book, never held an office, never went to church, but she kept the peace across the realm. More than any of the rest of us, she left her mark in time.

When she died, no Mass was said for her. They stuffed her into a burlap sack and buried her outside of town in the village dump. Her only mourners... a few flies happened to buzz by.

As I think back, I often wonder how cruel it is of people, who have brought so much misery into the world, to treat someone who had brought so much happiness into the world that way.

293

Luckily for Florence, a few of us dug her up and put her in a casket and buried her alongside a stream under weeping willows of greenery and shedding tears. We placed a small stone:

There once was a half-pretty harlot named Florence
No one thought her of any importance
But boy did she keep the streets clean
Of men who could only dream
Of things that could never be, without Florence

I'm not saying she was right or wrong, the way she lived her life.

What I am saying is that she had the right to have lived it the way she did, helping people. Isn't that what Jesus is all about?

How come the rest of us Hypocrites who profess to be holier than thou, have not helped so many people?

Isn't this what freedom is about? I think so.

Of all those who claim to be free, Florence is the only one who spent her life living up to the sign that hangs outside the golden door…

"Give me your tired, your huddled masses yearning to breathe free. The wretched refuse of your teeming shore. Send the homeless, the tempest-tossed to me. I lift my lamp beside the golden door."

Prostitution is a just function in a free society.

The alternative is a dangerous society—raping of women in alleys and preying on children in schoolyards. Countries in which prostitution is legal have immensely lower rates of rape, extortion, murder and other sex-related crimes than do countries where it is illegal. Too, legal prostitutes pay taxes.

In countries in which prostitution is controlled by the government, one will not find an under-aged prostitute. In the United States and Eastern Europe, where prostitution is illegal, trafficking of children in prostitution is rampant

In those few areas in the United States in which prostitution is legal, the practitioner must be of legal age, must submit to periodic tests for HIV other STDs and must present an updated card to clients evidencing they are free of disease.

In these areas, in the past quarter century—there has not been a case of a transmitted disease recorded and there has been no record involving prostitution related extortion, violence, murder or suicide.

The Great Meltdown

"This chalice holds one hundred and twenty of the world's most pristine diamonds while children all over the world starve to death, Do you really think this is what Christ meant by His Church?"

John Paul I, St. Peter's Basilica, Rome, September 27, 1978

When he became a bishop, Albino Luciani attended a festival. He was disturbed not a single handicapped child was to be seen.

The next day, he visited an institution where these children lived under terrible conditions. He came upon a ten year old boy.

The boy had been hit by a drunk driver when he was five years old. Paralyzed from the neck down, it was clear that his mind had survived unscathed.

The bishop of Vittorio Veneto asked the boy, "What is your name? What do you want for Christmas?"

"Giuseppe." The boy thought awhile. He told the bishop, "I want to live outside with the people." He looked around the room at others who were even less fortunate than he was. "I want all of us, each one of us, to live outside with the people."

The following day, the bishop ordered his two hundred and seventy priests to sell their gold crucifixes and other items of idol worship.

295

A newspaper carried the story of a rector who complained: "He would have us serve the Eucharist out of a paper cup."

The next day a package arrived from the bishop's castle. The priest eagerly ripped open the box. In it was a paper cup.

On Christmas Eve, the bishop showed up at the little house of horrors together with a shovel. Attached to the shovel was a ribbon with a small note: "Merry Christmas, Giuseppe. Welcome to the world."

The next day, Giuseppe looked on as his father took up the shovel and broke ground for a new kind of clinic, a halfway-house designed to take himself and his friends out of institutions and allow them to live together with the general population.

Yet, Moses stood in the way of the compassionate bishop. Many mothers and fathers didn't want their children exposed to boys and girls who were severely impaired. They picketed the workers with signs of God's holy instruction in their holy book *Leviticus*:

'...whosoever that hath a blemish, whether he be a blind child, or a lame child, or a broken-footed child, or a broken-handed child, or a hunch-backed child, or a dwarfed child, or a child of disease is not to approach the altar of the Lord.'

The bishop would not be deterred by the prejudices of a selfish God. On his eleventh birthday, scarcely aware of the crowds and the glare of flashbulbs all around him, Giuseppe picked up a specially made pair of scissors with his teeth and cut the ribbon.

Christmas Eve, many years later

It was nine in the morning. The Patriarch of Venice had overslept.

As was his practice, slipping into shorts and sandals, cup of coffee in hand, he headed out to his bench in the plaza.

The cardinal's bench was taken.

There, sat a severely retarded boy together with his father.

He thought of Giuseppe. For had Giuseppe not cut the ribbon which opened up the world to special children, this little boy would not be here. The cardinal would have his bench.

The boy looked up at him and asked, "Would you pose with me for a photograph?"

He motioned to kneel down beside the boy.

The boy held up his hand as to stop him. "Could you put on your beautiful clothes?"

Luciani loathed vestments. He thought them hypocritical. Yet, he disappeared into the palace and returned in his cardinal's robe, topped off with a golden miter and a stately staff.

As he knelt down beside the boy, he told the boy's father: "There are times we must shed our humility and put on our hypocrisy. This is one of them."

The following morning at Christmas Mass, priests and bishops sat outraged as the congregation applauded the little boy who sat all dressed up in a magnificent robe together with golden miter and staff on the cardinal's throne on the great altar of Saint Mark's Basilica.

Just outside, in the little plaza which fronts the Patriarch's Palace, a gentleman in shorts and sandals chuckled to himself.

The cardinal had his bench.

When Albino Luciani ordered his priests to melt down their golden chalices and other implements of idol worship to build a halfway house for the handicapped, was the first time he made world headlines. When he rose to the papacy, he motioned to sell Vatican treasures and employ the Vatican Bank to wage a war on poverty in Central America against the ruthless union of the ruling Juntas and the United States; See The Vatican Murders: The Life and Death of John Paul I

Ten years after Giuseppe cut the ribbon, Eunice Kennedy Shriver founded the Special Olympics and started the transition from dwarf, crippled, retard to the world's Special Children. Her brother, Ted Kennedy rose up as the driving force behind more legislature extending human rights to mentally/physically impaired children than any other person in the history of the world. Most of his legislation has been adopted by other nations.

Hence. When one sees Braille on a telephone, captions on a television screen, a ramp on a street corner, one will remember who put them there.

When one sees impaired children on that same corner, one will remember who put them there. When one sees them playing in a baseball game, one will remember who put them there.

Albino Luciani, Eunice Shriver, Ted Kennedy and other champions of human justice who chose to cease to be mortal men and evolved as Gods.

A Cross Dog Across the Street

"Thou shalt not be as Hypocrites; for they love to pray standing in public places that they may be seen and heard of men."

Jesus Christ. Gospel of Matthew

At one time, I lived near the Baltimore Basilica. My rooms looked down on this tree off to one side of the cardinal's mansion.

To the other side of the mansion, was a hi-rise which housed the homeless. The diocese decided it would get out of the shelter business; it would tear down the building and replace it with a multi-million dollar prayer garden dedicated to John Paul II.

In the ensuing summer came the shouts of protesters demonstrating to keep the shelter open. The diocese tore it down anyway.

The Pit Bull

The summer had come and gone and snow and ice had moved in for the winter. On Sunday mornings, I would sip my coffee and watch the churchgoers go out of my building. They would walk down to the corner and, though the basilica was on this side of the street, they

298

would cross to the other side of the street, walk the block, and then cross back over to the basilica. Every single one of them.

When Mass ended, they would pass through the prayer garden admiring the towering bronze of the Polish Pope. Then retrace their steps, crossing to the other side of the street, walking the block, then crossing back over to this side of the street.

"Strange." I muttered, "Must be a cross dog."

Slipping on my coat, I headed out to solve the mystery of the day.

Unlike the faithful, who would cross to the other side, I walked on the same side of the street as the basilica. I came upon what all those good Catholics had been going out of their way to avoid.

A store had gone out of business. Its doorway had been taken over by a homeless man of about fifty. One of those who had been thrown out when the prayer garden had replaced the shelter.

He had the usual makeshift roll of rags and was bundled up in an old dirty fatigue jacket which seemed to have weathered many more wars than it had actually fought. I hurried across the street to a coffee shop and returned with a bowl of soup and crackers.

As trembling hands grasped the bowl, my eye caught a soiled tattered row of ribbons. Having served in the military, I was able to read them left to right: "Silver Star... Bronze Star... Purple Heart..."

Here, on this side of the street, was the reason all those good Catholics were able to cross to the other side of the street and party in their magnificent basilica and enjoy their opulent prayer garden.

Headline photo: this tree dedicated to John Paul I in 1978 cost us $75. The multi-million dollar John Paul II Prayer Garden can be viewed on the Internet.

Both popes would be happy with their memorials. Driven by the doctrine *out-of-wedlock children have no souls,* both Poland and Italy suffered from immense orphan populations; two million in each country. In the twenty years they were bishops, John Paul I built 44 orphanages and not a single church. John Paul II built 53 churches and not a single orphanage. Two very different men who served two very different Gods.

The Worst of Children

"It was the plight of the orphans that made me realize my devout mamma was a sheep and my atheist papa was a lion. It was then I began to shed my wool and groom my mane."

Albino Luciani

…an occasional thud of a frozen tot broke the quiet of the dawn

The icicles poured like waterfalls from the rooftops all the way down to the walkways beneath them.

In the summertime, each house had had its own identity — red - green - blue – yellow - orange. Each had been a tiny splinter in a magnificent rainbow. Now in the wintertime, each was just one of an endless row of crystal figures in an enormous glass menagerie.

The parade of weather-beaten wooden carts moved through the tiny hamlet in the Italian Alps as they had every other morning. The snow was heaped so high on each side of the road, they passed unseen.

Yet, the shouts of the barkers broke the stillness of the morning air: "milk - milk - milk," "cheese - cheese - cheese," "lamb - lamb - lamb," "bread - bread - bread," "eggs - eggs – eggs." Their voices echoing through the white-capped rocky mountain gorge.

Yet, one had made its way before them—no wares—no barker— no echo. A silent one—a ghostly one—a hopeless one…

The cart rumbled along the snow-covered cobblestone streets in the wee hours of the morning; its chauffeurs, pausing, here and there, gathering their ghoulish haul—those of Italy's two million orphans who hadn't survived the wintry night. Only the creaking of the wheels and an occasional thud of a frozen tot broke the quiet of the dawn.

They were orphans because they were the worst of children—BASTARDS. Born-out-of-wedlock children. No one wanted them. No one in their right mind wanted them.

Everyone hated them. That is, everyone who went to church. In those days everyone went to church. Every priest, every nun, every monk, every devout parent, every brainwashed child, despised them.

Each time their frozen bodies would pass by in the cart, they all thought it right. The only hint of compassion every now and then: "They are better off dead."

Everyone thought there was something holy about it. After all, it was written in their book: 'A bastard child shall not enter the congregation of the Lord.' These were the worst of children—BASTARDS.

That is, everyone except Piccolo—the little boy Albino Luciani. He thought it was wrong. He didn't care if it was written in a book. In fact, he knew it was wrong. He knew it was wrong because his revolutionary socialist atheist father had told him it was wrong...

This is the introduction to the story of 'His First Mortal Sin' in the author's bio of the Pope: *The Vatican Murders* as related to the author by Albino Luciani when he was bishop of Vittorio Veneto. It is included to remind the reader until the middle of the twentieth century bastards were the most despised of all in Catholic countries.

When Albino was growing up, every village in Italy, Poland and other Catholic countries had a cart that went about the streets every morning picking up the frozen bodies of orphans who had not made it through the winter nights.

Deuteronomy 23: *'A bastard child shall not enter the congregation of the Lord.'*

In the 1940s and 1950s, Hollywood icons and other celebrities who owned up to their illegitimate status brought an end to the atrocity. Yet, the word 'bastard' continues to have a terrible connotation today despite the stigma is now dead.

Until the 21st century, an illegitimate child could not be legitimately baptized in Catholicism. A severe shortage of priests forced the Vatican to relax its rules. It had to choose between homosexual, women or bastard priests. It chose the latter.

The Little Girl in the Attic

"I still believe people are really good at heart..."

Anne Frank

The train pulled into Amsterdam Central Station. I found my way to the travel services booth and landed a room.

The clerk handed me a small slip with directions to the hotel. On it was the room rate "395 NLG." Unfamiliar with exchange rates, I was unaware I was splurging this first night in Europe.

As I stood on the sidewalk in front of the hotel, I counted the stars on its marquee, "One - two - three - four - five."

The clerk at the railway service desk must have noticed the 'Rolex' watch I had picked up on Times Square for ten bucks. Yet, thinking I may have already paid the bill, as the clerk had taken my credit card, I walked up to its grand entrance.

With ragged jacket, mildewed backpack, knee-torn Levi's and wear-and-tear sneakers, I came instantly under surveillance.

A uniformed sentinel off to one side was trying to reconcile the measurement between a bum off the street and an eccentric American millionaire. The most difficult judgment one can make.

Shuffling my sleeve to expose the Rolex, I evaded the guard. On reaching the desk, my credit card did the rest of the trick.

The room was magnificent—a four poster bed, a well-stocked mini-frig and a palatial marble bath with a whirlpool spa.

Two toilets. I surmised the funny looking one must be one of those things they call a bidet. I've been to Europe many times since and I have never been able to figure out what they use them for.

On the marble vanity, lined up like miniature soldiers standing at attention, a half-dozen bottles. As I read them, I realized I couldn't read them at all. "I will end up gargling with the shampoo. I'll have them take them off the bill."

"The bill?" I wondered what this was costing me. Taking out my translator, I checked the conversion table and exclaimed, "Wow!"

The next morning I enjoyed an exquisite breakfast. Crepes Suzette and all. Needless to say, I checked out.

I could write off one night at these rates over five years or so, but two nights might put me under forever.

I spent the day as a tourist, starting with the arts.

First to the Van Gogh Museum.

It synchronizes classical music with the great master's works. The music is tailored to the mood of the pieces exhibited on each level.

One starts at the top.

Here are the artist's lighter works, the blossoms, the wheat fields, the thatched roofed cottages... The music is light and airy. Mozart, Mendelssohn and Debussy make their rounds.

As one descends the winding slope, one passes through the romantic worlds of Stravinsky, Tchaikovsky and Rachmaninoff. Here, 'daisies' and 'the day on fire' dance under the midday sun.

Like a pair of stallions in quest for the roses, art and music run neck and neck, all the way down to the ground floor.

There starry skies are foreboding; people, cows, even flowers are brooding. Darkness reigns supreme. Beethoven, Wagner and Dvorak have their time under the midnight moon.

Then to the Rijksmuseum. *The Night Watch*. As immense as it is powerful, here, only here, among all of God's creation does quality and quantity end in a dead heat in time. So overpowering, ten minutes onto the street, I could not recall anything else in that great hall of art.

Finally, the Rembrandt Museum. As I wandered from room to room, I came to realize this man, this master, knew of man's greed more than any other who came before or after him. In a few brief moments, I would see more gold than adorns all of the great domes and altars in the Christian world. Perhaps, even more than is said to be held in Fort Knox and all the depositories of the world.

By midday, I had witnessed more money on canvas than I would see in all of my professional career, on all the balance sheets of all the corporate giants, I would have the privilege to work for.

The house on the canal

Later that afternoon, I happened upon a street which ran down along one of the city's canals. I came upon a house.

An old man stood there beckoning me. I followed him into the house. Up the steps. Then up some steps, again.

A bookcase stood along one wall. To my surprise, he opened the bookcase and I followed him up some steps, some more.

I found myself in a simple room, an attic, one end of which was a kitchen and at the other end, a kind of parlor.

The old man handed me a book with a picture of a girl with dimples on its cover. He told me in a quiet and reverent voice almost as if not to wake her: "This is what she was."

Moving to the center of the room and stretching out his hands: "This is where she lived."

Taking me to a window: "This is what she saw."

Taking me to a chair which sat in a corner: "This is where she spoke of things that used to be."

Taking me to a small table set against a wall: "This is where she wrote of things that were."

Taking me into a tiny room off to one side, his voice now edged in solemnity: "This is where she thought of things that had never been and dreamed of things that were to be."

Taking me to a wall: "The things she dreamed of were not to be," he whispered hopelessly, "this is where she was no more."

He pointed to a black and white photograph of a factory. A factory that could be any factory, except for the words 'Bergen-Belsen' painted on its wall and black smoke smoldering from its chimney.

I tucked something into his hand. The action was quick. That is all I can remember. Just that it was quick.

I moved toward the landing… staggered down the stairs.

304

Like a ghost, I emerged from the bookcase, and staggered down some stairs, some more. Stumbling out of the door and down the steps to the walk, moving hurriedly from the pursuit of it all. Like one who has just robbed a bank; escape, escape was my only desire. My only end, my only destination.

I took a bench and gazed for a while at a mother duck with a half-dozen of her children following her down the canal.

It was then, I heard it. I heard it for the first time.

From the screeching of the wheels, to the pounding on the door, to the hoof beats on the stairs, to the opening of the bookcase, to the scurrying in the attic, to the manacles fastened, to the banging of the boxcar doors, to the bedlam at its destination.

To the shouting of the guards, to the waving of the hands, to the chambers on the right, to the ovens on the left, to the smelling of the flesh, to the end of a little girl's life.

I opened the book the guide had given me. I read:

"I still believe people are really good at heart…when I look up into the heavens, I think it will all come right, and that peace and tranquility will return again."

"Not really what most people would call a vacation. Not exactly like lying in the sun with a Pina Colada by your side in the Caribbean.

"But it is necessary," I reminded myself. "It is necessary for her, it is necessary for me, it is necessary for all humanity. That what she dreamed of, those things that were to be, will come to be, for her, and for me, and for all humanity."

This story recounts an incident in the author's life. Anne Frank died in the concentration camp Bergen-Belsen in March 1945. She was fifteen. "The Diary of Anne Frank is the world's all-time bestseller other than the Bible.

The Dumb Dutch Farm Boy

"Our faith is why we cannot love our neighbor as ourselves"

Albino Luciani

The next day I took the train to Utrecht. Exiting the station, I took a spot at a sidewalk café, intending to people-watch.

As luck would have it, a waiter showed up mumbling in Dutch.

I drew out my Dutch-English translator. Flipping through the pages I uttered, "fles." Then, "wit - wijn." I followed it up in English with, "bottle - white – wine," augmenting my struggle with an assortment of sign language, from drawing the shape of a bottle, to flashing my white handkerchief, to lifting an imaginary glass to my lips.

"Fles - wit - wijn." Altogether, offering a fairly good impression of a tourist who already had too much to drink.

The boy's bewildered expression told me it was too much for him. The most strenuous challenge one can face, is to try to make sense out of a conversation with a dumb Dutch farm boy.

With a mischievous smile smothering his confusion, he headed back into the restaurant. I planned the strategy I would use when he would show up with a bowl of soup and a cheese sandwich.

Much to my surprise, he showed up with a bottle of white wine. Carefully, with a hint of professionalism, he uncorked the bottle and without a word started to pour the glass very slowly at first.

Then, suddenly, before I had the chance to stop him, he filled it all the way to the top. An abomination in the world of wine.

306

He gave me an ignorant smile of achievement and turned back into the restaurant. I consoled myself, "At least he got the order right, though he obviously knows nothing about pouring wine." I scoffed. "Particularly, white wine."

My eyes drifted out onto the street. Lots of people. Tall ones, short ones, old ones, rich ones, poor ones, beautiful ones, ugly ones, you name it. The wine was surprisingly good. I emptied the glass.

I had no sooner placed it on the table, he was on the job. This time, much to my delight, he filled it properly halfway.

Then, suddenly, before I had a chance to stop him, he brought it all the way up to the brim again.

I started to burn. He gave me a darting glance, once again housed in a suspicious mischievous smile, despite I had given him a look that could have brought down an elephant.

I pondered my fate, "Why is he doing this to me? Why is he torturing me so? He must know if he fills the glass to the top, the wine will get prematurely warm. I don't understand this."

As I struggled with the thought, he uttered something in Dutch and shot me another prankish smile as he moved away from the table.

He would get me many times more. While deeply engrossed in people-watching, he would quietly slither up to the table and fill the glass properly halfway, then suddenly bring it to the very top.

Alas, he showed up with the check. As the dumb Dutch farm boy stood over me with his leering grin, I thought to myself, "So now the time has come for revenge."

I knew if I under-tipped him, he would have won. So I over-tipped him, gambling it would drive him out of his mind.

Without a word, he gave me a receipt and, again, a mysterious, smile. As he turned away, I shot him one last look. One that could have very easily brought down a herd of elephants.

Roaming down the street, I stopped at another sidewalk café.

More people-watching. There were white ones, black ones, brown ones, yellow ones, and, "yes," I held the thought, "more than its share of gay ones." Slurs popped into my mind: "bitch, faggot, kike, chink, commie, nigger…" All of these had grown up in Christianity.

For 'bitch' one has to go back to the fourteenth century when sexual desire in a woman was deemed equivalent to a dog in heat.

If one steps up to the fifteenth century Spanish Inquisition, charred remains of homosexuals were tabbed faggots. Their God told them so: "If man lieth with mankind, as he lieth with a woman, both of them have committed an abomination: they shall surely be put to death."

'Kike' was born under the nose of the lady who lifts her lamp beside the Christian door. Illiterate Jews signed immigration forms on Ellis Island with a circle. 'Kike' is the Yiddish word for circle.

'Chink' was born a bit later, when the Chinese were struggling to build America's infrastructure: roads, rail and waterway systems

'Commie'—perhaps the worst slur one can be called in western civilization—was the brainchild of Adolf Hitler. He conceived the idea of conditioning his Christian sheep that the economic system of atheist nations is their enemy. In truth, atheist nations are the great enemy of Christian nations because they separate church from state.

For 'nigger' one has to go back to the seventeenth century when a Christian preacher had struck on the word in referring to slaves being unloaded from ships as animal dung. He had good reason to say so. His God told him so in many ways, 'The lord spoke to Moses saying, whosoever should he be with a...flat nose...is not to approach the altar of the Lord... 'Thou shalt not covet thy neighbors; property, including his slaves...'

It was then I first heard it:

From the shouting in the jungle, to the booming of the rifles, to the clanging of the chains, to the fastening of the shackles, to the creaking of the oars, to the snapping of the whips, to the stench down below.

Then, to the barking of the auctioneer, to the weeping of a child, to the pleading of a mother, to the terror in a father's eyes.

"This is supposed to be a vacation. I am paying for my sins."

Speaking of sins, with the wine starting to hit me, I went out of the café and started to look for a room. I wandered down the main avenue. A sign blinked 'Hotel' halfway down a side street.

As I moved toward the blinking light, I suddenly stopped dead in my tracks. Just to my left was a half-clad girl sitting in a window.

I looked first to my right, then to my left, then, again, to my right, and, finally, to my left, once more. I heard a door buzz.

I will not tell you what happened after that. After all, as I have said, my mother might get her fingers on this book.

Not so dumb, after all,

As I checked into my hotel room that evening, I emptied my pockets of the records of the day: a ticket to the toy museum, a stub for the train trip to Utrecht, two for the trolley, a large rather elaborate one for dinner, also true of the one for the wine...

There was a note on the back of the one for the wine.

My Dear Lucien,

Forgive me for calling you by your first name, as I feel I have known you all of my life. Also, please forgive my sense of humor. Sometimes I let it get away from me.

When I started to pour your wine, I noticed a look of great anticipation on your face, and having only a split second to make my decision, I decided to go for it. So I poured it to the very top. Forgive me, but I relished in your pain.

As I saw you deeply involved in people watching, I decided to go for it again. Here, I ask that you reach deep into your heart to forgive me. This time, I had time to plan it. The act was premeditated. As I, again, brought your glass to its brim, I saw pain in your face. Once more, I, took pleasure in it.

But, as I moved away from your table, I realized what I had witnessed was not pain, but hatred.

This is why I am writing you this note. I do not want to bring any more hatred into this world than is already in it.

I trust you will forgive me.

Thank you much for the generous tip. It will help me pay my way through graduate school where I am majoring in English.

Thanks for the lesson in Dutch. It will help me in my work.

Your mischievous waiter, Hans

That night, I dreamt not of the girl in the window, but of the little girl in the attic and of the child on the auctioneer's platform. Once more,

I endured the screeching of the wheels, to the pounding on the door, to the hoof beats on the stairs, to the opening of the bookcase, to the scurrying in the attic, to the manacles being fastened, to the banging of the boxcar doors, to the bedlam at its destination.

Then to the shouting of the guards, to the waving of the hands, to the chambers on the right, to the ovens on the left, to the smelling of the flesh, to the end of a lifetime, the end of a little girl's lifetime.

Then the booming of the rifles, to the shouting in the jungle, to the clanging of the chains, to the fastening of the shackles, to the creaking of the oars, to the snapping of the whips, to the stench down below.

Then to the barking of the auctioneer, to the weeping of a child, to the pleading of a mother, to the terror in a father's eyes.

Headline quote: subject of a paper written by fourteen year old Albino Luciani on display at the Seminary of Feltre until after his death in 1978 when it was removed to the Vatican. The paper demonstrated all prejudices are products of religion.

In World War II, excluding Japan, the Axis powers were entirely Christian. Not a Jew, Muslim, black, known atheist, Asian or other element of society. Germany split evenly between devout Catholics and Protestants and Italy entirely Catholic.

Reincarnated Courage

"...Until we can guarantee basic human rights to the tiniest minority, we cannot truthfully call ourselves a democracy."

Albino Luciani, Italian Parliament, January 16, 1961

Christopher Park

In a tiny borough just south of Sheridan Square in Greenwich Village, the streets run up and down and back and forth, now and then, crossing themselves, breaking them up into tiny fragments called 'places.'

So much so, if one follows one of these little places up in one direction, one will eventually find oneself coming down in the other direction, in the very same place.

In colonial days, these places had been paths from house to house. One could only go so far, until one had to turn back a bit, and cross a wooden bridge which spanned a small stream. Then, go, so far again, until one had to turn back a bit, and crossover the same stream, again.

Through the years, these little places have gone untouched.

No one—not a soul—has bothered to straighten them out. These little places—the sole surviving highways of yesterday.

311

Stonewall

It was the summer of nineteen hundred and sixty-nine. Halfway down one of these little places, stood an old stable; its massive wooden doors spilling out onto the cobblestone street before it.

Except for the placard above its door, 'McQuade's Tavern,' one could easily take it to be the car-barn which had once housed the carriage and horses which carried George Washington from Mount Vernon to New York for his inaugural address.

At the time, I lived with my roommate, one stop north on the MTA in Manhattan's Chelsea district. Each night, when the bell struck 11 o'clock, it was our custom to prowl out to the bars.

Hidden midway down one of these little places, it took us many months to find it, McQuade's quickly became our favorite haunt.

Like any other night, when the bartender called out "last call," we would pick up a pair of six packs at the door and head out into the darkness of the night, spotted by rows of make-believe gas lamps plotted along that little place just south of Sheridan Square.

Like many of its neighbors, the square is a misnomer of modern times. It isn't a square at all. It is a triangular strip of turf formed by two streets which rendezvous as they cease to exist.

Just a hair north of it, is Christopher Park. Another sliver of turf formed where two other streets meet their destiny.

As we came out onto Christopher Park, we were greeted by an angry mob gathered in front of the Stonewall Inn, a gay bar frequented by transgender types. You know, the obvious ones.

In the blink of an eye, we found ourselves hemmed in the gutter by the heavy iron fence which enclosed the park behind us.

A stone's throw before us, a squadron of cops were strung along the front of the bar. The vice squad as we called it in those days. A line of paddy wagons sneered hungrily off to one side.

An officer was clubbing a small-framed boy of twenty or so; his white shirt red with blood. It was apparent this helmeted legionnaire of the Lord was not going to let up. He had lost it.

The crowd outnumbered its adversaries a hundred to one. Not a single soul moved a single inch. Each one stood frozen in frigid fear.

My friend nudged me, "Hand me one of those six packs."

Ripping a can out of the pack, in a single motion, he threw it with every bit of strength God willed him. It struck the officer on the forehead, blood gushed just above his eye. Not enough to bring him down. Yet, more than enough to stop him.

Within seconds, a barrage of cans and bottles rocketed from the crowd. Instinctively, the officer in charge bellowed, "Hold your fire!" The brood disappeared quickly into the bar.

As I think back, I have often wondered whether that officer's action had been one of fear or one of courage. Yet, let's give him that. He did it out of courage. He was the hero of the day.

For had it not been for the swift action of that officer, much more blood would have been shed that day than had been shed by those at Concord who had ignited the great war to begin with.

What's more, some of it would have surely been mine.

Nevertheless, this was not an isolated incident. It was just one more battle in the longest and bloodiest war in the history of man.

Believe me, the American Revolution did not end when the French fleet trapped Cornwallis at Yorktown in October 1781.

One might choose to call it by different names: *Independence, Emancipation, Wounded Knee, Women's Suffrage, Integration, Civil Rights, Special Olympics, Stonewall,* and what have you.

To me, they have all been a part of what those brave young lads at Concord took those first bullets for in the spring of 1775.

They have all been a part, of those tears that, now, so very long ago, dropped… first, onto my shoulder…

> …then, ran down my back.

Headline quote: As a bishop, Albino Luciani defends the right of single persons including homosexuals to parent children in Italian Parliament, January 16, 1961.

In the nineteen-sixties, thousands of homosexuals were incarcerated for being caught in gay establishments. In the early morning hours of June 28, 1969, police raided the Stonewall Inn. For the first time, homosexuals stood up for their rights.

On a lighter note, I leave you with one more, one for the road…

The Story of Sam

I came upon a little creature,

as tiny as a mouse.

I saved him from the bitter cold,

and took him in my house.

I wrapped him in some swaddling clothes,

and lay him in his bed.

You'll never guess what Santa did,

when down the chimney he slid.

And under the tree was a miniature shed,

and a surprise that lay in its crib.

Christmas Eve, Baltimore Harbor

315

It was the coldest night of the year. No, it was the coldest night of the century. As I passed by the boarded-up carousel that sat on the southern edge of the harbor, I fancied I could still see its lights. I could still hear its music. I could still see its stampede of lions, and tigers, and pigs, and horses, and sheep.

I wondered where they were going? Wondered what was their destination? Wondered what was their dream?

As I looked up, the snow-laden decks of the nineteenth-century house, I called home, peered out hopelessly over the harbor.

A glistening menagerie of icicles poured from their edges, some masquerading as daggers and others as spears, as if they had gotten their dates mixed up and witches and goblins, not Santa, their aim.

I proceeded up toward the house. An icy rain was falling and as each drop reached the pavement, it added to the stalagmites hanging upside down from the sidewalk. Suddenly, I stopped.

Huddling at the edge of the cobblestone lane, was a tiny ball of fur.

At first, I thought it a small gray mouse. Then, noticing the length of its tail, I surmised it was, indeed, a baby rat.

I thought of the mother rat my carpenter had killed in my cellar a week earlier. Could this be one of her babies?

It was breathing heavily. Half frozen to the ice, obviously near death. "There is nothing I can do." With a somewhat weighted heart, I proceeded up the walkway and around to the front door of my house.

I went directly to the fireplace and stoked the coals a bit. Adding a couple of logs, I picked up a book and curled up in the overstuffed chair that flanked the hearth.

The light and the warmth of the fire felt good. The tree, which sat at the other side of the fireplace, told its tale, of light, of tinsel, of angels, of balls of silver, of crystal and snow.

Soon the chill I had picked up out on the harbor was gone and, as I turned a page, I thought of the creature, God's creature, I had passed on the way. "Perhaps it's over," I hoped. "Yes, it must be over by now. It's best. He's with his mother now."

Time for bed. Up the stairs I went. Entering the bedroom, I stopped at the fireplace, stoked the coals and added a log or two. Slipping into my flannel pajamas, I climbed under the covers and, with book in hand, proceeded to read myself to sleep.

But sleep was not going to come easily that night.

One of those things one calls tears climbed up out of my heart, started from the crevice of my eye, and crept toward the lid. I looked first to the right, then, to the left, then, again, to the right, and, then, to the left, once more. Not quite yet a man, I let it slip out onto my cheek. In my heart, nothing, no, not a thing was left in its place.

"Well, he could still be suffering? Got to be sure." Getting up, I donned my boots and mackinaw and went out into the night.

The freezing rain had made its transition to snow. Silent white flakes drifted down softly as if to sleep. Yet, a brisk wind crept about the ice covered ground keeping them very much awake.

As I proceeded down the walkway, I hoped it would all be over. Coming to where he lay, I saw that he was punishing me for what my carpenter had done to his mother.

His breathing was more labored now. Petals of snow clung to his whiskers. His hair frozen to the ice. He looked up at me, a sad look, one that seemed to say, "Help me. Please...please, help me."

With no other way out of my predicament, I made my way back to the house and scrambled down to my workshop.

Gathering up a putty knife, an old rag, a miniature basket, an old birdcage, I headed back up the stairs. Dropping the cage by the living room fireplace, I went back out into the bitter night.

Returning to where he lay, I chipped the ice around him; then, cautiously, that which was beneath him.

Having freed him from his prison, I picked him up with the rag. With the greatest of care, I placed him in the box.

Taking him into the house, I set him down by the fireplace and went about readying the cage.

I lined it with paper, added a jar-cover of water, a splice of carrot, and a crumb of cheese.

I stole up to the medicine cabinet and fetched a nose dropper. Then back down to the refrigerator for a tad of milk.

Returning to the chair beside the fireplace, I reached over and picked him up, his tiny body trembling nestled in the rag.

I warmed the milk with the heat from the fire. Then taking up the nose dropper, I began to nourish the baby rat.

Soon, his labored breathing ceased, I wrapped him in the rag in the basket. "His swaddling clothes," I smiled as I put him in the cage.

Placing it under the tree, I proceeded up the stairs and stoked the fire a bit. With book in hand, I climbed back into bed and...

Images of Santa soon danced in my head,
even Dickens could not guess what he did,
when under the tree was a miniature shed,
and a surprise that lay in its crib!

When I rose the following morning, Sam, as I would come to call him, was already up. Though slow from his experience, he seemed to be none the worst for it. The cheese was gone and he had made some inroads into the carrot.

As I sat there in the dining room sipping coffee, I looked out over the harbor and wondered what I could do now. The winter was still young. If I were to put him out now it would not give him a fighting chance. After all, his mother is gone. Thinking of his mother, "What if he has some brothers and sisters?"

Looking out at the alley which ran behind the house, I realized that I was beginning to toy with my sanity itself. After all, rats are wild animals, fugitives of everything that is civilized. Here, I was not only harboring one, but considering saving his siblings as well.

Nevertheless, knowing I was dealing with nature's creatures, God's creatures, I must do whatever I can.

Putting on my coat and boots, I proceeded down the stairs and out of the rear of the house and across the frozen garden. Unlocking the gate, I proceeded out into the alley.

Sure enough, I came upon another one, then another. Yet, too late; the night had taken its toll. God's tiny creatures, each one frozen in its tracks. I checked up and down the alley, once more.

My next door neighbor called out of his window: "What did you lose? What are you looking for?"

I yelled back: "Rats, baby rats, baby rats that might be suffering from the cold."

Going back into the house, sadly, I couldn't bring Sam good news. I tried not to look at him, that he might see it in my eyes.

Taking him out of his cage, I took my chair by the fireplace and began to comfort him in his great loss. Hoping, all the time, he would not notice the tears cuddling in the corners of my eyes.

Indeed, it was a long harsh winter. Each time I looked at Sam, I knew I had done right. As spring approached I thought I could keep him there all of his life. And now he was all full of life.

Yes, I would want to keep him there, for he was now my pal. But that would deprive him of the freedom to grow up and fall in love and bring others of his kind into the world.

With the winter gone, the day had come when I had to say goodbye to Sam. With cage in hand, I proceeded out of the house.

The day was glorious. The four golden federal stars, which adorned the weather beaten brick facade fronting the house, glistened in the sun. The air was brisk and a slight breeze was trying to charm the leaves on the trees. I crossed the street and climbed up the hill to Federal Hill Park which overlooks the city's inner harbor.

I set the cage down on the ground near some bushes that ran in a row up the slope. When I had first put him in it, I had some question, because of his tiny size, the cage might not hold him; he might squeeze out through its ribs. Now he was so big, I thought he might not be able to get out of its door.

Yet, when I slid the door open, he ran out of the cage and up along the edge of a row of bushes. Then, suddenly, he stopped.

He looked back at me with his eyes, as if to say, "Thank you, thank you from the bottom of my heart." He was gone.

As I passed my neighbor's house, with the cage in hand, he joked, "Out looking for rats again?"

"No, just sending one off to college." I scoffed.

319

Entering the house, I closed the door behind me.

One of those things one calls tears climbed up out of my heart, started from the crevice of my eye, and crept toward the lid. I looked first to the right, then, to the left, then, again, to the right, and, then, to the left, once more.

Not quite yet a man, I let it slip out onto my cheek. In its place, in my heart, was left something that would be with me all the remaining days of my life.

Later that evening I passed by the carousel. Now it was all lit up. Now all could see its lights, all could hear its music, all could see its stampede of lions, and tigers, and pigs, and horses, and sheep.

Yet, I still wondered what was their destination? Wondered where they were going? Wondered what was their dream?

And my neighbor? Well, after that. Whenever I would run into him on the street, he would pass with a downward glance.

I've never understood why? Perhaps, you know why?

'The Story of Sam' recounts an incident in the author's life. It demonstrates man's prejudice extends to animals.

↑ ↑

The carousel in Baltimore Harbor from the rear deck of the house on Federal Hill
The same house the author had once read Paul's letter in *Not Quite yet a Man*.

Epilogue

"The most fundamental weapon of war is faith, which conditions children of God-driven nations to hate children of atheist nations, so that when they grow up they will kill them in the name of God."[1]

Albino Luciani, July 22, 1928

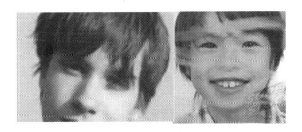

In the Basilica di San Marco in Venice on March 19, 1972, Albino Luciani quoted a letter written by an American soldier to his mother.

" '...it has been raining here in Vietnam for days now. The rain has washed the hatred out of the mud and turned it back to the color God intended it to be.

Including the blood of that boy who dreamt of things that were to be, which for him will never come to be.

Yet, it will never wash away the guilt of those who plotted his murder. It will never wash away the tears of the fool who carried it out.' "

The Patriarch's voice took a on a rare tone of bitterness:

"What's more, it will never wash away the evilness of the God who gave the order."[2]

Albino Luciani, March 19, 1972

"Never be afraid to stand up for what is right, whether your adversary be your parent, your peer, your teacher, your politician, your preacher, or even your God." [3]

Albino Luciani, March 5, 1973

"God is an assumption we are born into…" [4]

Albino Luciani, March 11, 1973

Albino Luciani = John Paul I

The lion—as opposed to sheep—stands for his atheist father who taught him right from wrong. The three stars stand for the three attributes his father built into him:

Compassion - Courage - Change

The six mounds stand for the six Italian peaks for which he held the speed record.

[1] *Povera Tigre Feltre* 22 July 1928. He was fifteen when he wrote this article. Though the influence of his atheist father it was published in this activist journal
[2] *Messaggero Mestre* 20 Mar 1972
[3] *Messaggero Mestre* 11 Mar 1973. Albino Luciani speaking to a youth group a week earlier in Venice on the day he became a cardinal.
[4] *Messaggero Mestre* 11 Mar 1973. He made this follow-up statement to a reporter who questioned his first statement: *"God is an assumption we are born into or picked up along the way."*

Image Bibliography

Shutterstock license ID 4EF4DD3C16029726C712D6106F2EB514393D541F 12/23/11 & 5/8/2015

Cover front: cross: *shutterstock.com /Sean Liew* 'A': *shutterstock.com /Kannanimages*
Cover back: coat of arms: *shutterstock.com /Atlaspix*
End of each chapter footnote '?' figure: *shutterstock.com /Lyudimyla Kharomova*

Page
1 frame: *shutterstock.com /robybret* coat of arms: *shutterstock.com /Aylaspix*
5 boy with book: *shutterstock.com /Ruslan Guzov*
6 forest: *shutterstock.com/Andreinc*
7 butterfly: *shutterstock.com/Ambient Ideas* moth: *shutterstock.com/Circumnavigation*
10 spaceship: *shutterstock.com /wire-man*
11 bike: *shutterstock.com /Hamurishi*
14 manhole figures: *shutterstock.com /Palto*
15 ball: *shutterstock.com /Maximus Art*
16-20 letter: *author creation*
23 open book: *shutterstock.com /silverjohn*
24 soldier & baby: *shutterstock.com /Kletr & Andreas Gradin*
29, 124, 128 ghost & flames: *shutterstock.com /Jonystckphoto & Nata-Taka*
32 magnifying glass hieroglyphic: *shutterstock.com /V-Krv*
36 Hieroglyphics: *shutterstock.com /Andrey Burmakin*
37 List of Pharaohs: *author creation*
40 Jewish Temple at Elephantine: *shutterstock.com /Florin Stana*
43 German cemetery: *shutterstock.com /LENS-68*
44 Hitler: *shutterstock.com /Toniwhim* Holocaust: *shutterstock.com /Javi-Indy*
45 Pius-Spellman & Spellman-Eisenhower: *shutterstock.com /Petr Jilek* posters: *author*
46 Vietnam (3): *shutterstock.com /Viet Rhino*
47 Vietnam (2): *shutterstock.com /Viet Rhino* Chinese soldiers: *Paul Tseng*
47 Mideast: *shutterstock.com/Moham-id*
48 Asian Youth *shutterstock.com /Rose Ng*
48-49 soldier's letter /author rendition
50 Pius-Spellman: *shutterstock.com /Petr Jilek*
51 eye: *shutterstock.com /Bruce Rolff*
53 vigil: *shutterstock.com /Lukas Maverisk Greyson* tug-of-war: *shutterstock.com/Orla*
59 sheep: *shutterstock.com /Arnica*
60 hate signs: *shutterstock.com /BamBax*
65 lamb: *shutterstock.com /Henk Hennuin*
66 Ghost: *shutterstock.com /Lehigh Prather*
67 List of Popes: *author drawing*
72 Holy Trinity *author drawing*
75 Hindu & Christian Trinity: *shutterstock.com /Rachelle Burnside & Zvonimir Atletic*
77 Changing Times: *shutterstock.com /iQncept*
82 History book & magnifying glass: *shutterstock.com /Jeri Flogel*
85 figure w/magnifying glass: *shutterstock.com /YamatoHD*
87 spotlight: *shutterstock.com /Vlue*
90 clay tablet: *shutterstock.com /Fedor Selivanov*
94 Abraham & Isaac: *shutterstock.com /Zvonimir Atletic*

95-96 animal sacrifice: *shutterstock.com /Kirsz Marcin*
96 turtle doves: *shutterstock.com /Renata Sedmakova*
98 evolution: *shutterstock.com /Miceking*
99 heart: *shutterstock.com /Alex Malikov Beam: shutterstock.com /Bruce Rolff*
100 fetus: *shutterstock.com /Sebastian Kaulitzki*
104 Eucharist: *shutterstock.com /Fabio Lotti* steak dinner: *author photo*
105 eagle: *shutterstock.com /Draw Home* Dove: *shutterstock.com /Teschinko*
107 flying saucer: *shutterstock.com /sgame*
108 weeping willow: *shutterstock.com /Markoski.*
109 *shutterstock.com:* tower/church:*/Natalia Bratslavsky/nhtg* - caskets: */Jtole*
110 child: *shutterstock.com /Jtole*   Fatima: *shutterstock.com /Meunerd*
112 hungry children: *shutterstock.com /W Garcia* Eucharist: *shutterstock.com /Fabio Lotti*
113 church: *shutterstock.com /tillen.* hands: *shutterstock.com /Maksim Slmeljov*
114 wine cellar & Vatican Museum: *author photos*
117 Jesus/Father in carriage: *Artwork by Ben Vogelsang/exclusive property of the author*
118 lightbulb: *Clip Art license 7771920-GR*
120 caricature of pope: *Artwork by Ben Vogelsang/exclusive property of the author*
121 stove: *shutterstock.com /Penpix*
122 bodies in snow: *shutterstock.com /RoncalliII*
125 ruins: *shutterstock.com /Morpit*
125, 129 girl/ghost: *shutterstock.com /Kuco Jonystckphoto*
129 *shutterstock.com:* Goldilocks: */Anton Brand* Pumpkin: */Ann-Mei* Pinocchio: */5ciska76*
131 All creatures: *shutterstock.com /nem4a*
133 Globe: *shutterstock.com /rtGuest* JPI *shutterstock.com /Javi-*
134 God: *author photo* Earth: *shutterstock.com /jon*
135 Lice: *shutterstock.com /pxAye* Embryos: *author drawing*
136 Mite: *shutterstock.com /D. Kucharski & Kucharska*
137 Bacteria: *shutterstock.com /Sarans*
138 Atom: *shutterstock.com /Sean Cladwell*
139 Diamond/human molecules: *shutterstock.com /Denis Urublevski*
140 little men: *shutterstock.com /Strejman*
141 boy with toy soldiers: *shutterstock.com /bikeriderlondon*
145 boy in cellar: *shutterstock.com / Ruslan Guzov*
146 boy/girl in snow: *shutterstock.com /Rosin*
156 boy/girl in snow: *shutterstock.com /Rosin*
157 soul-cot: *shutterstock.com /Distant Mystic*
158 soul-hand: *shutterstock.com /smoke1*
161 crown: *shutterstock.com /sabdra zuerlein*   Hieroglyphic: *shutterstock.com /GIS*
168 cavemen: *shutterstock.com /Santiago R.C.*
171 baseball: *shutterstock.com/ RetroClipArt*
175-176 brain: *author drawings*
185 Jekyll & Hyde: *shutterstock.com /Neftali*
190 LOVE: *shutterstock.com / Balandina G*
192 Hindu Temple: *shutterstock.com /Steve Estvanik* Adam: *shutterstock.com /K Wong*
195 dice religion: *shutterstock.com /Almagami* ?:
196-229 dice four dimensions of man: *shutterstock.com /Almagami*
203 icon Jesus: *shutterstock.com /Olga*
203, 205 Manson: *shutterstock.com /Trobbin*
209 mummy: *shutterstock.com /Brizo*
211 chopsticks: *shutterstock.com /Ljupco Smokovski*
218 hands: *shutterstock.com /Maksim Slmeljov*
241 violin and bow: *shutterstock.com /Robert B. Miller*

242 pond: *shutterstock.com /TJThomason*
249-250 Paul's letter: author creation
251 violinist: *shutterstock.com /re-bekka*
261 popes in bed: *Artwork by Ben Vogelsang/exclusive property of the author*
263 icicle: *shutterstock.com /ThadeusC*
264 boy in bed: *Artwork by Ben Vogelsang/exclusive property of the author*
269 prejudice monster: *shutterstock.com /Seamartini Graphics*
270 teacher: *Artwork by Ben Vogelsang/exclusive property of the author*
275 soldiers: *Artwork by Ben Vogelsang/exclusive property of the author*
278 cemetery: *Artwork by Ben Vogelsang/exclusive property of the author*
279 helmet: *Printmaster 11 license PR-2623271*
282 *shutterstock.com /fashcool*
286 transgender: *Artwork by Ben Vogelsang/exclusive property of the author*
288 totem /cross Indians: *Printmaster license PR-2623271* cardinals: *shutterstock.com /legg*
291 Supreme Court at Mass: *author photo*
292 statue of liberty: *shutterstock.com /Miroia*
295 boy on throne: *Artwork by Ben Vogelsang/exclusive property of the author*
298 John Paul I tree: *author photo*
300 cart with bodies: *shutterstock.com /Yannahlit*
302 Anne Frank: *shutterstock.com /HansL*
306 wine bottle: *shutterstock.com /Sands*
309 Hans' letter: author creation
311 Christopher Park: *author photo*
315 harbor: *shutterstock.com /Alex Sun*
318 mouse/branches: *shutterstock.com /Suzanna Fonaryova*
320 house & Baltimore Harbor: *author photos*
321 boy: *shutterstock.com /Sabphoto* Asian boy: *shutterstock.com /Sanmonckhol*
322 Albino Luciani coat of arms: *shutterstock.com /Atlaspix*
326 gift: *shutterstock.com /Garsya*

© Artwork attributed to Ben Vogelsang was commissioned by the author specifically for this book and is protected under its copyright.

Author's Books

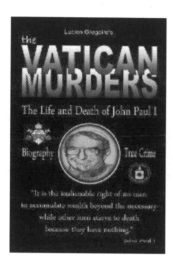 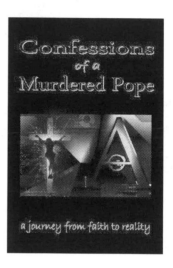

Printed in the United States, Milton Keynes UK & Scoresby Australia

Dealers, book clubs & others representing themselves as booksellers. 48% discount:

Email: channelsales@authorsolutions.com Phone: 1-888-728-8467 ext. 5022

The Vatican Murders: The Life and Death of John Paul I

ISBN: 978-1-4918-3525-8 (sc)
ISBN: 978-1-4918-3527-2 (hc)

Confessions of a Murdered Pope: a journey from faith to reality

ISBN: 978-1-5049-1772-8 (sc)
ISBN: 978-1-5049-1773-5 (hc)

E-books are available on Amazon, B&N, iBooks and all marketing sites

Author

Born and raised in New England, *George Lucien Gregoire* completed both his undergraduate and graduate work in Massachusetts schools.

As an international figure in cooperative education and as founding trustee of organizations providing education to impaired children, he has served on boards of secondary schools and universities.

He was a NATO intelligence officer when he made the acquaintance of Albino Luciani when the little known bishop of Vittorio Veneto was leading the priest-worker movement which gave rise to the Communist Party in Italy.

In addition to scrutinizing thousands of leaves of scriptural, archeological and scientific accounts in exacting his knowledge of world religions and traveling to the origins of key faiths, this Catholic-born author has been an active participant in synagogues, mosques, Orthodox, Protestant and Evangelical sects, Hindu temples and Buddhist meditation centers. He gathered much of his practical understanding of religion from members of these congregations.

He is the author of the only biography of John Paul I written by an acquaintance of the 33-Day Pope: *The Vatican Murders: The Life and Death of John Paul I.*

Through the years, friend and foe have contributed to the accuracy of my work. Should you find any tidbit—no matter how small—in which I deviate from the truth, I appreciate your bringing it to my attention.

I am especially appreciative of those who take the time to review my work in journals and on the Internet.

Thank you for recommending it to others.

I am hopeful, it lives up to something a bookstore owner once told me.

"Lucien, many people come into our shop and pick up your book. Though not all of them buy it, each one of them leaves here thinking things they never thought before." [1]

George Lucien Gregoire

George Lucien Gregoire
University of Maryland
38 South Paca Street #403
Baltimore Maryland 21201
Tel: 410 625 9741 Email: vatican@att.net

[1] Giovanni's Room Bookstore, Philadelphia